Acting Hollywood Style

D1193706

Foster Hirsch

Acting Hollywood Style

With Photographs from The Kobal Collection

Harry N. Abrams, Inc., Publishers
AFI Press

Foster Hirsch has written fourteen books on theater and film subjects.
He is Professor of Film at Brooklyn College of the City University of New York.

Editor: Margaret Donovan
Designer: Dirk Luykx
Photo Editor: John K. Crowley

Frontispiece: Irene Dunne on the set of *Life with Father* (1947)

Library of Congress Cataloging-in-Publication Data
Hirsch, Foster.
    Acting Hollywood style : with photographs from the Kobal
collection / by Foster Hirsch.
    288 p. 22.8 x 30.2 cm
    Includes bibliographical references and index.
    ISBN 0-8109-2685–7 (pbk.)
    1. Motion picture acting   I. Title.
PN1995.9.A26H5   1991
791.43′028—dc20   91–307

Text copyright © 1991 Foster Hirsch
Illustrations copyright © 1991 Harry N. Abrams, Inc.

Paperback edition published in 1996 by Harry N. Abrams, Incorporated, New York
A Times Mirror Company
All rights reserved. No part of the contents of this book may be
reproduced without the written permission of the publisher

Clothbound edition published in 1991 by Harry N. Abrams, Inc.

Printed and bound in Japan

Contents

Previews

TWO CLOSEUPS.

Greta Garbo's famous offscreen gaze at the end of *Queen Christina* (1933). What does she see? What do we see?

1. On the prow of her ship the former monarch stands like a statue. Her lover, for whom she has abdicated, lies behind her, slain in a senseless duel; now, without a country to rule or a great passion in which to shelter, she gazes deeply into offscreen space. What does she see? What do we see?

As if lying in wait for revelation, the unmoving camera stares at the woman's face. In the absence of dialogue and with no protection from the peering camera, it is through her face alone that the actress must "write" this climactic scene.

At first her face seems frozen, as unyielding as her posture. "I will not show you anything you want to see," her mask seems to tell us. "I will not cry—I did that for you before; I will not grieve, for isn't that what you expect from me, a queen who has lost her kingdom and her count? I will not, I will not . . . " And yet as the camera remains in place, her mask flickers, emitting almost subliminal signals of strength, pain, resignation, the memory of an exalting love, the fleeting implication that for her the world has been well lost.

In this famous closeup at the end of *Queen Christina* (1933), Greta Garbo's face, tantalizingly, is both open and closed, legible as well as veiled. It is available, yet mysterious—her face contains the imprint of her character's inner life as thoughts seem to pass *behind* her eyes. "What should I think of? What should I do?" Garbo is supposed to have asked her director, Rouben Mamoulian, before shooting the scene. "Think of nothing, empty your face of thought," Mamoulian is supposed to have answered. Those watching her on the set that day may indeed have thought she was a blank slate, but the actress and her director knew that her "empty" look was addressed to the transforming eye of the camera. Nearly sixty years later the message it sends is still potent. How to speak to the eye of the camera—often, as in this scene, without words or without any visible assistance from the camera—is the task of all screen players, and few in the history of the art have understood the language as shrewdly as Garbo.

2. The woman in the flower shop laughs at the Tramp she sees through the window. Impulsively she steps outside to hand him a flower, and as her hand touches his, she realizes that this odd-looking fellow is her benefactor, the mysterious man who gave her money for an operation that restored her sight. At first she's dismayed—the Tramp is so different from the savior she had imagined him to be—and then she is moved. As the camera looks at the Tramp, he smiles as his eyes light up with an expression no one who has seen it is ever likely to forget. For the Tramp bestows on the object of his charity a look that all at once exposes his love, his vulnerability, his bravery, his tentativeness, and his

Inciting audience response: like Garbo, Charlie Chaplin in closeup at the end of *City Lights* (1931) creates a face that seems to pierce the screen's flat surface.

hope. Placing the gift of the flower between his teeth, he is transformed from an adult male into a shy girl and then, in a flash of his eye, back again into a grown-up luminous with feelings that have been accumulating throughout his story.

Like Garbo's gaze into infinity, this closeup of Charlie Chaplin that concludes *City Lights* (1931) is a high-wire test of a movie actor's skills. In the space between his face and the camera, Chaplin is undefended; yet, with his eyes and the set of his features as his only linguistic tools, Chaplin "writes" an eloquent poem that fittingly crowns *City Lights* but also transcends it to become a timeless tribute to the human spirit.

Two long shots.

1. Dancers in a deserted hotel room, framed by an ocean view seen through tall glass windows. As the strains of "Night and Day" float onto the empty polished circle that is to be their stage, the man pushes his unwilling partner into motion, coaxing her into following his sinuous arabesques. At first resistant, she gradually yields to the power of his danced enchantment, conforming the arch of her back, the sway of her hips, the placement of her legs, to his, until what was initially an uneasy duet slides by degrees into a vision of danced unity. Through his movement the man has courted and bewitched a disapproving woman—at the end of the dance she glances up at her seducer with a look of dazzlement, as if she can't quite believe what has just happened to her. Her response is both echo of and cue for our own: like her, in the sort of vicarious thrill that is one of the reasons we go to movies, we too have been swept off our feet.

Through dance Fred Astaire acts as powerfully as Garbo and Chaplin do through their eyes. While Garbo and Chaplin perform in closeups, Astaire requires that the camera remain a distant witness to his gliding movements—once he claims the gleaming floor as his performing space, the camera dare not intrude. With his dance Astaire conquers the camera, the spectator, and (here in *The Gay Divorcee,* 1934) his reluctant partner, Ginger Rogers.

2. Dressed in black, the masked man leads his pursuers on a wild chase. He scales walls, jumps from balconies, vaults from a hitching post into a window, leaps over horses, carts, and sacks, turning each obstruction into a display of his athletic prowess and all the while flashing a dazzling smile. So assured is this roustabout that he even has time for a break, lounging momentarily on a ledge to eat an apple.

As Douglas Fairbanks, Sr. (in *The Mark of Zorro,* 1920), moves through space defying objects and gravity while converting the world of the film into a gigantic jungle gym, the camera stares in rapt fascination. The only movement in the frame is that of the actor, as if camera choreography might detract from Fairbanks' acrobatics. As in *Gay Divorcee* the "invisible" camera and editing—the respectful long shots and the long takes—establish a unified time/space framework that assures us that the performers are really doing what we are seeing.

Like Astaire's dance, Fairbanks' conquest of walls and balconies is linked to story and character; as Zorro, he is Robin Hood in early California, rising up against oppression. His movements define an agile, liberating "heroism," as Astaire's embody a suspended state of "being in love." Both stars thus adapt the skilled movement of their bodies through space into a performance art ideally suited for movies. Fairbanks' leaps, like Astaire's steps in time, exemplify some of the special requirements of screen acting.

In the preceding examples the actors were on their own as they performed for the camera's scrutiny. In the following scenes the actors receive help.

1. Rain slashes against the car windows. Lights from passing cars pierce through the fog. There's a blare of offscreen horns and the swell of discordant music as the driver, losing control of the car and of herself, slumps over the steering wheel in hysterics.

This famous scene of a crack-up (Lana Turner in *The Bad and the Beautiful,* 1952) is often used as evidence that glamorous movie stars can also (sometimes) act. Goaded by her demanding director, Vincente Minnelli, and exhausted by numerous retakes, Turner claims that her breakdown was the real thing. But placed into such a charged framework, in which image and sound—the flickering lighting, the rain smashing against the car window, the hammering score—create a mise-en-scène that shrieks "crack-up," how much acting was Turner really required to do?

2. Framed by two well-lighted colleagues, novice newspaper editor Charles Foster Kane (Orson Welles in *Citizen Kane,* 1941) steps into a shadow and, draped in a premonitory darkness, begins to read his idealistic declaration of principles. In this shot, in which the declamatory lighting does most of the "acting," Welles the ingenious director has upstaged his own performance.

Expressive eyes, faces that invite attention, liquid bodies—these are essential tools of the film actor's craft. And since 1927 acting on film has required a knowledge of how to inflect words as well as faces and limbs. Here's a sampling of the Hollywood actor's way with words.

1. "What was your childhood like?" one con asks of another (Clint Eastwood, in *Escape from Alcatraz,* 1979) as they sit in the prison yard during recess. "Short." Eastwood knows how to give a monosyllable the illusion of being a full declarative sentence—he makes that one word tell us all we need to know about his character's past.

2. "Oh Charlie, Charlie," Terry Malloy (Marlon Brando in *On the Waterfront,* 1954) says when in the back seat of a taxi his brother pulls a gun on him. An interjection and a name, softly repeated: the words seem unimportant and yet the actor endows them with eloquence. Throbbing with subtext, Brando's voice contains at once Terry's love for and disappointment in his brother as well as his acceptance of his own failure. It is right after this moment that Terry makes the most renowned speech of self-recognition in American movies: "I coulda been a contender, I coulda been somebody, instead of a bum, which is what I am."

3. In the previous examples, wariness with words seems to define the Hollywood actor's relation to language, yet in the thirties and forties particularly, movies often revel in talk. James Stewart's final oration in *Mr. Smith Goes to Washington* (1939), for example, is a Hollywood aria as demanding as a soliloquy of the classic theatre. On the Senate floor, Jefferson Smith (Stewart), a David risen up from the plains to slay the Goliath of a corrupt political machine, triumphs through his command of language. Listening to Mr. Smith's impassioned words, a crooked senator cries out, "I'm not fit to live—every word that boy says is the truth!"

4. Dialogue in the preceding examples carries a special jolt. Most of the time, however, actors in movies have a more relaxed speaking style, as in a scene in *San Francisco* (1936) in which a priest (Spencer Tracy) talks to a police officer about a boyhood friend who slipped into a life of crime. Talking casually while he prepares coffee, Tracy turns us into eavesdroppers. His plain speaking, which creates an illusion of behaving in a true-to-life fashion, as if the camera isn't there, is what film actors are usually required to do.

Following through on the hints contained in these "previews" about what we need to be on the lookout for in order to evaluate screen acting, I have divided my book into five sections: Tools of the Trade, which considers the ways that film technique enhances and sometimes competes with or even replaces the actor's work; Body Language; The Landscape of the Face; The Rustle of Language (a phrase borrowed from Roland Barthes); and Starstruck: Hollywood acting as star acting.

In examining parts of the actor—bodies, faces, voices—as they interact with the filmmaking process, I suspect I will seem to be a determined deconstructionist ripping apart performers like an overzealous grammarian parsing a sentence. But I hope by the end to put all the pieces together and to leave the reader with some tips on how to analyze as well as enjoy acting in the movies. This is a book about resources on either side of the camera: the actor's, on the one hand; the filmmaker's and the spectator's, on the other.

This is also a book about a particular style of acting, the one developed within the commercial American filmmaking system. I have limited my focus to Hollywood rather than attempting to consider performance practices from other cultures or traditions—German expressionism, for instance, or the acting in avant-garde or documentary films—because "Hollywood" acting has had the greatest worldwide influence. Though it is by no means uniform or monolithic, the Hollywood Style, which favors the techniques of star acting, established the basic conventions of screen performance.

Proceeding topically rather than chronologically, my approach favors practice over history. As I choose samples from the work of representative actors—Garbo, Chaplin, Marlon Brando, and Bette Davis are the most frequently cited performers—I make no attempt to include every major player in American movies; many of your favorite actors (indeed, many of mine) make no appearance. Nor do I follow the complete career of any one performer. This is not a roll call of great performances, and not all my selections are of great or even good acting; some players are included because their work is representative of the Hollywood Style rather than because it is peerless.

Although it's possible to be reasonably objective about how a performance on film is constructed, I don't see any point in maintaining a deadpan reaction to individual performers. Acting *should* elicit a personal response, and as I propose a set of suggestions for how screen acting operates, my own preferences will be amply evident.

While this is not, then, a history of film acting, I would nonetheless like to introduce my dramatis personae—the actors from the early silent period to the eighties whose work I will draw on for examples—within something of a historical framework. Two major influences have shaped the evolution of acting in Hollywood: the first, the ability to record sound on film, is technological; the second, the studio system, is industrial.

Al Jolson's boast, "You ain't heard nothin' yet!" in *The Jazz Singer* (1927), heralded a Great Divide in the history of screen acting. After they heard voices issuing from the screen, the general moviegoing public began to regard speechless acting as obsolescent: acting at half mast. In its demands on both performers and spectators, silent acting is indeed different from acting in the "talkers" (as talking pictures were first called). To act without speech is after all a fundamental violation of human reality, and actors who must communicate without a heard voice are clearly not "one of us." Their voicelessness turns them into figures on display: spectacles.

In the absence of verbal language, the most common mode of communication in the offscreen world, silent actors must speak with the language of their faces and bodies. To eyes, hands, arms, shoulders, legs, and torsos fall the burden of conveying thought and feeling.

The careers of the major silent actors after the coming of sound indicate the chasm between acting on screen with and without a voice. Throughout the teens and twenties, as film was developing its narrative and technical grammar, these fifteen performers had a significant impact on acting: Theda Bara; Douglas Fairbanks, Sr.; Lillian Gish; William S. Hart; Mary Pickford; Charlie Chaplin; Gloria Swanson; Rudolph Valentino; John Barrymore; Buster Keaton; Harold Lloyd; Lon Chaney, Sr.; John Gilbert; Clara Bow; Greta Garbo. Each of these actors was an early version of a type that has continued to be redrawn and reinterpreted. Bara was the original vamp, a femme fatale deadlier than the male. Fairbanks was the movies' first great action hero, an athlete whose body, placed generously on display, assured his stardom. Stern-faced and weather-beaten, Hart was the first major Western star. With their blazing eyes, Valentino and Gilbert embodied the prototype of the dark lover, the man who lives and dies for romance. Chaplin, Keaton, and Lloyd created three comic masks while discovering the kind of comic performance that was best suited to the new medium of silent movies. Gish was the first major artist of movie melodrama, Swanson the movies' first clotheshorse. Domesticating a sex appeal that Bara had made exotic and otherworldly, Bow was the first contemporary sex kitten, a saucy twenties flapper. Delighting in appearing in makeup and costume, in altering their faces and the way they used their bodies, Barrymore and Chaney suggested options for character acting on film. Garbo updated Bara's image of Woman as Temptress. Only Pickford's persona—a grown-up playing a plucky adolescent—left little legacy for later actors to borrow from.

Of these fifteen architects of screen acting only Garbo, Chaplin (a special case), and to a qualified extent John Barrymore (usually a ham actor who spoke in a plummy theatrical diction and who played ham actors, often to the point of self-parody, throughout the thirties) held on to their star status in talking pictures. The others lost their place in the industry they helped to create.

Well before the end of the silent period the careers of Bara and Hart had been exhausted through repetition and overexposure. Valentino died in 1926 and Chaney in 1930; while Valentino would surely have had to modify his image to have survived on the other side of the sound barrier, Chaney in his one sound film, *The Unholy Three* (1930), a remake of one of his silent successes, spoke in a gruff, contemporary-sounding voice that would have been usable in the gangster films of the early thirties.

Except for Garbo, the players who had become stars in the silents were diminished by speech. John Gilbert, the most famous victim of the talkies, spoke in a hollow, high-pitched voice marred by elocution-school overarticulation that made the Great Lover of the silent screen sound prissy. While revisionists have tried to blame Gilbert's fall on L. B. Mayer, who in this scenario is accused of having tampered with the way Gilbert's voice was reproduced, to anyone who has seen Gilbert's talkie debut, *His Glorious Night* (1929), the actor's discomfort with the new medium is palpable. Adding a voice to his image seems to have dried up his actor's instincts; having to speak freezes his body and deadens the eyes that distinguished his silent performances. (Though Gilbert improved, he was never more than passable in talking pictures.)

Gish's suffering heroines, Pickford's high-spirited and often comic child-women, Fairbanks' heroes, Chaplin's Tramp, Keaton's stone-faced manchild, and Lloyd's be-spectacled buffoon were all protected and embraced by silence. Speech would only have undercut the poetry of their mime and the size of their personas. Moreover these performers had voices that contradicted their star images. In silence they are outside time; with voices they sound merely mortal.

As a character actress later in her career and on stage, Gish has of course been effective—indeed she has the longest sustained career of any performer in this century—but, except for her magnificent performance in *Night of the Hunter* (1955), she is a great actress only in the silents. Her crusty voice—the voice of American common sense—does not match the lyricism and vulnerability of her silent characters. Speech was an acting challenge Pickford was never able to master. Dialogue impaired her movements and dimmed her eyes, and her thick, unmusical voice exposed America's Sweetheart as the tough businesswoman she was in real life. Fairbanks' high-pitched voice could not keep pace with his supple leaps and vaults, and shades of a New York accent tainted his swagger. But for Fairbanks, international playboy and friend of royalty, who by 1930 was too old to continue to play parts like Robin Hood and who never wanted to play anything else, the loss of his screen credibility was not the catastrophe it was for Pickford.

For Chaplin, as for the other silent clowns, the spoken word did not have the same comic possibilities as mime. Chaplin's crisp, clear, British-accented voice is not intrinsically funny, the way Mae West's is, for instance; it becomes a comic instrument only when the actor demolishes language, as in the gibberish song at the end of *Modern Times* (1936) or in *The Great Dictator* (1940) when he orates nonsense German in his parodies of Hitler's maniacal platform forensics. Chaplin resisted dialogue longer than anybody else and as his own boss with a large international following he was in a unique position to do so. When he finally spoke up he became an ideologue who delivered sermons on politics, war, morality, and art and offered autobiographical revelations. The act of speech altered and sometimes threatened Chaplin's comedy, and in his four full-talking pictures (*Monsieur Verdoux*, 1947; *Limelight*, 1952; and *A King In New York*, 1957, in addition to *The Great Dictator*) mime is either reminiscence or respite.

Bidding farewell to the Tramp and reworking his comic style, Chaplin in his own way adapted to talking pictures, and if by design he was less funny he nonetheless continued to be a skilled film actor. Keaton and Lloyd, on the other hand, had nothing to say with words that they couldn't say more trenchantly without them. When he spoke Lloyd had a nondescript voice. And when he added sound to his routines—grunting and wheezing as he scales a building in *Feet First* (1930)—the extraneous realism threatened to ground him. Keaton's heavy, slow, melancholy voice, steeped in the alcohol that helped to ruin his career, needed a distinctive vehicle, a tragicomedy or one marked with black humor. Instead, working as a hired hand at M-G-M he was reduced to playing second banana to Jimmy Durante, a talking comic, the gruff-voiced majordomo of malapropism.

Unlike the homespun and everyday voices of Bow, Gish, Pickford, and Swanson, Garbo's low, sultry tones and the musical rhythms of her Swedish accent enhanced her aura. Alone among the great silent icons Garbo sounded the way she looked; with a voice she was even more vivid than in silence. And so she alone maintained an unbroken career across the Great Divide represented by the arrival of the talking picture.

In outlining ways in which silent acting differs from the performance requirements of sound film, I don't meant to isolate the silents to the realm of the prehistoric or to overlook the substantial continuities between acting techniques on either side of the phenomenon of sound on film. Indeed, talking actors speak with body language and faces and eyes, and silent actors used their voices even if they were unheard. Throughout my discussion, examples drawn from the silents will intermingle freely with those from talking pictures.

The studio system dominated American filmmaking from the twenties more or less through the fifties, with the middle decades of the thirties and the forties now commonly referred to as the Golden Age of the classical Hollywood style. (Television and the 1948 court ruling that required studios to sell off the theatres in which they had shown their products helped to unravel the studio system.) Through their program of developing and promoting stars, the studios exerted a lasting impact on screen acting.

In the Golden Age of the studio era, the machinery of starmaking was more firmly in place than it is ever likely to be again, and each studio orchestrated the careers of its in-house stars. In the thirties, often with protests from the hard-worked actors, Warner Brothers maintained the careers of, among others, Bette Davis, James Cagney, Edward G. Robinson, Ruby Keeler, Dick Powell, Joan Blondell, Paul Muni, Errol Flynn, Olivia de Havilland, Humphrey Bogart; Twentieth Century Fox launched Will Rogers, Shirley Temple, Alice Faye, Henry Fonda, Tyrone Power, Loretta Young, Don Ameche; M-G-M promoted Joan Crawford, Greta Garbo, Spencer Tracy, Clark Gable, Jeanette MacDonald, Jean Harlow, James Stewart, Mickey Rooney, Judy Garland; RKO boosted Katharine Hepburn, Fred Astaire, Ginger Rogers, Cary Grant, Irene Dunne; Paramount helped to advance the careers of Mae West, the Marx Brothers, Maurice Chevalier, Marlene Dietrich, Claudette Colbert, Gary Cooper, W. C. Fields, Bing Crosby, Charles Laughton; Universal made stars of Boris Karloff, Bela Lugosi, Abbott and Costello, and Deanna Durbin; while a "minor" studio like Columbia gave career boosts to Jean Arthur, Barbara Stanwyck, James Stewart, Irene Dunne, and Gable and Colbert.

In the forties and fifties these stars, among others, were added to the studio payrolls: Betty Grable and Marilyn Monroe at Fox; Lana Turner, Elizabeth Taylor, Paul Newman, and Grace Kelly at M-G-M; Alan Ladd, Veronica Lake, William Holden, and Audrey Hepburn at Paramount; James Dean at Warner Brothers; Rita Hayworth and Kim Novak at Columbia. By the fifties, however, as the system began to be dismantled, a new star like Marlon Brando could avoid long-term contracts and a prolonged association with a particular studio. Throughout the decade, Brando worked at Warner Brothers, Columbia, M-G-M, Paramount, and Fox, setting a free-lance pattern that has continued to be the norm.

Major actors in the post-studio era from the sixties to the present—performers like Robert De Niro, Dustin Hoffman, Jane Fonda, Robert Redford, Meryl Streep, Jack Nicholson, Barbra Streisand—are more likely to sign contracts for particular projects rather than with a studio. Close ties between a star and a studio, like Eddie Murphy's with Paramount and Bette Midler's with Touchstone, are rare.

Since the sixties, studios have no longer had individual identities, whereas house style in the Golden Age was so sharply defined that it was possible to trace differences between the Marx Brothers at Paramount and at M-G-M; between Katharine Hepburn at RKO in the thirties and at M-G-M in the forties; between Joan Crawford at M-G-M in the thirties and at Warners in the forties; between Jeanette MacDonald's image at Paramount in the early thirties and in her later cycle with Nelson Eddy at M-G-M.

Tension between studios and stars has always been a part of the business of filmmaking. In the earliest period producers didn't even want their hired hands to have names. In 1919 Hollywood's leading stars, Douglas Fairbanks, Chaplin, and Mary Pickford, formed United Artists with D. W. Griffith in order to become their own producers, anticipating a trend of the post-studio era. Actors under regulation seven-year contracts, particularly those at Warners, where Bette Davis, James Cagney, and Olivia de Havilland waged landmark battles with their employers, often complained about being overworked, underpaid, and frustrated by their inability to choose roles.

But in a hazardous profession studios provided a security and continuity of exposure rarely achievable once actors became their own brokers. And in the matter of taste, or in judging their own capacities, stars on their own have seldom proved to be more astute than the studio front office. I don't want to fall into the haziness induced by nostalgia and claim that no latter-day actors are as talented as the stars of the Golden Age—that simply isn't true. And regardless of changes in the mode of production there will always be a pool of performers who know how to act on film. However, because of industry overhauls, the starmaking machinery isn't as systematic as in the "old days," and few post-sixties actors are seen as frequently or promoted as carefully as the contract players were.

The stars trained by the major studios in the thirties dominated movie acting for the next thirty years. Studios marketed actors as types, and the ones who graduated to star status became in a sense their own genres, wielding a potent influence on the stories as well as the look of their films. As defined by the studios, "star quality" can often be reduced to a quintessential characteristic—Bette Davis' willfulness, for instance—and in promoting a star, once the kernel of his or her personality was discovered, studios faced the challenge of providing variations on a theme: in how many ways, and in how many different kinds of settings, can the willful Davis heroine be presented?

As in the silent era, in which acting styles arose in response to the kinds of stories that silence and contemporary taste demanded, so in the generations of the sound film a connection can be made between the needs of genre and the formulation of acting types. If the silents needed (among others) slapstick clowns, swashbucklers, victimized heroines, and saucy flappers, the first decade of sound, for instance, called forth actors who could terrify (the horror film), be zany (screwball comedy) or "swell" (drawing-room comedy), sing and dance (musicals), talk tough (gangster stories), and suffer and fall in love (melodrama, the "woman's film"). The dominant style for early sound films was contemporary, rapid-fire, immediate, with actors like James Cagney, Edward G. Robinson, Joan Blondell, and Barbara Stanwyck impersonating molls and sharpshooters who spoke a slangy urban diction popular audiences could identify with.

The average, representative, idealized American; the rebel; the emperors and empresses of sex; the action heroes; ladies and gentlemen (the Hollywood and Vine version of New York's "400"); the entertainers (singers, dancers, comedians); the triumphant victims and sufferers—these are among the most persistent types generated by Hollywood storytelling, the types needed to construct and to maintain the basic movie myths. In the light of genre and type, the history of Hollywood acting constitutes an ongoing repertory company, with enduring, variably elastic categories to be filled by a vast rotating cast. New actors add to or subtract from the qualities that define a particular type, either by conforming to or countering tradition. A few stars successfully negotiate a change of type, or create a new mold. But by and large the typology established early in the sound era continues to dominate.

From the beginning, film actors have performed under the realist imperative, molding their work to the strong illusion of reality created by the medium itself. Realism, however, is still a style, the largest and perhaps most demanding of all performance modes, and no matter how real it may seem, movie acting depends on artistic heightening and selection, on skillful fakery.

"Realism" dates. Stars not only reflect cultural history, they are trapped in it: clothes, settings, narrative and moral conventions, styles of movement and speech, inevitably age and what once seemed modern and familiar to contemporary audiences gradually passes into a time warp. Screen acting thus offers historical markers in fashion and taste and values and in what it means to be human. Yet in looking at hundreds of performances from every period of Hollywood filmmaking, I've discovered that beneath the dated externals good acting endures. A strong performance leaps over time zones to stir us still.

Both literally and figuratively larger than life, screen actors have always had an intoxicating sway over their audiences. Representing more than the roles they play, they both embody and help to shape the values, the consciousness, the wishes and anxieties and fantasies, the ideals and fears, of the culture that pays to see them. The massive popularity of America's Sweetheart, Mary Pickford, or of Betty Grable's pinup girl or James Dean's tormented adolescent tells us as much about three different eras (America in the teens, during World War II, and in the mid-fifties) as about three different styles of movie acting. In tracing the outlines of communal desires, screen acting is always about more than acting.

Tools of the Trade

Watching: Acting as the Audience Sees It

AT THE MOVIES WE'RE ALONE IN THE DARK, SUSPENDED IN A SEMI-dream state as we look at moving images projected onto a screen. What we watch is what the camera has already looked at and recorded, and as it speaks to us it's our job to connect, respond to, and interpret a series of fragmented messages.

Actors are usually the primary focus of what the camera sees. If we factor in the looks that actors often throw at each other, then the screen performer is often the center of a triple gaze: the camera's, the spectator's, and a fellow player's. While the stage actor is of course looked at, looking within a play—the glance of one character at another—is not likely to command the attention editing gives it on screen; and in the theatre there is no mediating camera. The presence of the recording, glaring, probing camera transforms the actor into an object, a commodity to be scrutinized. And aren't film actors praised precisely for being photogenic, for having qualities of face and figure "the camera loves"? High cheekbones, large eyes, a Dick Tracy jaw, full lips, a noble nose, a dazzling smile, women's wasp waists and creamy complexions, men's broad shoulders and ruddy faces, all are attributes the camera embraces.

Film actors perform for the camera's invisible eye—not the same kind of audience the stage actor must play to. Regardless of who else is in the scene or watching them on the set, film actors act with and to the camera as they gauge how much, or more often how little, to give it. Sometimes the link between actor and camera is so intimate that co-workers during filming have felt excluded or puzzled because the actor facing the camera didn't seem to be doing any acting at all. During the filming of *The Prince and the Showgirl* (1957) Dame Sybil Thorndike, a stage actress, thought Marilyn Monroe's acting was so small and private that it could never register. When she saw the completed film, however, she realized that Monroe had known exactly what the camera needed. Gary Cooper was another star who often seemed blank to his co-workers on the set, yet in his best work the camera translates his apparent idleness into a strong screen presence.

I've been talking about the camera as if it had an identity and a psychology. If the camera is a "character," whom does it represent? For whom does it speak? Some feminist critics have argued that it represents a distinctly male heterosexual view, that of the traditionally male crew, the usually male camera operator following the instructions of the usually male director. Sexy stars like Monroe "make love" to the camera and thereby engage the male spectator in a make-believe ritual of seduction. But is the camera really gender-specific? That putative male crew who filmed Monroe also shot Valentino's heaving breast and Marlon Brando's muscular back. Rather than being exclusively heterosexual and male, isn't the camera remarkably ac/dc, capable of revealing the lure of male as well as female bodies, faces, eyes, lips, voices? Hollywood acting contains something for everyone, and isn't it in fact part of the creative artist's temperament (and I include cine-

Acting to and for the camera: Garbo on the set of *Queen Christina*, being coached by her director, Rouben Mamoulian (with pipe), for the last shot.

17

FROM LEFT
Watching: Tom Ewell appraises Marilyn Monroe in *The Seven Year Itch* (1955), Jean Peters eyes Marlon Brando in *Viva Zapata!* (1952), as the camera turns us into voyeurs who share the admiring gazes of the on-screen observers.

matographers along with writers and directors) to be able imaginatively to identify with perspectives and desires other than his or her own?

While it's possible to see the camera's penetrating gaze as phallic, as an invisible projection of maleness, it is also possible to see it as an ambisexual privileged observer. In the back-and-forth, angle/reverse-angle editing and the over-the-shoulder shots traditional in Hollywood, the camera affords us the best possible viewpoint, treating us in effect as lucky invisible witnesses. Often the camera discloses the scene as we would have wished to see it if we had been there.

Like the camera, the screen on which the image is shown is an aspect of moviegoing audiences usually take for granted. But also like the camera, the screen has an identity, a presence, that influences the actor's work and the way we receive it. Theorists have tended to describe the film screen in one of two ways: as either a mirror or a window. Watching the mirror-screen, audiences see versions of themselves; actors on the mirror-screen become substitutes for the spectator, idealized versions of representative American types like Gary Cooper, Spencer Tracy, Henry Fonda, John Wayne, Eddie Murphy, Woody Allen, Clara Bow, Jean Arthur, June Allyson, Judy Holliday, Barbra Streisand, Shelley Winters, Ellen Burstyn.

Looking "into" the mirror-screen, audiences thus see a made-up world that approximates their own shared reality. Peering "through" the window-screen, they see something different, a view into forbidden and "other" scenes that turns them into voyeurs or time-travelers. Although in Hollywood moviemaking some of these "other" scenes—fantasies, biblical and historical epics, tales of horror and the supernatural—are often acted as though they were examples of contemporary naturalism, a few performers on the window-screen like Garbo, Marlene Dietrich, Valentino, and Boris Karloff are distinctly different from real life, exotics who are not just like us.

Neat separation between the two screens as between the kinds of performers who fill them is of course not possible. Tinting realism with fantasy, Hollywood acting like Hollywood storytelling frequently blends the mirror with the window, and players like Bette Davis, Katharine Hepburn, Marlon Brando, Joan Crawford, and Humphrey Bogart straddle both screens simultaneously, being stranger than life while also embodying drives audiences can immediately recognize.

Both mirrors and windows "screen" us out; our participation in the on-screen world remains vicarious rather than actual. Encased within and behind the screen, actors act in a world apart—a separate place. Their voices may fill the theatre auditorium, but their images remain sealed within the frame. And consigned to an endless mechanical reproduction of their actions, they are both more and less than their own real-life selves, both more and less than the real people who sit in the dark watching their shadow play. Film actors are literally absent, yet they can move us even with a mere trace of themselves.

Unlike performances in the live theatre, film acting is frozen, a mechanical memory of what the camera recorded at the moment of filming. But if celluloid arrests actors it does not do the same to the audience. Spectator response to acting changes according to the size of the audience, the screen, and the theatre—what I call the exhibition effect.

In the twenties and thirties studios and theatre owners built a chain of movie palaces that constituted one of the glories of twentieth-century architecture. Most of the theatres were designed as combination vaudeville and film houses, and after the unexpectedly premature demise of vaudeville (the form was virtually extinct by the early thirties) the palaces continued on a films-only policy throughout Hollywood's Golden Age. With their vertical signs announcing the name of the theatre, their marquees iced with flickering neon, and their high, wide, and deep auditoriums, these palaces of entertainment dominated the streetscapes over which they hovered majestically. Blinking marquees beckoned customers with the promise of excitement within; entering a palace was to be immediately embraced in a world of make-believe that provided the ideal setting for watching movies.

Ornate, playful stage sets that offered a papier-mâché splendor, picture palaces were an architecture of fantasy. In the twenties Oriental, Arabian, Moorish, Egyptian, neoclassical, and French and Spanish baroque were popular exotic motifs; deco delights followed in the thirties. Atmospheric theatres, with stars twinkling overhead and clouds moving across the ceiling, and an assortment of turrets, balconies, minarets, and lighted windows along the sidewalls, created the impression of being in a grand Spanish courtyard or an Arabian bazaar. "We sell tickets to theatres, not to shows!" theatre owner S. J. ("Roxy") Rothafel announced proudly in 1930.

Part of the intoxication of seeing a movie at a picture palace was the sheer magnitude of the house, which could seat from 1,500 all the way up to 6,000. At a palace the actor as well as the spectator commanded a monumental space, one now available only in the handful of remaining palaces still showing movies. New York's Radio City Music Hall, the largest of them all, no longer shows films on a regular basis, but whenever they have had special screenings I have gone eagerly, as much to recapture a sense of what it was like to see movies in a great theatre as for the films themselves. Sitting in the center of the last row of the Hall's third mezzanine, I have a lordly bird's-eye view of the 6,000-seat, deco-sunburst auditorium. Once, from the Music Hall's vast screen, Judy Garland in *A Star Is Born* (1954), Lillian Gish in *The Wind* (1928), Garbo and Gilbert in *Flesh and the Devil* (1926), the entire cast of *Gone With the Wind* (1939), filled the house, performing with an impact attainable only on a large screen in a large theatre. When seen in the vast darkness of a luxurious movie palace, the work of all movie actors is given a jolt, the kind of dimension that helped turn Golden Age actors into legendary stars.

Over the last thirty years, as television has inflicted a permanent dent in the size of the moviegoing public, palaces have been gradually replaced by multiplexes. Anonymous shoeboxes, tunnels and shooting galleries with dinky screens and a complete absence of architectural flair, these mini-screening rooms disguised as theatres devalue movies and the ritual of going to see them. They are to movie exhibition what fast-food emporiums are to a gourmet restaurant; they're the theatrical equivalent of shopping malls, which is where they are usually located. Seeing films in them is little different from watching pictures at home on a videocassette recorder; indeed, "I'll wait to see [that new movie] on my VCR" is a common refrain. And since even big hits are usually available on video in a matter of months after their initial release, why bother to go out to the movies at all, when, in most cases, they aren't presented the way they used to be and deserve to be?

The Look

When Sarah Bernhardt, one of the great stars of the nineteenth-century theatre, filmed *Queen Elizabeth*, she had nothing to offer the movies—and, significantly, the medium had nothing to offer her. Released in 1912, Bernhardt's film of one of her stage hits was the first feature-length narrative shown in America, the first of Adolph Zukor's projected series of famous players in famous plays. True neither to its theatrical source nor to its new placement on celluloid, *Queen Elizabeth* was a star vehicle presented in a medium that had barely begun to learn how to make acting work at all.

ABOVE AND FOLLOWING PAGE
Remembrance of things past: moviegoing as it was, when large, luxurious, fancifully designed theatres provided an ideal environment in which to observe actors.

In 1912 Bernhardt was a stout matron with an amputated leg, a doughy face, and a large stomach, but even if she had been a half-century younger and in the full ripeness of her art, she would have been betrayed by her technique. When the queen has a thought, Bernhardt points to her head; when Elizabeth is pained, she grasps her heart. Imperious, she extends her arms wide, either vertically or horizontally; frustrated, she grips her head; terrified, she throws out her arms as if to ward off the devil. In the code she is using, borrowed from the traditions of late-nineteenth-century stage acting, each gesture and stance indicates a generalized emotion. Love, fear, rage, queenliness, are indicated with her hands and arms and with the line of her body rather than her eyes and facial reactions. Her overembellished, external style contains no trace of either the performer's or the character's inner life.

Even if Bernhardt's technique had been more realistic, however, she would have had no chance to make an impact. Acting on screen needs help from the camera and from the entire filmmaking apparatus, yet in *Queen Elizabeth* the immobile camera stares at the actress in a series of identically placed long shots. Surrounded by an entourage whose task in many scenes seems to be to assist Bernhardt to the nearest available chair, the star dominates only by the largeness of her gestures. When she waves her arms, she seems to be fighting for the kind of attention closeups provide.

21

In this early period closeups were avoided on the assumption that audiences, used to seeing an actor in full figure on the stage, might feel cheated by glimpses of parts of the actor's body, as if such fragmentation would be an assault on both the actor's person and the spectator's right to see. D. W. Griffith was the first film director fully to realize that partial views, pieces of the actor, are often more powerful than full-length shots. When (in *Intolerance*, 1916) Griffith inserted repeated closeups of Mae Marsh's hands twisting and knotting in feverish anxiety as her husband is tried for murder, he carried to an extreme degree ideas he had been working on since 1908 about how to film the work of the actor. The closeups of Marsh's hands forcibly demonstrated that guidelines for acting on screen could not be based on theatrical models.

Griffith's experiments with closeups pinpointed the difference between the artifice of stage acting (which is acting conceived in long shot) and the greater intimacy and naturalism possible on film. Closeups are the film actor's basic acting tool, the primary means by which the apparatus helps the actor to build a performance. The best movie performers are the ones who know what to do and what not to do when the camera moves in to explore their faces.

Knowing how to take a closeup, how to turn the prying eye of the camera into a co-creator, is the supreme test of screen actors' skills. How do actors command the space within the frame? How do they connect their own closeups to characters or objects outside the frame? How do they use closeups to deepen characterization through nonverbal means? How, in short, do accomplished screen performers employ closeups to woo both the camera and the audience? Although the following examples of actors who know how to seize the opportunities uniquely offered by the closeup are from different periods and cut across a number of genres, a basic motif links them: in silence or with the aid of dialogue, in high drama or slapstick, these actors demand our attention by the way they act with their eyes.

The pioneers of screen acting had to discard the theatrical tradition Sarah Bernhardt represented. They had to invent a new art form, a playing style that had no rules or precedents, and many of their intuitive responses supplied the foundations on which all later screen performance has been built. Closeups gave them particular acting challenges, and here's how some of the shrewdest silent players met them.

In *Cobra* (1925) Rudolph Valentino plays his usual male version of the femme fatale. "In scrapes or out of them, there was always something magnificent about the young Count Torriani," an opening title announces, followed by a closeup of Valentino smoldering as he sips a drink. In our first view of him the star peers offscreen with hooded eyes and a loaded look: what is he gazing at with such intensity? "Women and trouble... that is my inheritance," he explains to a friend.

Valentino's rapt offscreen gaze reappears throughout the film, compelling us to read the imprint of memory or desire in his eyes. In these closeups Valentino faces either slightly to the right or left of the lens, whether Count Torriani is contemplating another character, an object, even his fate, all located beyond the frame. Looking offscreen, Valentino projects his performance into the audience—the look into offscreen space, which Valentino helped to construct as part of the basic syntax of the film actor, continues to be one of the ways performers break through the flatness of the screen to play to and involve the spectator.

Like all good movie actors Valentino has his secrets, which he shares with us alone; in his closeups he often binds us to him as he divides the action into a kind of double focus. Always "on" when women are near, the count plays up to a rich lady who clearly finds him irresistibly attractive, but when she momentarily turns away from him, he shrugs, a gesture intended only for us. When the cobra (Nita Naldi) comes in for the kill, Valentino turns away demurely as she embraces him; as he faces away from her and toward the camera, he signals his turmoil and his gradual submission. Valentino thus plays two scenes at once: one with Naldi, the other for the camera.

The count's renunciation scene at the end is a virtuoso example of the actor's use of asides. Self-convicted as being unworthy of the love of Mary, a pure woman, the count puts on a mask of decadent bravado while in sidelong glances aimed only for us Valentino lets us in on his character's true feeling about relinquishing the "one pure, clean love" he has ever known. As he faces the camera and slowly exits from Mary's office, Valentino's eyes grow moist as the count contemplates an arid future. The actor's premeditated, statuesque style is dated, but his sense of how to use his closeups to reveal thought and inner conflict, to speak privately to the audience, to expose his character's duplicity, and through his penetrating offscreen glances to extend his acting space beyond the frame remains an essential part of the screen actor's arsenal.

OPPOSITE, FROM LEFT TO RIGHT, TOP TO BOTTOM
Mayfair Theatre, Asbury Park, New Jersey, 1930; Avalon Theatre, Catalina Island, California, 1929; Aztec Theatre, San Antonio, Texas, c. 1927; Russell Theatre, Maysville, Kentucky, 1930; Grauman's Egyptian Theatre, Hollywood, California, 1924; Grauman's Chinese Theatre, Hollywood, California, c. 1927.

Lillian Gish's costar in *The Wind* is an offscreen sound. In the film's symbolic scheme the wind is nature unleashed, sex on a rampage, life in all its potential stark terror, which Gish's innocent character needs to confront before she can become truly womanly. In the closeups that punctuate the action Gish stares offscreen, wide-eyed with fear, as the wind howls with increasing ferocity outside the cabin in which her character is isolated. Her blazing eyes, cocked head, and twisted posture conjure an image of the wind as a personal threat: the Furies in relentless pursuit. At the height of the storm she rolls her eyes and swoons as a rapist pounds on the door. After she shoots her attacker she cowers on her bed trying to shut out the wind's incessant screech.

In a silent film Gish's offscreen looks make us both see and hear her adversaries, the desolate sand and the wind that hurls it against the cabin. Looking just to the right or left of the eye of the camera, Gish thrusts her character's fear out into the audience as she enfolds us in her reactions to offscreen sounds.

In their failed talking film of *The Taming of the Shrew* (1929) Douglas Fairbanks and Mary Pickford remain sly manipulators of the offscreen look. When they get the chance to use it, they command the camera with just as much confidence as in their silent-movie heyday, upstaging Shakespeare in the silent splendor of their mime. Their first telling moment occurs on their wedding day when Petruchio arrives late, ill-dressed and eating an apple. As he's taunting the shrew, he shoots asides to us to let us know he's just putting on an act. Kate narrows her eyes, sending daggers to her offscreen tormentor. In their closeups, isolated within the frame, the two stars control the camera with a bravura that dissipates when they start to talk.

After the wedding Petruchio puts on a show of being a domestic tyrant who beats his servants, throws tantrums, and prevents his new wife from eating the meal that lies temptingly before her on the groaning table. After each of his outbursts Fairbanks looks away from the scene to smile to himself as he includes us in his game. Those smiles, from the actor with the most captivating grin in American movies, are irresistible, a display of screen presence that overrides Fairbanks' discomfort with Shakespeare.

OPPOSITE
Not to be the Hollywood Style:
Sarah Bernhardt in *Queen Elizabeth* (1912), emoting in a stylized
nineteenth-century theatrical tradition too grandiose for the requirements of the new narrative
medium.

LEFT
Looking beyond the picture
frame, in Rembrandt's *Portrait of
a Lady with an Ostrich-Feather Fan*
(c. 1660; National Gallery of Art;
Widener Collection). Films add
movement and time to a visual
convention of portrait painting.

Pickford charms us too, when she plays to us in the next scene after Kate has overheard Petruchio confessing to his dog that he has been putting on an act. Now, when he tries to prevent her from sleeping, as he had earlier kept her from eating, she puts on a show of docility while answering his tirades with mute asides to the camera that express Kate's true feelings of anger and resentment. Pickford recites the climactic speech of wifely submission in a childlike, singsong rhythm. And then, finished talking, she throws a wink to her offscreen sister Bianca, letting her and of course us know that she has been enacting a charade, that in fact this shrew has decidedly not been tamed. It's an enchanting grace note, Pickford in closeup using her large, expressive eyes to speak in the language of screen acting she had helped to originate. In a flash the actress subverts the spoken text and her own uncertain rendition of it to claim the last word for mime.

Bette Davis in *Dark Victory* (1939), Charlton Heston in *Ben-Hur* (1959), and Peter O'Toole in *Lawrence of Arabia* (1962) provide prime examples of how charged, wordless offscreen looks function in talking pictures. In each case the look is the visual center of the performance and also carries the story forward. In these moments of heightened intimacy between player and camera, actors in effect become coauthors.

Bette Davis' strongest performances are permeated with offscreen looks in which the actress, her large eyes locked onto a person or object or filled with anger or memory, seizes the frame. In *Dark Victory* the story of her character's eyes is actually the dramatic focus, and all of the film's big moments depend on Davis' offscreen gazes. Judith Tra-herne (Davis) suffers from a mysterious incurable disease that begins with failing vision. "I'm young and well and you can't make an invalid out of me," she warns the doctor she has been reluctant to visit. But then her sight momentarily blurs and as she looks offscreen Davis subdues her usual voltage—her look doesn't reach out as far into the audience as it normally does. Trying to cover her loss of sight, she lights a match, then has trouble bringing it up to the cigarette in her mouth. When the doctor cuts through her facade to tell her the truth about her condition, she lowers her head, averting her eyes from him and from us.

Five masters of the offscreen gaze: Rudolph Valentino playing to the audience as he resists Nita Naldi in *Cobra* (1925); Lillian Gish reacting to the sound of the gale in *The Wind* (1928); Mary Pickford, more comfortable looking than speaking, in *The Taming of the Shrew* (1929); Marlon Brando edgily glancing away from Eva Marie Saint in *On the Waterfront* (1954); Bette Davis transfixed by thoughts of a bleak future in *Dark Victory* (1939). The throw of their concentrated eye movements seizes space within the frame and also projects the drama out to the audience.

After she has been told that an operation is required, she stares at her reflection in a mirror: the look doubled, the object of its own gaze, and kept for once within the frame. After the operation, when she discovers the truth in her doctor's file (the operation was a failure), she stands still and looks offscreen into a dark future. Her gaze into the unknown goes even deeper when at a party she listens to a song, "Give Me Time," as the camera moves in to isolate her in a tight closeup as her hooded eyes are riveted to a terrifying elsewhere. In the finale her vision begins to fade just as her husband is about to leave for a conference where he is to be honored. She sends him off, pretending to see, but after he leaves, her eyes empty. "I want to be left alone," she tells her best friend, and reclining on her bed with only the camera to see her and no longer needing to conceal what is happening to her, she looks off one last time as we see her vision noticeably dim.

At key points throughout *Ben-Hur*, the hero (Charlton Heston) is illuminated by his visions of Christ, present on screen only in shadow, or as a figure seen from the back, or a hand extending into the frame. We see Christ exclusively through the hero's eyes. In chains in a kneeling position, for example, Ben-Hur glances up as he receives a cup of water. What he sees fills his eyes with light: the look *in excelsis*.

In *Lawrence of Arabia* Peter O'Toole uses offscreen looks as a means of completing Robert Bolt's cryptic screenplay. These silent offscreen communions, the heart of O'Toole's performance, beckon us into the turbulent inner life of the possessed antihero. Staring off into the desert, Lawrence seems to divine his destiny. After he has led a massacre against the Turks, he gazes off, a bloodied knife held in his upraised hand, horrified by the violence he has instigated. At the end, leaving Arabia at his own request,

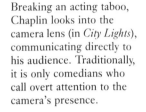

Breaking an acting taboo, Chaplin looks into the camera lens (in *City Lights*), communicating directly to his audience. Traditionally, it is only comedians who call overt attention to the camera's presence.

A performer who did not befriend the camera: Broadway entertainer Al Jolson needed a big stage and a full house he could work up into a frenzy. His physical discomfort before the prying, closeup camera is apparent in this still from *The Jazz Singer* (1927).

he sits in a car gazing offscreen as he seems to be looking within to weigh the magnitude of his failure. At each of the story's major passages, then, O'Toole deepens his characterization with offscreen looks that take us inside Lawrence's thoughts to reveal moments of prophecy, self-accusation, and moral uncertainty.

As he did with other aspects of screen acting, Marlon Brando supplied his own inflections to the offscreen look. In *On the Waterfront* his character repeatedly looks away from a scene and into offscreen space. Like touching his ear, rubbing his chin, chewing gum, opening his jacket and scratching himself, Terry's furtive sidelong glances are one of the tics that give the character a vibrant physical life. Brando's offscreen look, unlike those of the other actors mentioned, is a fleeting, seemingly improvised gesture that has multiple uses. First it is simply a way of alleviating the character's agitation, a means of breaking up the tension in a scene: Terry's darting eyes aren't looking at an offscreen object or person, they are merely looking *away* from his partner. (Since *Waterfront*, shifty sidelong looks and roving eyes that don't seem to be seeing anything have become a common device for naturalistic actors.) The jumpy looks off scattered through the performance complement the character's fractured speech patterns, the stammerings, backtrackings, repetitions, that signal Terry's discomfort with words and with his own inability to choose the right ones.

The real action in the film is an inner one as Terry comes to realize how he has been used by the union bosses, and for key moments in the character's growing self-awareness Brando finds another new use for the offscreen look. Traditionally actors use the look to suggest what their characters already know; Brando's looks off signal his character's confusion, his lack of focus. Brando often looks off *just before* Terry has a moment of realization. The action is a private moment as the character tries to collect his scattered thoughts; when his eyes center firmly within the frame, Terry is ready to act. In the taxi scene, when his brother pulls a gun on him Terry's eyes momentarily dart to someplace offscreen—what moment from their past does he see?—before he gently pushes Charlie's gun away. Now, in full understanding, Terry's eyes face front; he doesn't have to look away now and he begins to speak in a voice that's as steady and straight ahead as his glance.

As he boxes his larger-than-life-sized opponent, the Tramp (Chaplin in *City Lights*) shoots an occasional glance directly into the eye of the camera. It's the kind of direct look, almost subliminally quick and flashing with wit and aliveness, that Chaplin had been aiming into the lens since the beginning of his career—a great film actor's intuitive way of conquering a machine and of speaking directly through it to his audience.

In eyeing the camera, Chaplin was breaking the visual barrier erected from the origins of acting on film: the prohibition against looking into the lens is a way of preserving an illusion of the camera's invisibility as well as the actor's reality. To look into the camera is after all to give the show away, to tell the viewers that what they are watching is indeed a performance: playacting. Chaplin violates the unwritten rule, and wins. His actor's bravado is a gesture of high-wire daring that compels rather than collapses credibility. When he looks at us from the ring, he's telling us he's in trouble, asking for our sympathy, and assuring us that he's going to make it.

Except for rare stunts—Laurence Olivier as *Richard III* (1955), for instance, courting the eye of the camera as he summons us as conspirators in his Machiavellian schemes—only comedians and Douglas Fairbanks, who winks into the camera, employ direct address. Groucho Marx, Bob Hope, Woody Allen, use the camera at times as an audience as they break through the screen to offer asides, whisper confidences, or deliver stand-up routines. There's a charming moment in *Ferris Bueller's Day Off* (1986) when Matthew Broderick looks directly into the lens to express comic frustration. His "comment" removes us momentarily from the action while at the same time winning us over: just like Chaplin.

When in *Taxi Driver* (1976) the demented hero Travis Bickle (Robert De Niro) asks a question of an imaginary enemy—"Are you talkin' to me?"—the actor places his offscreen look daringly close to the camera's eye. "Are you talkin' to me?" Travis repeats as his eyes lock with the presumably accusatory eyes of his phantom adversary. Then Bickle breaks contact as he glances distractedly off to the side, casing his barricaded apartment. The scene is set up to make us wonder if De Niro will challenge the rules by looking directly at us, thereby making us the objects of his character's growing homicidal rage. Yet in narrowly missing the lens, the actor conforms to the Hollywood tradition in which ripping the realist illusion is permitted only for comics.

Filling the offscreen look is a crucial test of craft. Here are two actors who failed it. The first star of talkies, stage star Al Jolson needed a big performing space—nothing less than a full stage—and a large, responsive audience to grab hold of. When only the camera was there to reflect his glory, he was dispossessed. In *The Singing Fool* (1928), a part-talkie that reprised the maudlin self-glorification of *The Jazz Singer,* Jolson misplays a scene that a good film actor would have hit a home run with. When his character learns that his son has died, the camera moves in for a closeup, and what does Jolson do? Instead of quietly absorbing the emotion of the scene, he disperses his energy by randomly roving his eyes from side to side as if he's trying to escape the camera's gaze. Instead of grief, he projects shiftiness.

In his musical numbers as well, Jolson needs room. When he sings "There's a Rainbow Round My Shoulder," in what the story presents as a triumphant onstage performance, Jolson doesn't adjust his style for the too-close camera. Rotating his arms and legs as well as his eyes, he exudes far more than he has to. Only in the finale, when in long shot he sings "Sonny Boy" in his trademark black-face makeup and gives full vent to the tear in his voice, does his fabled showmanship light up on screen.

Jolson never relaxed or became still or indrawn enough to make his closeups work. If the object of his offscreen look was only a film crew rather than a full house at the Winter Garden Theatre he could whip up into a frenzy, he was thrown. Other stars fail the look test because they arrive without inner resources. For example, here is Kim Novak in a big star vehicle, *Picnic* (1955), dancing with a sexy wanderer (William Holden). When the object of her offscreen gaze is Holden, she is passably steamy. But the real challenge comes in the next scene when she's alone in the frame and standing off by herself and has to register what the dance has meant to her wistful small-town character. As Novak moves into position for the offscreen look on which the rest of the action pivots, lights from the picnic twinkle in the distance, giving her a halo, and the image is blurred to connote a misty romanticism. What do we get? A gaze emptied of any readable content: Kim Novak, a beauty queen as movie star, posed for the camera, creamy of complexion, full of figure, and dead of eye.

Acting in Film Time

In tight closeups actors are in charge: the throw of their offscreen looks binds them to the audience. But after the shot is over, actors cede control of their performances to the machinery of filmmaking. Unlike stage actors, who typically build their performances in long, unbroken arcs, screen players act in pieces, in fits and starts that are assembled after the fact into an illusion of wholeness. And to satisfy the condensations of film time, the actors' originally fragmented performances are subject to further ruptures: snipped, scissored, punctured, their work is heavily edited as it is shaped by others.

In the classical Hollywood style the actor's work is cut to the measure of simple continuity or "invisible" editing, which through angle/reverse-angle shots, eyeline match, and alternating over-the-shoulder shots sustains the impression that consecutive images of talking heads are seamlessly linked. The back-and-forth movement of continuity cutting strokes audience desire to see around the action, without breaking an illusion that the time and space of the scene remain intact. This is the traditional editing style we're so used to that we don't—we aren't meant to—pay any attention to it.

But editing the actor's work isn't always this low-key. Sometimes it can significantly alter a performance, changing its rhythm or intention or enhancing it through suggestion. Whether declamatory or invisible, the sleight-of-hand of editing stitches actors into the world of the film as it underlines their responses to a character or object or event that does not appear in the same frame and that may not even have been present during filming. Editing converts the actor's work into a series of reactions.

In Russia in the twenties, at the height of the montage fever that swept through Soviet film schools, a young director named Lev Kuleshov conducted a test that reveals the possible deceptions of the edited image. Telling his actor to empty his face of any expression, Kuleshov filmed a prolonged closeup of Ivan Moskvin, a celebrated actor from the Moscow Art Theatre, looking offscreen. At a separate time and place Kuleshov shot three additional closeups, of a plate of soup, a young girl skipping rope, and a coffin. When he intercut these images with the actor's blank face, audiences unaware of the circumstances of the filming supposedly praised Moskvin's subtle range as he communicated hunger (face and soup), grandfatherly joy (face and young girl), and grief (face and coffin). Kuleshov's editing bound the actor to three objects he never actually saw and through simple succession "framed" spectators into seeing things.

Kuleshov's experiment highlights the fact that an actor's performance is filmed in isolated fragments, that all screen acting is subject to the codes of editing, and that editing can create the illusion that the actor is emoting when in fact, like Moskvin, he is simply having his picture taken.

For his own contemporary full-length experiments in montage, Sergei Eisenstein claimed that he did not need professional actors. When he made *Battleship Potemkin* (1925) and *Ten Days That Shook the World* (1927) he hired mostly nonactors who looked the part—a casting method Eisenstein called typage. And indeed in his films the drama is not carried by the actors, who are reduced to bit players propelled by the force of historical events. Movement within and between shots, rapid shifts in the direction of movement from shot to shot, the counterpoint between long shot and closeup and between horizontal and vertiginous angles—these visual collisions produced by Eisenstein's terse virtuoso cutting by and large "act" the stories.

If in the twenties Soviet filmmakers gave priority to montage over acting, in the American narrative tradition editing has rarely been allowed to replace the work of the actor. Nonetheless, simplified to angle/reverse-angle cutting, the Kuleshov approach is a common Hollywood procedure and one, moreover, that doesn't substitute for the actor's need to act but is often a steep test of the actor's mettle. Unlike Moskvin, actors in Hollywood movies can't do "nothing" but must often act and react on a dime, in the space of a glance or a blink.

James Stewart's performance in *Rear Window* (1954) is as pure an example of Kuleshovian acting as I know of in American films. Stewart plays a man with time on his hands—a broken leg has confined him to a wheelchair in his courtyard apartment. As a photojournalist who specializes in scenes of catastrophe, Jeffries (Stewart) is a professional observer who in his enforced idleness closely monitors the comings and goings of his rear-window neighbors. When he thinks he has discovered an act of violence in one of the windows across the way—he suspects a man of having killed his nagging invalid wife—he becomes a determined sleuth.

Restricted to his apartment, and separated from the murder scene by a courtyard, he must conduct his investigation in long shot. We virtually never see more than the character does, and so his reactions cue our own. In closeups, Stewart responds to what he sees through his window: he reacts to newlyweds with a slow smile; for a lonely spinster whom he names Miss Lonelyhearts he has a look of sorrow; the gyrations of a nubile dancer, Miss Torso, produce a sly smile of sexual pleasure; while tracking the activities of the man he suspects is a murderer prompts a range of responses from initial neutral interest, to surprise, anxiety, glee, and ultimately fear.

The heart of Stewart's performance and of the film is in these reaction shots as, isolated in his own frame, the actor scrutinizes the world beyond his window. In what order were the closeups filmed, and how much of what he is responding to did Stewart actually see at the time of filming? On their own, detached from their sequence in the master plan of the film's director, Alfred Hitchcock, Stewart's responses would be inexpressive; they acquire dramatic meaning only through being edited into an image sequence. Indeed, if Hitchcock had been a dadaist, he could easily have dismantled his actor's performance, making of those subtle smiles, widened eyes, parted lips, increasingly alert and alarmed gazes, a shadow play of dotty incoherence. The acting challenge is enormous, though with

his customary skill Stewart makes it look effortless, as in such close quarters it has to be; acting in fragments and on his own, Stewart is specific and low-key—he acts in a style that matches the "invisible" editing.

In *Rear Window*, as in most screen acting, drama becomes articulate in the relations between shots—the film is really as much about how film performances are constructed as it is often said to be about moviegoing itself, with Jeffries' desire to see and hear his neighbors' stories a reflection of our own voyeurism in front of the screen. The way Stewart's performance depends on editing is extreme but nonetheless typical. Film actors often have to act in closeup, within a frame that separates them from whomever or whatever they are responding to. Often the object of their gaze is not actually present. For a crucial closeup in the taxi scene in *On the Waterfront*, for instance, Rod Steiger had to play to Elia Kazan, the film's director, sitting in for Marlon Brando, at that moment at his therapist's office. For a key scene in *Close Encounters of the Third Kind* (1977) the director, Steven Spielberg, needed a child actor (Cary Guffey) to react to a spaceship landing in the field outside his house. Since there was no spaceship on the set (special effects were added at a later point), Spielberg brought in a clown to entertain the child and to get the reaction he wanted, a laugh of wonderstruck, bubbling delight. (Like *Rear Window*, *Close Encounters* is a film about looking, with the observers often separated from the object of their curiosity,

ABOVE AND OPPOSITE
Acting in closeup: James Stewart in *Rear Window* (1954), responding to the actions of a character (Raymond Burr as a possible killer) across a courtyard. Reacting to a character, an object, or an action not present within the frame and perhaps not even on the set during filming is a frequent screen-acting challenge.

a procedure that heightens the act of watching and mirrors the audience's own drive to see.)

All screen acting is steeped in the fragmentations and disruptions of film time. How a performance is edited—whether it is frequently interrupted, as in *Rear Window,* or allowed to unfurl in longer sweeps of unbroken time—places different demands on the actor. Acting in long takes, which approximates the challenge of stage performance, requires sustained force, while acting in short takes requires absolute precision, for the performer has to be saturated in the moment and charged with the proper response. Unlike stage players, film actors have more than one chance to get it right, and if numerous retakes don't yield a winning shot, editing can sometimes cover the actor. Acting inadequacy is easier to disguise the shorter the shot.

"Short-take" acting is the primary mode of the present, as it was of much of the mature silent films. "Long-take" performances dominated the first two decades of talking pictures. The shifting pattern is closely linked to the place of the spoken word on film. "I like the speech in the old films," I overheard a patron comment as he emerged from a showing of *Freud* (1962) at a New York revival house. What this college-aged filmgoer in the late eighties seemed to notice and to enjoy about the "old" film was the mere presence of a significant amount of dialogue. The "speech" in *Freud* may not be prizewinning but the characters do talk more than most characters in contemporary films, and to listen to *Freud* required a level of concentration the filmgoer clearly found unexpected.

In the "old" films, as opposed to the leaner dialogue tradition of the last twenty-five years, characters had more to say and the films allowed them the time to say it as dialogue scenes were typically shot with long takes and a sedentary camera. From the time that television began to provide viewers with the daily experience of processing words and images projected from a screen, the pace of film narrative has quickened and the quantity of dialogue has diminished. Exposed to ever-speedier commercials and the frenetic fragmentation of MTV videos, audiences today get the point faster than ever. Quite unlike the studio era tradition, in which audiences were expected to be and often were seduced by dialogue, films since the sixties rarely stand still in the presence of the word.

If in the *ancien régime* actors often delivered passages of sustained dialogue in front of a stationary camera, today's actors are more likely to speak in terse phrases popped into a jumpy, fractured time sequence. Here are three masters of screen acting—Barbara Stanwyck and Henry Fonda in *The Lady Eve* (1941) and Meryl Streep in *A Cry in the Dark* (1988)—in performances that exemplify the demands of "long-take" and "short-take" acting.

In *The Lady Eve* (written and directed by Preston Sturges) Stanwyck plays a sophisticated con artist traveling on a cruise ship with her equally slippery father. As soon as she spots a rich rube who's been up the Amazon for a year (Fonda), she's determined to snare him. They meet when she trips him as he walks by her table. He falls for her, literally and figuratively, and takes her to his stateroom, where he shows her a snake he collected on his expedition upriver; she runs screaming back to her own room. In the next scene, the one I want to pause over—a long-take medium closeup with the camera remaining in place, observing—Stanwyck proceeds to seduce her quarry, nuzzling his face and purring into his ear. As she rubs her face against his, her voice growing ever cozier and more intimate, Fonda melts; if he were standing, the effect she's having on him would buckle his knees. "I'll be able to sleep now," she says, becalmed, her fright over the snake forgotten. "I can't say the same," he whispers faintly. This is a seduction scene conducted entirely in words, and through the power of the actors' imaginations. Their presence and their colliding voices—Stanwyck's Brooklyn accent brushes tellingly against Fonda's Midwestern prairie drawl as they deliver Sturges' spiced dialogue—command the still, spying camera.

Performing in a radically different handling of film time, Streep as a lower-middle-class Australian housewife accused of killing her infant daughter doesn't have a single sustained scene or speech. Like the film itself, the performance is presented in disjointed fragments. Unlike Preston Sturges' clean, classical style, Fred Schepisi's direction is hyperactive, with rapid alternations between long shots and closeups and a dense sound track that often deliberately muffles dialogue. The film's terse, modern syntax—snatches of dialogue played off against layered on-screen and offscreen sounds and restless intercutting—places Streep within the action as a participant rather than a star. Typical of the contemporary style, Streep works in quick brushstrokes. We read her acting the way we read a pointillist painting, connecting the separate dots to form a coherent, integrated image. In *The Lady Eve,* as if bewitched by the actors, time seems to stand still; in *A Cry in the Dark* the star is caught up in the temporal spin.

Cues for Passion

Film acting is, of course, more than a series of closeups. To widen the scope, let's consider the ways in which elements of film style enhance and sometimes undermine the actor's work. How can the powerful sound and light show, the subtle manipulation of space and time, within which movie acting is framed variously invigorate or camouflage the performer's contribution? Are the following scenes, for instance—each an example of celebrated Hollywood craftsmanship and similar in effect to Lana Turner's famous car scene in *The Bad and the Beautiful*—moments of great acting or of great filmmaking?

Faced with the doom of her family and their land, Scarlett O'Hara (Vivien Leigh) goes up to a hill overlooking Tara and, digging her hands into the earth that her father has taught her to cherish, cries out, "As God is my witness, I will never be hungry again!" And then, as she repeats her vow, the camera cranes up to a high-angle long shot in which Scarlett is silhouetted against a perfervid orange-tinted studio sky, a lone figure balanced against a stark tree with Tara looming in shadowed deep focus as Max Steiner's music pours over the image in swelling crescendo. The lighting, the camerawork, the music, the placement of the scene at the climax of the thrilling first act of *Gone With the Wind*—this is surefire filmmaking, but how much does the actress herself contribute to the scene? How much does she need to? It may be sacrilege to say so, but I've always felt that in her delivery of these charged lines Leigh's voice doesn't vibrate enough and her body doesn't quiver enough—she seems to me a little too poised considering the high emotion of the moment. At any rate, the "film" at this moment carries her.

"Ladies and gentlemen, this is Mrs. Norman Maine," Judy Garland (in *A Star Is Born*, 1954) announces from the stage of the Shrine Auditorium as the camera moves up, up, and away (the film sneakily cuts from the real Shrine to a studio process shot) over the heads of the wildly applauding on-film audience to an extreme high-angle overhead shot that gives the theatre the dimensions of the Babylonian forecourt in Griffith's *Intolerance*. Garland's trembling voice and tensed posture convey her character's inner rumbling as Vicki Lester pays public tribute to her dead husband, whose once-bustling career her own has eclipsed. But even if Garland didn't act the scene as truly as she does, wouldn't it still play, given the heroic camera movement, the stirring exit music, and that on-screen audience whose responsiveness is a summons for our own?

In deep focus and surrounded by inky blackness, Charles Foster Kane (Orson Welles in *Citizen Kane*), a newspaper tycoon desolated by the departure of his second wife, stands with his head bowed and his body slumped in a narrow doorframe that seems to squeeze his voluminous figure. In the following scene Kane walks dejectedly in front of a mirror that breaks up his image into an infinite regressive series. In these overloaded compositions, lighting, space, a doorway, and a mirrored maze "perform" as much as the slumped-over actor.

The film "acts": composition, color, lighting, and Max Steiner's lush score enhance Vivien Leigh's performance in this climactic moment from *Gone With the Wind* (1939).

These scenes from *Gone With the Wind, A Star Is Born,* and *Citizen Kane* are extreme cases, but film acting is frequently encrusted with similar cues for representing the actor's and evoking the spectator's emotions. Angles, lighting, music, all the bric-a-brac of the filmmaker's mise-en-scène, collaborate with and sometimes steal the show from the actor. When the sound and image speak as powerfully as in the previous examples, when the frame is so dense with signification, how much acting is required? To what extent is the actor dependent on his or her own resources? To what extent is he or she required to function as a kind of supermodel, a figure in the filmmaker's erector set around whom the impact of the scene is designed?

In the rhetorical high points of these landmark movies, the actors are placed within highly controlled environments typical of the studio era, when most films were shot on sound stages and even films shot on location had studio-made segments. The world created within the studio is a protected place. In the studio, filmmakers could mold light and space for dramatic emphasis—the reality outside the studio wasn't so much copied as it was shaded and interpreted according to the needs of the story. Here are two representative scenes in which studio lighting and settings enhance acting.

About a quarter of the way through their cross-country journey, a journalist (Clark Gable) and a runaway heiress (Claudette Colbert), in Frank Capra's beloved screwball comedy *It Happened One Night* (1934), spend the night in a field. Up to this point, despite a mutual attraction we can spot at once, they have squabbled and complained about each other. But now their attitudes begin to change as the film itself moves into a new mode. Although much of the movie has been shot on location, giving it an almost documentary texture, that of a road picture about backwoods Depression America, here the story moves into a closed-off place, a not-real studio world that glows with romantic backlighting. In silhouette against a studio night sky and a studio hay field, with glinting lights bouncing off hair and bodies, the actors are bathed in a romantic haze as they speak their lines in a seductive whisper. The fabricated studio quality is quintessential Old Hollywood: it's in scenes like this that the filmmaking machinery lifts actors beyond themselves (and us) into a world apart, a world in which lighting and space, the "earth" and the "sky," are made to reflect what the characters are feeling. This is Hollywood expressionism, in which reality is remade as a frame for stars.

Settings charged with symbolism memorably boost Henry Fonda's performance in John Ford's *Young Mr. Lincoln* (1939). Following a courtroom victory, the young lawyer enters a studio-made hallway which, photographed in deep focus with Lincoln's shadow thrown across it, looks like the corridor of Destiny. After Lincoln converses briefly with

CLOCKWISE FROM LEFT
Creating worlds for actors to act in: setting up shots for *Dr. Jekyll and Mr. Hyde* (1932) and *You Only Live Once* (1937); the created world as it appears on screen in *You Only Live Once,* with Henry Fonda and Sylvia Sidney.

Studio lighting often lifts actors into a separate realm, a world upholstered expressly for movie stars: Clark Gable and Claudette Colbert in *It Happened One Night* (1934).

Mary Todd and Stephen Douglas, two characters who will have prominent roles in his future, a door at the end of the hallway opens, washing Lincoln in a dazzling light as he goes out to face the crowd assembled to cheer him. He says good-bye to the Clay family, whom he has defended, then stands facing a lowering studio-made sky before announcing that he will walk up to the top of the hill. Looking off into the light streaming out of the clouds, he seems to confront history. As his solitary silhouetted figure moves in long shot up to the rise of the hill, storm clouds break.

In these scenes studio craftsmanship takes over the work of the actors and completes it, turning Fonda's lawyer into a Man of Destiny, endowing the new lovers in *It Happened One Night* with an irresistible charm. Rather than simply recording acting, these representative samples of studio artifice powerfully help to shape it. If by and large the studio look is a bygone convention—contemporary audiences want the real thing, and scenes that may actually be filmed in studio conditions are made to look as real as possible—it was the ideal frame in which to present such stylized Hollywood genres as musicals, horror stories, and *noir* thrillers.

"Venice" in *Top Hat* (1935) is a Big White Set that makes no pretense of capturing the real city. The film's "Venice" is a vast stage on which Astaire and Rogers can dance; it's an airy, fanciful environment that's just the right cradle for the film's light-comedy story. In *film noir*, as in musicals, actors are encased in a sealed-off mise-en-scène, a dark rather than light world that groans with looming shadows and with banisters, windows, and mirrors that create claustrophobic frames within the frame. The intensities of chiaroscuro lighting suggest an inner as well as an outer darkness; light and space rumble with sinister portents as they reflect the characters' guilt and paranoia. In *Double Indemnity* (1944) Fred MacMurray and Barbara Stanwyck, in a fatal rendezvous, shoot each other in

a house of tomblike darkness while the high-key lighting gives their faces an eerie, masked quality. A victim awaiting his executioners in *The Killers* (1946), Burt Lancaster hovers in the inky shadows of a dingy rented room. As crazed silent star Norma Desmond, Gloria Swanson cowers like a black widow in the cobwebbed light of her Gothic mansion in *Sunset Boulevard* (1950). On the run, a con artist at the end of his rope, Richard Widmark in *Night and the City* (1950) emerges out of the darkness of a real London alleyway that Jules Dassin has transformed into a studio-like *noir* maze into the glare of a spotlight that makes him look like a trapped animal.

Even in stories set closer to home than a *noir* nightmare, a horror fantasy, or a musical that takes place over the rainbow, the "reality" created within the studio is typically manicured, conventionalized, merely partial. "New York" in many Golden Age films is manifestly *not* the real thing but a backdrop of painted skyscrapers seen through a window. Homes in screwball comedies like *My Man Godfrey* (1936) and *Holiday* (1938) look like mausoleums; they're dwellings of the rich made to order to satisfy the fantasies of Depression audiences. Even modest typical homes, like the one that *Mildred Pierce* (1945) lives in at the beginning of her rise to riches, have a slightly artificial veneer. Like studio-made city streets, they're too clean to be true.

The studio look both embraced and promoted the acting conventions of the movie-star tradition, which has dominated Hollywood filmmaking. Studio sets mirror the distance from reality of shimmering stars. Together sets and acting in many Golden Age

Shot composition tells us that the figure on horseback is a Man of Destiny: Henry Fonda as *Young Mr. Lincoln* (1939), riding into legend.

films double the same message: that movies after all are only imitations of life.

Most of the time in studio filmmaking, performance and background are made for each other. But sometimes studio artifice—sets that look like sets, rear-screen projections behind the foreground figures, ragged shifts between studio and location textures that give the film a visual schizophrenia—can betray actors trying to act truthfully, or who should be trying to act truthfully.

Consider the case of *The Sea of Grass* (1947) with Spencer Tracy and Katharine Hepburn unhappily directed by Elia Kazan. The story requires location shooting; it needs the look and the feel of the land, the sea of grass, which dominates the characters' lives. But the land is real only in location shots periodically inserted into the action—the stars themselves are never actually on the land. When, early on, Tracy introduces his new city wife (Hepburn) to his land, the actor and his sea of grass never appear in the same shot. When she's riding on a wagon with the land projected onto a screen behind her, Hepburn's hair remains rigidly in place. Coming inside from a raging snowstorm, Tracy arrives in immaculate condition, miraculously untouched by the harsh weather. The film keeps reminding us that the actors are cut off from the real outdoors where the story is set, that they are on a Culver City back lot pretending to be on the plains. Occupying a realm of their own, a world unto themselves, was the recipe for some of Tracy and Hepburn's beloved tandem performances, but here in one of their flops it is fatal. Miscast—Tracy plays an archconservative cattleman who dispossesses ranchers; Hepburn is his neglected wife, a character who is banished from the story when she conceives a son out of wedlock—the stars give small, unventilated, narrowly self-protective performances as remote from reality as the studio sets. They act as if indeed they aren't really there. Even with these problematic roles that play against their personas, if they were out on the open range and photographed in a robust style as opposed to the static interior shots here, they might still have rallied.

Music and screen acting have had a close connection since the silents, when the image was always accompanied by a continuous score, played in deluxe first-run theatres by a full symphony orchestra and in the nabes by lonely, overworked pianists or organists. Film music, now as then, mirrors the emotion on screen and is also designed to elicit Pavlovian responses from the spectator. Sometimes music completes the emotions welling up within a scene; sometimes it clobbers them.

Some performances, like those of Anthony Perkins and Janet Leigh in *Psycho* (1960), are virtually inconceivable without the music that accompanies them. Bernard Herrmann's score has a rapid pulsing beat, like strings (or nerves) snapping, that reflects the agitation not only of the psycho (Perkins) but also of the Everywoman secretary (Leigh) who becomes a criminal when she makes the fateful decision to steal money from her boss. Leigh, an actress with a bland, unflappable surface, needs Herrmann's score to help her convey what is going on inside her character; the music helps in creating the illusion that she is giving a distinguished performance. She's just right for her role, in fact, as actors in Hitchcock films almost always are, but Herrmann is a true coauthor of her work.

Although the actor doesn't need assistance, Leonard Bernstein's driving, declamatory score completes the force of Brando's final action in *On the Waterfront*, when Terry Malloy stumbles bashed but undefeated to work. Alive with the power and tension of the moment, Bernstein's music enhances the character's tortuous walk past his coworkers.

Bette Davis' vitality, her eagerness to act, need only sparing musical comment or support. Often, though, she received far too much, as in *Beyond the Forest* (1949), the last film under her Warners contract, an overripe melodrama with an insistent score that duplicates the messages Davis herself hurls at us. As Rosa Moline, Davis plays a hotblooded housewife trapped in a stifling marriage in a small-minded small town. For Rosa the Promised Land is Chicago and whenever she expresses her desire to go there the song "Chicago" whines away. In a typical scene, Davis pants in closeup as a smokestack belches behind her. With music added to the already overloaded image, we are inundated.

Films from the forties—and particularly the woman's film bristling with *Sturm und*

A typical *film noir* strategy, graphic arrangements of light and shadow to evoke an aura of menace and entrapment. "Imprisoning" Victor Mature on the stairs in *I Wake Up Screaming* (1941) and "framing" Yvonne de Carlo in the window in *Criss Cross* (1948), the virtuoso lighting in these two shots notably enhances the work of the actors.

What kind of acting would you expect from a character who lives in a house that looks like this? The kind Joan Crawford provides in *Mildred Pierce* (1945). "Reality" in most Golden Age movies was notably cleaner and more orderly than the real thing.

Drang—are notably guilty of overscoring. Too often the acting in these melodramas isn't allowed to breathe, as practically each gesture and emotional reaction is musically annotated.

CLOCKWISE FROM LOWER LEFT Versions of the studio look: "New York" in *How to Marry a Millionaire* (1953, with Marilyn Monroe, Betty Grable, and Lauren Bacall), like "Venice" in *Top Hat* (1935, with Fred Astaire and Ginger Rogers), is a fabrication, a not-real place that appropriately suspends the characters in these stylized films in a world of their own. Sometimes, however, as evident in the stills from *The Petrified Forest* (1936, with Bette Davis and Leslie Howard) and *Sea of Grass* (1947, with Spencer Tracy and Katharine Hepburn), the manufactured studio look of the Golden Age undercuts believability: these stories needed to be placed in the real outdoors.

Like the presence of the camera, then, editing, set design, lighting, and scoring collaborate with the actor. At full tilt, as in *Citizen Kane* and in other peak moments throughout the Hollywood canon, shrewdly used tools of the trade either complete the actor's work or construct an illusion of strong acting. If sometimes an overzealous sound-and-light show tramples acting, actors on screen nonetheless need the support of fluent, expressive filmmaking; when the film is dry, the actor is likely to seem equally parched. A quiescent apparatus, as in the scene from *The Lady Eve* previously discussed, can work only if acting and dialogue have exactly the right pitch and only if the scene is surrounded by shots of varying length and movement. *The Lady Eve* succeeds on both scores.

Some of the worst acting in American movies is to be found in the transition period between silents and talkies, from 1928 until 1930 or 1931, when the medium was adjusting to the technological shock of sound on film. The spectacle of talking heads seemed to paralyze the camera and the actors. And while it is true that the earliest sound cameras were bulky and made such a racket that they had to be enclosed in booths, even after lighter and quieter equipment was available the actors remained frozen in place at the center of the frame as the immobilized camera stared at them. As in the primitive one- and two-reelers, when films were only beginning to learn how to tell stories, the scenographic model of the early sound film was clearly theatrical. In observing the actors from a fixed middle distance, the camera attempted to duplicate the vantage point from a good seat in the theatre orchestra. If in the pioneer early silents actors imitated a heroic nineteenth-century theatrical style, in the early sound film they simply stood still and talked. And talked. And talked yet some more.

As if they realized that *The Jazz Singer* was the summons for their last hurrah, the most accomplished silent-film actors and directors performed at the height of their powers in the late twenties: Victor Sjostrom's *The Wind* with Lillian Gish, Raoul Walsh's *Sadie*

Thompson (1928) with Gloria Swanson, F. W. Murnau's *Sunrise* (1927) with Janet Gaynor, Jacques Feyder's *The Kiss* (1929) with Greta Garbo, are works of dazzling plastique in which acting and film technique exude a sensuous confidence that disappears in the early talkie (or part-talkie), which had yet to discover how dialogue needed to be written, photographed, and acted. To introduce sound on film, most studios produced revues filmed on a stage, as the camera stays rooted in the "audience." M-G-M's *Hollywood Revue of 1929,* in effect a series of screen tests for its contract stars, is typical. Jack Benny and Conrad Nagel (whose sturdy voice made him one of the first stars of talking movies) are the hosts who introduce, among others, Joan Crawford in her flapper period performing a leaden tap dance and warbling wobbily; Laurel and Hardy as magicians for whom every trick misfires; Buster Keaton in drag as a clever acrobatic Salome; Norma Shearer and John Gilbert performing two versions of the balcony scene from *Romeo and Juliet,* the first straight and stiff, the second, with much more verve, in contemporary slang; and Marion Davies dressed as a soldier in a klunky song and dance routine. The quality is variable, from the heavy-footedness of Crawford and Davies up to Keaton's comic ballet, but all the performances are stranded in a no-man's-land between the stage and the screen. Except for perfunctory high-angle shots of geometric dance formations at the end, the camera sits in a glum stupor, while the "turns" are entombed in a sonic black hole because the filmmakers eliminated an on-screen audience and applause. Who are the hapless entertainers performing for?

If the medium had to learn how to film speech, actors had to learn how to talk on film. Panicked by the inadequate voices of many silent stars, studios in the crossover period raided the Broadway stage for actors who spoke well and whose trained, resonant voices projected. But as they soon found out crisp diction and volume are not prerequisites for good film acting, and the stage-trained performers often sounded and looked as stiff as the films. George Arliss, a British theatre actor who speaks in an immaculate upper-crust style, could have become a movie star only in this uncertain transition period, when the movies didn't yet quite know the kinds of voices they needed. Arliss is well-spoken to a fault, but like his wiry body his voice has no life on screen. In *Disraeli* (1929), one of his many prestigious biographical films, he delivers epigrams—"The less a prime minister does, the fewer mistakes he makes"; "In politics nothing is insignificant"; "War is never a

Too much: "burning up" the frame and placed against a belching smoke-stack, Bette Davis in *Beyond the Forest* (1949) doesn't need musical annotation, yet music inundated the image, as it often did in overscored melodramas of the forties.

The camera stares at Garbo in her first talking role, *Anna Christie* (1930), and the sound-recording equipment hovers ominously overhead. The flat mise-en-scène is typical of the early talkie period, when there was more dully filmed dialogue and less visual interest than at any other time in the history of Hollywood filmmaking.

solution, it's an aggravation"—with rhetorical gestures and in a measured, juiceless style. Yet to many contemporaries Arliss represented a model for the new talking screen. At the time, he was considered a more legitimate film actor than ill-spoken plebeian American types like James Cagney, Jean Harlow, and Clark Gable, then pushing their way to stardom.

The dead camera and inert mise-en-scène of a stillborn, theatre-bred project like *Disraeli,* which matched Arliss' own reserve, were fatal for genuine film actors. One of the most telling examples of how an immature sound-film apparatus betrayed a real movie performer is Clarence Brown's underbaked version of Eugene O'Neill's *Anna Christie* (1930), Garbo's talkie debut. ("Garbo talks!" the film's ad campaign promised.) Emerging out of the waterfront fog and framed by a doorway, Garbo makes a delayed star entrance that is powerful. Slumped over, in the hunched posture already a part of her iconography, she strides into the waterfront bar dragging her character's history of despair. And when, after sliding into a chair, she at last speaks, barking the most famous bar order in theatrical history—"Gimme a whisky—ginger ale on the side. And don't be stingy, baby."—contemporary audiences could be relieved that Garbo would not be joining the silent star casualty list. Startlingly low-pitched, husky, deep, and lustrous, Garbo's voice complements her image of bewitching sexual power and ambiguity. When a few lines on she utters another famous line, "I'm *so* tired . . . ," the weariness of a misspent lifetime is in the dying fall of her voice.

So far, so (very) good—but then Brown seems to have no further ideas about how to present his star in a talking film of a well-known play. His blocking is stage-bound; the camera rarely crosses a "proscenium" line for closeups; there is little intercutting to underline conflict or reaction. Scene follows scene in visual and rhythmic monotony. The mute apparatus does little more than put Garbo on display, and, displayed, she poses, arching her back and shoulders like a high-fashion model and intoning rather than speaking her lines. Abandoned by the film and noticeably insecure in speaking English, the star gives an external performance—pushing her voice and expressing anguish by placing her hands on her head—which the staring camera does nothing to mitigate.

"I'm getting to like the sea," Anna says, standing in the doorway of her father's barge, but the sea she's drawn to seems far away, an image projected onto a screen behind her. Like the static camera setups, the rear-screen sea suspends Garbo in an enclosed, theatre-bound space, while an extraneous sequence shot on location in Coney Island in a loose, open style only heightens the artifice it interrupts.

Canned transcriptions of famous plays like *Anna Christie* were a staple of the early sound period. Retaining a structure as well as dialogue conceived for the stage, these potted works gave actors little chance to develop a speaking style, terse and off-the-cuff and slangy, more suited to movies. M-G-M's flavorless rendition of Noel Coward's *Private Lives* (1931) is another uneasy transplant filmed in a succession of stodgy, medium-distance two-shots with few closeups and a virtual absence of camera movement. M-G-M contract players Norma Shearer and Robert Montgomery, Hollywood's answer to Gertrude Lawrence and Noël Coward, who originated the roles of Amanda and Elyot on stage and for whose arch style the piece was conceived, deliver their lines hollowly from center "stage" as the uninvolved camera looks at them. (Scenes of the characters mountain climbing, like the trip to Coney Island in *Anna Christie,* are dragged in for misconceived air-conditioning.) Shearer is too genteel and Montgomery too genial to enact Coward's acidly witty characters, but even if they had been properly cast, as Garbo was in *Anna Christie,* the film's primitive rhetoric would have insured their failure.

The Director's Touch

Some film directors have been hazards to their actors; most have followed a policy of minimum interference. The few who have had a major impact on screen acting have confronted with notable success problems of how to place acting within film space and time and how to make dialogue reach out from the screen to enfold the spectator.

Sharing the frame: restrained by William Wyler's canny mise-en scène in *The Little Foxes* (1941), Bette Davis is forced to give a tight-lipped ensemble performance rather than a blazing star turn.

William Wyler, Elia Kazan, and George Cukor, three Zen masters to whom grateful actors regularly pay tribute, have each had strong ideas about where to position their actors within the frame. Wyler directing Bette Davis in *The Little Foxes* (1941); Kazan working with James Dean in *East of Eden* (1955); and Cukor guiding Judy Holliday in *Adam's Rib* (1949) suggest ways in which mise-en-scène has been enlisted to help the actors look good.

Collaborating with his cinematographer, Gregg Toland (who had photographed *Citizen Kane*), Wyler developed a style of deep focus and long takes that allows for interplay among a group of characters. Wyler's method favors placement of actors within the shot over editing, which, as in *Rear Window,* breaks up acting into reaction shots, a series of negotiations between the individual actor and the camera. Wyler's group shots contain the kind of tips on how to read subtextual currents that intercutting and closeups customarily supply. As a technique for filming *The Little Foxes,* Lillian Hellman's melodrama about the battles for economic and psychological dominance among a rapacious Southern family, deep focus and long takes are especially apt. Observed in deep focus, characters spy on each other, eavesdropping from the top of stairs or from behind drapes or peering through windows. Clashes of will and power struggles are filmed with all of the participants within the same shot.

Where does this leave the star? Exactly where Wyler wanted her, sharing the screen with her co-players rather than giving a bravura star turn. Davis wanted to play her juicy role at full throttle as the bitch of all time, as Tallulah Bankhead had done on stage, but Wyler's technique slyly binds the star to the ensemble. And as Wyler understood, the star's power is in fact intensified by being leashed. With few closeups and forced to share the spotlight, Davis internalizes the character's rage and her own. Suppressed by her director and the mise-en-scène, she gives a tight, brittle, murderously subdued performance.

Wyler's staging thus harnesses the star's thunder. To suggest divisions, characters are spatially separated within the frame: Regina (Davis) on one side, her estranged daugh-

Decentering the star: Elia Kazan suggests James Dean's neurotic, quicksilver presence by frequently placing the actor in the corners and edges of the frame or in the background, as in this scene from *East of Eden* (1955, with Raymond Massey and Julie Harris).

ter on the other; Regina at the top of the stairs, the domain from which she issues commands and oversees her adversaries. Battles between Regina and her two brothers are filmed mostly in three-shots, with the character at that moment holding the trump card dominating the playing space. At the end, in the last turn of the screw as she claims the ultimate victory over her brothers, Regina sits on her chair—the empress on her throne—with her victims placed on either side of her.

Significantly, Wyler allows Davis one-shot closeups only for Regina's private moments, when in effect the character is "offstage": looking at herself in a mirror and measuring her reflection against a younger portrait hanging nearby; putting on her face as she prepares to greet her husband, returned from the hospital; in the last image, looking out a rain-splashed window at her daughter's departure. Showing the character with her mask removed, these shots temper Davis' performance. Like Wyler's cunning setups in group shots, they are insurance against overstatement.

The first time we see James Dean as Cal, the unloved son in John Steinbeck's modern biblical parable, he's seated on the side of the wide CinemaScope frame huddled on a curb. Throughout the first part of the film, Cal is often in the rear of the shot or off to the side, eying other characters through trees or out of windows, eavesdropping behind blocks of ice, skulking at the end of a long hallway in the whorehouse run by his long-lost mother. Frequently placing Cal at the margins of his own story, Kazan signals the character's imbalance and introversion; the blocking presents him as a lurking figure, a moody stranger who emerges out of and returns to a world of shadows.

As in all his best work (*A Streetcar Named Desire*, 1951; *On the Waterfront; Baby Doll,* 1956), in which naturalistic performance fuses with an intermittently expressionist mise-en-scène, Kazan places his star in frames charged with neurotic tensions that seem to exude from the character. As if responding to Cal's agitation, the camera tilts when Cal and his remote father are seated in stony silence at opposite ends of a long dining-room table; when Cal pins his father against the wall, as if trying to squeeze a response from the old man after he has given him a birthday gift; when Cal, on a swing, announces that he's not his brother's keeper.

Kazan's intuitions about how to film Dean influenced the way Nicholas Ray in

FROM LEFT
On the job: Elia Kazan coaches Karl Malden and Vivien Leigh for a scene in *A Streetcar Named Desire* (1951); George Stevens creates an intimate atmosphere for Montgomery Clift and Elizabeth Taylor in *A Place in the Sun* (1951); George Cukor mesmerizes Bill Travers and Ava Gardner on the set of *Bhowani Junction* (1956).

Rebel Without a Cause (1955) and George Stevens in *Giant* (1956) directed him. Ray opens *Rebel* with a startling closeup of the actor sprawled on a street clutching a teddy bear and weeping. During explosive confrontations with his parents, the camera tilts. In *Giant* Dean is again frequently off-center. His character, Jett Rink, is an alien presence who for most of the film does not claim his own place in the frame but hunches off to the side or at the back, in half-visible deep focus, mysteriously biding his time.

In a key scene in *Adam's Rib* Judy Holliday, as a character in prison for having attempted to shoot her two-timing husband and his doxie, is placed in the right corner of the frame as she talks to her lawyer (Katharine Hepburn) across a bare table, while in deep focus through an open door prison traffic passes unobtrusively. Cukor sets the camera at an eye-level medium shot, and as Holliday delivers a long monologue he neither moves the camera nor cuts away. There are no distractions whatever from the core of the scene: Holliday's acting. And in her attentive posture and concentrated gaze, Hepburn throws the scene to her partner, making sure we focus on Holliday rather than her. Playing the scene with the poignant humor that became her trademark, Holliday fulfills her director's faith. (The scene helped to convince Columbia head Harry Cohn to allow Holliday to recreate her original stage role of Billie Dawn in his film version of *Born Yesterday* [1950].)

Cukor's taste in this scene is typical of his work. The least imposing and restrictive of the great Hollywood directors of acting, with none of Kazan's or Wyler's visual ingenuity, he simply provided a clean framework for his performers. Cukor put emphasis on the actor rather than the medium, assuming that with most of the big stars he directed—Hepburn, Garbo, Tracy, Crawford, Cary Grant—the medium didn't have to do more than whisper. Sometimes his uncluttered style doesn't disguise the theatrical origins of much of his source material, and sometimes his characters seem like chatterboxes. But when his method works, as in the scene in *Adam's Rib*, it's because Cukor knew how to place his actors—the ongoing movement behind his two performers adds a crucial touch of realism—and how to make them sound like people talking to each other rather than like actors delivering dialogue. It's his eye for realistic detail that separates his work from that of the early sound directors, who also had a no-frills approach to filming talking heads but who stranded stiffly spoken actors in a sound-stage vacuum.

Like Cukor a few directors have had a notable impact in helping actors turn dialogue into the sounds of real speech. Frank Capra, Howard Hawks, John Ford, George Stevens, Orson Welles, Woody Allen, and Robert Altman are all directors who appreciate the naturalistic, plain-spoken style suited to most movies. Actors in their films typically deliver dialogue so that it sounds like overheard conversations in which words collide and overlap as characters interrupt each other the way people do in life. To help fuse actors to their roles, Allen and Altman actually employ improvisational techniques, but all of these directors work for qualities of spontaneity, ease, and intimacy. Their way with words can be heard in James Stewart's delivery in Capra's *Mr. Smith Goes to Washington, You Can't Take It with You* (1938), and *It's a Wonderful Life* (1946); in Gary Cooper's in Capra's *Mr. Deeds Goes to Town* (1936) and *Meet John Doe* (1941); in the ensemble performances in Welles' *Citizen Kane* and *The Magnificent Ambersons* (1942); in Ford's Westerns like *Stagecoach* (1939) and *Fort Apache* (1948); in Allen's comedies like *Annie Hall* (1977) and *Manhattan* (1979); and in Altman's group portraits like *McCabe and Mrs. Miller* (1971) and *Nashville* (1975).

These directors enforce a distinct verbal rhythm on their actors. Replacing Diane Keaton with Mia Farrow as his leading lady, Allen has coached Farrow so that she has echoes of Keaton's fractured, whispery, off-the-cuff verbal style. In *The Lady from Shanghai* (1948), Rita Hayworth sounds like the ingenues in other Welles films and is more relaxed and natural than at any other time in her career. Although Allen and Welles had intimate offscreen relationships with their actresses, it doesn't require an affair or a marriage to produce the muted conversational style they elicit.

In Hawks' screwball comedies like *Bringing Up Baby* (1938) and *His Girl Friday* (1940) all the actors speak at a rapid-fire, helter-skelter pace. In George Stevens' films, dialogue is often slowed down to a luminous hum. In *Alice Adams* (1935) and *Woman of the Year* (1942) Stevens uncovered a lovely naturalness beneath Katharine Hepburn's usual hauteur; pairing her with straightforward, homespun actors like Fred MacMurray and Spencer Tracy, Stevens released her from her mannerist excesses. Elizabeth Taylor, another performer who can slip into verbal affectation, has never been more at ease than when she was directed by Stevens in *A Place in the Sun* (1951) and *Giant*.

For a taste of the bewitching quietism of Stevens' style, consider two bedroom scenes, in *The More the Merrier* (1943) as housemates Joel McCrea and Jean Arthur lie in separate beds talking softly to each other through a thin partition that divides them and in *Giant* as the Benedicts (Elizabeth Taylor and Rock Hudson) talk over problems concerning their children. While the conversation between McCrea and Arthur, who are just on the verge of intimacy, discovering to their surprise that they may be falling in love, is flecked with sly little pauses and hesitations, Taylor and Hudson talk to each other like people who have had a long, intimate relationship, completing each other's sentences as their voices blend together. The delicious intimacy of the acting in both scenes turns us into privileged interlopers.

To measure the influence a director can have on an actor, I want to look at two performances by Anne Baxter, in Orson Welles' *The Magnificent Ambersons* and in Cecil B. DeMille's *The Ten Commandments* (1956). In both assignments Baxter is clearly following orders. As the ingenue in *Ambersons*, a small-town flirt more attached to her father than her beau, she gives a quintessentially Wellesian performance, and as the conniving Princess Nefertiri in the biblical epic she is *echt*-DeMille; in the former she is absolutely terrific, in the latter she is pure papier-mâché. Even as early as 1940, playing a posing writer opposite John Barrymore in *The Great Imposter*, Baxter acted with the cloying artificiality that became her trademark (her style ultimately became so congealed that the only role she could play, as in *All About Eve* [1950], in which she scrapes by by the skin of her teeth, was that of a phony actress). Yet Welles takes the "acting" out of her voice and makes her speak with a bantering conversational ease that is utterly beguiling. In scenes with her father (Joseph Cotten) Baxter takes on Cotten's low-key simplicity. If Welles' visual style is often baroque, his way with actors clearly proceeds from the conviction that, on screen, less is decidedly more.

While Cotten retained what Welles taught him about how to act on film, Baxter misspent her career disregarding it. In *The Ten Commandments* she's a howl. "Oh, Moses, Moses, you stubborn, adorable fool," she croons archly to the hero, vamping the Old Testament leader in a tinny, fake-theatrical, modern style. Quite unlike Welles and the other directors who treat speech as natural utterance, DeMille coached his actors to pose and declaim in a remote, pageant-like manner. And while a larger-than-life quality is needed for his epic subjects, a typical DeMille performance, like Baxter's as Nefertiri, is pure tableau (hardly) vivant—stilted, stentorian acting containing no indication that people in the ancient world had inner lives. In *The Ten Commandments*, as in the director's other epics, the dumb-show acting is overwhelmed by decor and spectacle.

Directors have sometimes had a substantial influence in helping a performer to ripen or in developing a star persona. Would, for instance, "Grace Kelly" have been born on screen without Hitchcock to guide her, or would "Marlene Dietrich" have emerged without Josef von Sternberg?

The Kelly-Hitchcock partnership offers some clear-cut evidence of a director's role in shaping a performer's imprint. In both her pre- and post-Hitchcock movies, Kelly was a variable actress whose work ranged from bland to Brechtian. Hiding out beneath the chiseled perfection of her icy Celtic looks and bearing, she could be a cool cucumber. Kelly registers when directed by John Ford in *Mogambo* (1953) and by George Seaton in *The Country Girl* (1954), in which she's cast extravagantly against type as the dowdy title character, but in *High Noon* (1952) as a Quaker bride who objects to her husband's use of violence to defend his honor, as a princess in *The Swan* (1956), a year before she moved to Monaco, and in the Katharine Hepburn role in *High Society* (1956), the flat-as-a-pancake musical version of *The Philadelphia Story* (1940), she is notably lackluster. But directed by Hitchcock in *Rear Window* and *To Catch a Thief* (1955)—in *Dial M for Murder* (1954) Hitchcock does not disturb Kelly's aristocratic aura—she's enchanting, a new Hollywood icon: an ice maiden with blood in her veins.

Amid regal settings and wearing an Arctic-blue gown, Kelly is introduced in *To Catch a Thief* as an untouchable goddess. Her nouveau-riche mother announces to the hero (Cary Grant), a retired thief masquerading as a lumber baron from Portland, that she's sorry she ever sent her daughter to "that finishing school; I think they finished her there." As he escorts La Divine back to her room at the palatial Riviera hotel where they have met, she continues to maintain her glacial demeanor. Entering her room, she turns to give him an appraising glance, then moves toward him and kisses him hotly on the lips; withdrawing, she regains her hauteur before giving him a sly smile and then closing the door. The thief smiles to himself in quiet delight.

Stooping to conquer, a princess stepping down from her pedestal, in this moment Kelly, with Hitchcock's collusion, wins us over. The rest of the film cleverly exploits Kelly's duality, the spicy humor rumbling beneath her lacquered facade. Wearing white gloves, she drives recklessly on the hairpin curves of the Grande Corniche. She eats hungrily as she explains how she found out he's a fake: "You don't talk the way an American tourist ought to talk." "Give up, John, admit who you are," she says, her eyes smoldering as a fireworks display outside the window reflects her rising sexual excitement.

If in the story Kelly unmasks Grant, Hitchcock performs a parallel operation on his actress, uncovering a fun-loving, high-spirited American flirt beneath the pseudo-British speech and the finishing-school posture. "You should be spanked," her mother chastises her at the end. That's exactly what the film has done to her, "spanked" her for being too-too, an American lass who puts on the airs of British royalty. Cutting through her off-putting accent and making her accessible to the general movie audience, Hitchcock democratizes his star. *To Catch a Thief* is minor Hitchcock but (thanks to Hitchcock) major Kelly.

"Are you warm, are you real, Mona Lisa?" asks the lyric in the song that is composed during *Rear Window*. Since Kelly plays a character named Lisa, the question is not an idle one. As in *To Catch a Thief* here too Hitchcock has framed Kelly's performance around her object status, her sheer physical perfection, only to cut his sleek goddess down to delectable human size. Kelly plays a smart fashion editor who helps her seemingly

mismatched fiancé (James Stewart) solve the rear-window mystery. As in *Thief* she's a good sport.

Using slow motion when Lisa leans over Jeffries to kiss him, framing her dressed in a nightgown in a doorway, having her turn on the lights in the hero's darkened apartment in a three-step process timed to the announcement of her triple name, Lisa Carol Fremont, Hitchcock makes a spectacle of his star's sexual allure. (It's her sexuality, not the class differences between them, that causes the isolated hero to hesitate about marrying her.) But even as he shows off her body, Hitchcock remains protective; tempering her eroticism with humor, he directs Kelly to deliver her lines in a droll, teasing tone in which she kids but does not castrate her already disempowered beau confined to a wheelchair. And Hitchcock gives her the last laugh. After the crime has been solved and Lisa seems to have moved in on Jeffries, Kelly is casually dressed in sneakers and jeans and she's seen in a reclining position, an Odalisque in the film's "Greenwich Village." For show, to impress Jeffries that she can come down to his world, she pretends to be reading an adventure story, but when she's sure he's asleep, and aiming a private smile in our direction, she takes out a copy of *Harper's Bazaar.*

Like Hitchcock helping to release "Grace Kelly," Josef von Sternberg molded Marlene Dietrich's screen image over the course of the seven films they made together between 1930 and 1935, as in their collaborations between 1973 and 1983 Martin Scorsese provided a spectacular showcase for Robert De Niro. I don't mean to suggest any connection between these two actor-director teams beyond the fact that these paired artists helped to ignite each other's talent. Shaping vehicles for their stars helped the directors to develop their own idiosyncratic styles; working with their directors, Dietrich and De Niro added new twists to the rhetoric of acting on film.

Beginning with *The Blue Angel* (made in Germany in 1930) and then proceeding to Paramount for six of the most peculiar of all major studio productions—*Morocco* (1930), *Dishonored* (1931), *Shanghai Express* (1932), *Blonde Venus* (1932), *The Scarlet Empress* (1934), *The Devil Is a Woman* (1935)—von Sternberg was Pygmalion to Dietrich's Galatea. Or was he Svengali to her Trilby? "All of us Germans want a leader, someone to tell us what to do," Dietrich confesses to Maximilian Schell, the interviewer and director of

CLOCKWISE FROM LEFT
Grace Kelly listens intently to her director, Alfred Hitchcock, on location for *To Catch a Thief* (1955). Compare her relaxed appearance in *Rear Window*— the audience can readily appreciate the evident pleasure James Stewart takes in her—with her remoteness when she is not directed by the Master, as in this scene from *The Swan* (1956, with Louis Jourdan).

Marlene, a 1984 documentary. "I followed directions, I never argued with von Sternberg," she says, adding, "I used nothing of myself in those parts—I hate psychological acting."

An actress who obeyed the boss's orders yet who wasn't really involved ("I never took my career seriously; what interested von Sternberg when I auditioned for the part of Lola-Lola in *The Blue Angel* was the fact that I wasn't interested")—her enigmatic presence enticed the director, whose work with Dietrich is preoccupied with his star's passive-aggressive aloofness, her double-edged persona. While on the one hand Dietrich is intensely conscious of being looked at—she seems more aware of the camera than just about any other star—on the other a part of her doesn't seem to be there at all, as if her attention is on some private matter that is none of our business. "I wasn't erotic, I was snotty," the Dietrich of 1984 comments on her celluloid alter ego of a half century ago, and indeed there is a kind of resentment in her acting, as if von Sternberg and his camera are intruding on her. She poses dutifully enough, but she is also elusive.

Constructing his films around his star's provocative mask, von Sternberg wants both to pay homage to it and to penetrate it. The director honors, while attempting to control, his star's defiant ambiguity by reducing her in film after film to an object to be looked at, an icon placed on a par with the things, the bric-a-brac, that clutter his famously dense frames. He adorns her with veils, hats, masks, and feathers that partially cover her face. He places her in crowded, smoke-filled rooms crawling with shadows and photo-

LEFT
A legendary team: director Josef von Sternberg and his star, Marlene Dietrich. Was she the Trilby to his Svengali or the Galatea to his Pygmalion?

OPPOSITE
Dietrich on display in two typically lush, Byzantine von Sternberg compositions: framed by palms and shadows in *Blonde Venus* (1932) and in disguise in a nun's habit in *The Devil Is a Woman* (1935).

graphs her with objects—imprisoning, thronelike chairs with sculpted heads and hands (in *The Scarlet Empress*), stuffed animals (in *Morocco*), a music box with rotating figures (in *Blonde Venus*)—and with dangling ropes, nets, confetti, gauze, drapes, barred windows, and banisters that seem to take on a bewitching screen life of their own. Exquisitely lighted, she is presented to the peering gaze of the camera and the spectator to be admired for her exotic beauty and, in about every other film, to be punished for her intransigence.

Dietrich typically plays characters in hiding. In *Morocco, Dishonored,* and *Shanghai Express* she is a woman with a veiled past. In *Shanghai Express* she announces, unforgettably, that "it took more than one man to change my name to Shanghai Lily." In *Dishonored* she's a spy. In *The Devil Is a Woman* she's the masked queen of the carnival, a trickster out of Lope de Vega. In *Blonde Venus* she poses as a prostitute. *The Scarlet Empress* is about how her young German princess, chosen to marry a half-witted prince who becomes emperor of Russia, learns to mask her feelings as she grows shrewd in the ways of the corrupt Russian court. Other characters often can't penetrate her motives or are too conventional to decipher the code of honor by which she operates.

If in some roles Dietrich conquers Aphrodite's darts while herself remaining aloof

Dietrich as a human gargoyle in von Sternberg's *The Scarlet Empress* (1934), and performing in upscale drag in *Blonde Venus*.

from them and in others she behaves like a gentleman toward men she doesn't love, sometimes von Sternberg attempts to crack her mask by making her give all for a love that isn't necessarily returned. At the end of *Morocco*, smitten beyond resistance by a randy legionnaire (Gary Cooper), her character kicks off her high-heeled shoes to join a band of native women who follow the legion. In *Dishonored* she faces a firing squad because love for a Russian overcomes her patriotic duty as a spy for Austria. In these roles von Sternberg assures us that beneath Dietrich's glacial facade beats the heart of "a real woman."

Significantly, in none of their American films does von Sternberg allow his star to be as merciless a femme fatale as in *The Blue Angel.* In his own delirious way he gives her the Hollywood treatment, softening and glamorizing her to counteract her native astringent irony. Even so their work was tainted by an un-American exoticism, which Dietrich finally had to escape from in order to prolong her career. In *Destry Rides Again* (1939) she successfully democratized her image, as she continued to do in the forties in a series of potboilers with John Wayne. Being a good sport opposite such homegrown icons as James Stewart (her *Destry* costar) and Wayne earned her goodwill, but she was never again as arresting a screen presence, or so original a film actor, as in her work with von Sternberg, in which in tandem the performer and her mentor evolved a style of enameled self-consciousness.

Von Sternberg's mise-en-scène is the ideal frame in which to present Dietrich's sculpturesque acting, her languorous poses, gestures, and speech, her frozen, ambiguous offscreen glances. Their films are strictly sound-stage extravaganzas faithful only to the world within the director's imagination—objective reality would violate the dreamlike insularity of the improbable plots and of Dietrich's essential artifice, her otherworldly style.

Could Dietrich act, or did she, with the collusion of her director, merely trick us into thinking she could? Could she really sing, or did she simply know how to put over the songs in her limited repertoire? Was she, for that matter, really pretty? If film acting is rooted in the ability to project a vivid persona (and it is) and to command the interest of the camera and the audience, then indeed Dietrich was an exemplary screen artist. With von Sternberg's help, particularly with his eye for lighting and decor, she turned herself into an icon of glamorous polymorphous-perversity who had the knack of keeping her audience speculating about her role within a film as well as about her own real-life identity beyond it. Through her own instincts of self-protection and the lessons of her director, she mastered the craft of playing cat-and-mouse with the camera, offering enough to quicken curiosity before withdrawing into her privacy.

Dietrich is a minimalist with an enticingly layered style. Though she holds on to her secrets, we can nonetheless feel their presence even if we can't read them clearly. She remains one of the shrewdest practitioners of the art of film acting as modeling, yet almost subliminally, beneath her veiled face and the veils of von Sternberg's mise-en-scène, she conveys the impression that both she and her characters have a rich inner life. Von Sternberg felt he was making art, Dietrich thought she was doing a job, and their clash produced an original type in the history of Hollywood acting, the mannequin with a vivid personality.

The style Dietrich developed working with von Sternberg has had little influence on American acting; the nervous urban realism ignited by the Scorsese–De Niro partnership, on the other hand, sprang from an honored Hollywood tradition, the Actors Studio naturalism of such Kazan-Brando films of the fifties as *A Streetcar Named Desire* and *On the Waterfront* (in an explicit homage in *Raging Bull* [1980], De Niro as Jake La Motta, prizefighter turned cabaret comic, recites Brando's taxicab speech from *Waterfront*). Like the von Sternberg–Dietrich vehicles, the Scorsese–De Niro films—*Mean Streets* (1973), *Taxi Driver, New York, New York* (1977), *Raging Bull*, and *King of Comedy* (1983)—are a unified series in which the director explores his star's persona. "He's a punk kid, the biggest jerk-off around"—this comment about Johnny-Boy, De Niro's character in *Mean Streets*, might serve as the epitaph for each of the characters the director and his actor have created. All five are big-city losers, crackpots on a collision course toward self-destruction.

A "punk kid" who courts his own death by refusing to pay off a $2,000 debt to a Mafioso (*Mean Streets*); a taxi driver, filled with rage at the "scum" who clog the streets, who exterminates lowlifes in an orgiastic bloodbath (*Taxi Driver*); a saxophonist who willfully wrecks his career and his marriage (*New York, New York*); a prizefighter crazed with jealousy who destroys his professional and private life (*Raging Bull*); a no-talent comic aching to become famous who kidnaps a TV comedian and holds him hostage in order to get a crack at the big time, a spot on the comic's late-night talk show (*King of Comedy*)—these are the outsiders Scorsese and De Niro are drawn to. Netherworld characters insulated in urban ghettos as well as in their own fantasies, they're creatures of the night, quixotic, explosive, emotionally and sexually violent. In giving them life on screen, De Niro's jittery hyperactivity fuses with Scorsese's.

In *Mean Streets*, the two stake out an urban underground and a character type—a sociopath who slips from eerie calm to manic eruptions and back again—they have continued to be infatuated by. In contrast to the comparatively restrained style of *On the Waterfront*, Scorsese presents his story in a jerky, fragmented rhythm as he mixes *cinéma vérité* with sudden expressionist injections. His hand-held camera breaks into the action, hurling us right into the middle of brutal confrontations. De Niro's Johnny-Boy is part of the film's erratic and seemingly spontaneous movement; he bounces on the balls of his feet as

he walks with a loping, shifty gait and waves his hands and arms in a nonstop Saint Vitus' dance while his eyes dart offscreen Brandoesquely, casing the turf as he keeps on moving.

Johnny-Boy talks in circles, and his rap, layered with wisecracks and sentences that trail off into unintelligibility, is often drowned out by the noise of the city or by other characters. De Niro and Harvey Keitel (as Johnny-Boy's protector) bat words back and forth, pummeling each other verbally as well as physically. Their jabbing, feinting voices and their staccato rhythms have a family resemblance; the two actors sound like people who have been talking to and at each other for a lifetime. We're not meant to understand every word the characters speak, just as we're not meant to follow the story point for point. Indeed, Johnny-Boy's speaking style is matched by Scorsese's narrative shorthand, his determination *not* to tell his story smoothly.

De Niro's characters have abrupt explosions. Propelled by his own demons, Johnny-Boy opens fire from a tenement rooftop, an action that is introduced as quickly as it is then dropped. Ushered out of a campaign office in *Taxi Driver,* Travis Bickle assumes a threatening karate pose that paralyzes onlookers into a stunned silence. Later, in a sudden outburst, Travis smashes in his TV and then grips his head, shaking it back and forth in helpless amazement at what is happening to him. "I got some bad things in my head," Travis confides to a fellow taxi driver, which is as far as he can go toward defining his inner world. In *Raging Bull* Jake La Motta smashes a table when his first wife serves him dinner late, and then becomes ominously still. After he lashes out at his second wife, accusing her of cheating on him, he says to her in a whisper shadowed by mania, "Don't leave me, I'm a bum without you and the kids." In the film's climax Jake pounds his head against the wall in his prison cell, shrieking in a rage that he is not an animal. In *New York, New York,* De Niro begins in low gear; he's almost charming as he tries out a pickup technique at a stage-door canteen. But even in the context of what at first promises to be a romantic comedy set in the forties, De Niro's presence is unsettling right from the start. His edgy voice and his clenched posture anticipate his character's later flareups.

In a variation on the De Niro characters who lurch into madness, as Rupert Pupkin

Made for each other: director Martin Scorsese instructs Robert De Niro, on location for *Raging Bull* (1980), one of their numerous collaborations.

in *King of Comedy* the actor keeps his cool while his partner-in-crime, a psychotic auto-graph hunter (Sandra Bernhard), does the cracking up for both of them. This time his character's mania is withheld, suppressed beneath a sugared smile, a manner of fake bonhomie. Rupert's quiet, wheezing voice is lined with menace.

For each of these roles the actor uses his body fully. He gives Johnny-Boy a dim-witted, absentminded walk. Travis Bickle is taut and wiry as he trains himself to be ready for his imaginary Armaggedon. In *New York, New York* his saxophonist moves his body sensuously in symbiotic response to the music he makes. Astonishingly, in *Raging Bull* De Niro embodies both the lean, trim prizefighter of 1941 and, with a blubbery stomach that plops over his belt, the bulging wreck that Jake La Motta became by 1964. In *King of Comedy* he apes the external mannerisms of stand-up comics, pointing fingers and raising his arms to put over punch lines.

Scorsese's kinetic direction—his tortuous camera choreography and terse edit-ing—complements his star's intense physicality. And also like De Niro, who paints his characters with sharp contrasts in mood, Scorsese employs jolting shifts in technique. Slow-motion scenes, classical music, home movies in color (within the film's grainy black-and-white photography), and a biblical quotation, "Once I was blind and now I can see," from the Book of John rupture the surface of *Raging Bull*. In *New York, New York* the visual split-focus between realism and obviously fake backdrops—a snow-covered forest, a cy-clorama sunset—that are an homage to the studio style Scorsese grew up seeing and admiring echoes the swings in De Niro's performance from stylized romantic comedy to overwrought naturalistic melodrama. Eliminating sound in crucial moments (usually of violence, as in *Raging Bull* and *Mean Streets*), layering in offscreen noises to smother dia-logue, bleeding sounds from a previous scene into the following scene, or cutting off the sound before a scene is completed—Scorsese's dense and often unexpected sound tracks fully support De Niro's visceral characterizations.

Scorsese and De Niro have done their best work as a team, and neither has ever worked entirely successfully outside their cherished world of urban blight. As Irving Thal-berg in Elia Kazan's half-baked *The Last Tycoon* (1976) or as a priest in the jungle in *The Mission* (1986), De Niro is startlingly bereft. Outside the New York underbelly he often seems stranded, an actor without a persuasive voice or body. So far his most authoritative work without Scorsese is as the young Don Corleone in Francis Ford Coppola's *Godfather II* (1974), in which, speaking mostly in Italian, he imitated Marlon Brando's characteriza-

CLOCKWISE FROM LEFT
De Niro in eruption, galva-nized by Martin Scorsese, a director who fetishizes vio-lence: aiming to kill in *Taxi Driver* (1976); getting shot up in *Mean Streets* (1973); beating and getting beaten in *Raging Bull*.

tion in *The Godfather* (1972). Far from home, in *The Last Temptation of Christ* (1988), Scorsese's choppy modernist direction was as disconcerting as the fact that his Judas (Harvey Keitel) hailed straight from the Bronx.

In *GoodFellas* (1990), Scorsese and De Niro return to the New York Italian underworld. The film is both more comic and more violent than Scorsese's earlier crime pictures—murders are committed with unnerving casualness. But despite its schizophrenic attitude to its subject and Scorsese's obsessive preoccupation with low-life characters, the movie is made with a verve and attack that sweep us along into its lower depths. De Niro, however, is remarkably pallid, washed-out. In a modest supporting role he melts into the background.

Actors in Charge

After they have been photographed, performances are taken away from actors to be placed within and sometimes swept up by the finished product. Editing and scoring variously enhance, comment on, or interrupt the work of the actors, and more often than not they are servants rather than masters of the frame. Yet a few performers have such a strong presence and timing that is so specific that they compel the medium's subservience. Forcing the apparatus to slow down or to speed up, they seize control to become the ultimate *auteurs* of their own films. Most of the great screen comics, from Chaplin and Keaton to Mae West, W. C. Fields, and the Marx Brothers, "silenced" the medium into looking quietly at them as they performed their turns. I'd like to consider here, however, the work

of two noncomics (Cagney and Brando) and a dancer (Fred Astaire) who had a tougher job in claiming control of the screen. Cagney's staccato rhythm, Brando's brooding pauses, and Astaire's fluent dancing required the cooperation of the filmmaking machinery to a degree few stars have achieved.

Cagney's rat-a-tat New York accent offset by his hyperactive thumbs and semaphoring arms introduced a new style into early talkies: he set the prototype for the big-city mug whose voice and body created a quick vernacular music. In harsh, nasal tones Cagney spat out words like shots from a gun while jabbing the air and springing up and down on the balls of his feet. His dancer's grace was always a part of his work, lending a subversive appeal even to the most antisocial of his hoodlum roles.

In his heyday in the thirties, after *The Public Enemy* (1931) had made him a star, Warner Brothers designed films to showcase his crackling urban energy. Two modest vehicles, *Lady Killer* (1933) and *Jimmy the Gent* (1934), demonstrate the way Cagney's rhythm becomes a narrative as well as visual focus—actually, what the films are all about. In both pictures Cagney plays a con artist who works a wide terrain in a short narrative space. In *Lady Killer* he segues from a misbehaving movie usher to a card shark to a movie star who rejects his former cronies. In *Jimmy the Gent* he specializes in locating missing heirs to huge fortunes. Fueled by coincidences, the stories are quick, ramshackle, and episodic. House policy at Warner Brothers in the early thirties prized terseness, but Cagney's films clocked in at record speed: both films run little over an hour. As his characters drive the plots, crashing into the entertainment big time in *Lady Killer* and manufacturing alibis while outsmarting the competition in *Jimmy the Gent*, film style—the wipes, the brisk forward march of the stories—takes its cues from the actor. Both B pictures simply provide a frame in which Cagney's characters can display their live-wire ingenuity.

At the end of *The Wild One* (1954), Johnny (Brando), carrying a trophy, enters the cafe where much of the action has taken place and where he has conducted his offbeat courtship of the proprietor's daughter. He slinks over to the counter, then lingers over a cup of coffee in tense silence. Trying to read his thoughts, the girl, like the camera, looks at him as he remains hunched over his coffee. Will he give Mary the trophy, or will he leave town, keeping it himself? Johnny gets up and starts walking to the door; then, having made his decision at last, he turns and pushes the trophy toward Mary. He smiles. The action in the scene is an inner one, what Johnny is thinking, the choice he struggles to make, and

CLOCKWISE FROM LEFT
Actors who command the medium: James Cagney's pep propels *Jimmy the Gent* (1934); Marlon Brando's pregnant silences periodically retard *The Wild One* (1954) and *One-Eyed Jacks* (1961, with Karl Malden and the Mona Lisa).

Brando plays the moment with his own deliberate pace as he fills what in effect is one long sustained pause.

If Cagney is the speedy whiz kid of American film in the thirties, Brando is his fifties antitype, an actor who slows down his movies with resonating caesuras and contemplative offscreen gazes. Where Cagney collapses film time, Brando extends it. Where Cagney compels his movies to trot along at a clipped pace, Brando demands a languorous syntax. No film with Brando can be action-packed; no film with Cagney can be anything else. And when Brando stars in an action-oriented genre like the Western, he converts wide open spaces and shoot-outs into props for brooding Method psychodrama. In *One-Eyed Jacks* (1961) Brando himself directs a Western with a standard revenge plot as an epic frame against which to set his introspective style. Stately and poetic, filled with scuttling clouds, fog, twisted trees, and waves crashing against boulders with just the proper expressive intensity, the film has an aura as moody as the star's. Brando plays Rio, a charming rogue bent on exacting revenge against a former partner-in-crime who years ago betrayed him. Laying his plot as he pretends friendship for his enemy and courts the man's daughter, the character says little but vibrates with subtext. Beneath his heavy silences and long-held glances, we can feel Rio's busy inner monologue as he begins to realize that he loves the daughter of the man he must kill.

Directing himself, Brando slows down and sometimes entirely stills the filmmaking machinery in order to capture the charged undercurrents of his characteristically measured acting. Lyrical, self-indulgent, and reverberating with an emotional heft that outstrips its subject, the film is a monument to Brando as the slowest gun in the West.

Fred Astaire made hard work look easy. And to insure this illusion of grace without pressure, he worked out his own method of how to film dance. Using the camera solely as a recording mechanism, a means of capturing his fluid movements, Astaire compels its undivided attention. The camera maintains a discreet distance from the dancer as it gives him the space he needs, and in all the classic Astaire dances, camera and editing are used only to provide continuity and to record the movements of the dancer's entire body. The clean, spare style—long takes and long shots and a camera that moves only to follow the dancer—which Astaire enforced on the medium is a way of paying proper tribute to his talent; film language is never allowed to steal the spotlight. Quick editing, closeups of feet or legs, variety of point of view, dizzying overhead or low-angle shots—the tricks employed, for example, in the kaleidoscopic production numbers directed by Busby Berkeley—are outlawed. Astaire's movements rather than the camera's are the ones that create excitement. When Astaire starts to dance, space opens up and empties out, floors gleam, and the camera watches as it provides the spectator with a view from the best seat in the house.

In a gazebo in a park during a rainstorm, a place that seems specially chosen for lovers (and dancers), the shiny, empty round floor beckons Jerry Travers (Astaire in *Top Hat*), a song and dance man determined to woo a reluctant lady (Ginger Rogers). He turns the gazebo into a stage on which the camera captures but never interferes with his performance of "Isn't It a Lovely Day To Be Caught in the Rain?" As his moves become wider and as he quickens the pace of his spins and swoops and leaps, the camera softly retreats to give him more room. Hesitant at first, then despite herself swept up by his dance, Rogers begins to mirror his movements. But the camera never imitates Astaire: it observes, and moves only when it needs to in order to preserve the flow of the dance.

Acting is a human activity; filmmaking depends on machinery. Though the two sometimes clash they are not inevitably antagonistic. Nonetheless, actors have had to adjust the scale and the rhythm of their work to the camera and to editing, the two basic ingredients of the filmmaking process. Unlike stage actors, screen players do not have the luxury during performance of living through a story from beginning to end. They must emote in bits and pieces of time and often with their faces cut off from the rest of their bodies. And to protect themselves against the machines that "steal" and ultimately shape their work, film actors have had to develop a particular mode of performance—the Hollywood Style.

Another master of the medium: Fred Astaire's dances, as here with Ginger Rogers in *Top Hat*, compel the camera to remain at a respectful distance in order to record his full-figure movements.

Body Language

Mannequins and Live Wires

SHE IS REVEALED TO US IN FRAGMENTS: ANKLE-STRAP SHOES, SHAPE-ly stockinged legs, arms with jangling bracelets, a perfectly proportioned face with a firm jaw, high-altitude cheekbones, full painted lips, and oversized, heavily mascaraed, batting eyes: Joan Crawford as Sadie Thompson in *Rain* (1932). The camera examines the star as if she were a prize racehorse who has already won the race, having been chosen to play the plum role of a trollop in Tahiti. "Here she is," the camera in effect says. "This is the one who's been chosen. Do you like her?"

A blare of trumpets. A circus platform. A predominantly male audience lines up eagerly to get a good view of the star attraction. The camera travels slowly down a picture of the star plastered over the curtained stage before it comes to rest at eye level to await the teasingly delayed appearance of the star herself: Mae West in the flesh, sashaying onto the stage to the cheers and whistles of her admirers. Making her gala entrance in *I'm No Angel* (1933), La West parades her hourglass figure in form-fitting attire as she accepts the tribute of the crowd.

These two famous star entrances highlight a kind of display that is a crucial part of film acting. Screen actors are not only subjects—what the film is about—they are also objects appraised by the camera and the spectator.

In *Ziegfeld Girl* (1941) Lana Turner is an elevator operator in a department store who cracks gum, drops her final *g*'s, and has a working-class trucker boyfriend. On the job she is discovered by a Ziegfeld scout and along with other chosen ones Hedy Lamarr and Judy Garland, she is trained in how to wear exaggerated costumes and in how to walk up and down elaborate staircases. Made by M-G-M, the film is really a sustained metaphor for the studio's own starmaking prowess: being picked by Ziegfeld is equivalent to being groomed for stardom at M-G-M; standing on a Ziegfeld stairway is like being put on display for the camera.

As Stanley Kowalski in *A Streetcar Named Desire*, Marlon Brando displays a back and torso that speak a potent language Vivien Leigh's Blanche du Bois clearly knows how to read.

THIS PAGE
Presenting the bodies: the camera scrutinizes Sadie Thompson (Joan Crawford in her first scene in *Rain*, 1932); the on-screen audience greets Mae West, making a typically grand entrance in *I'm No Angel* (1933).

OPPOSITE
Starmaking movements: Lana Turner's mannequin walk down the stairs at the end of *Ziegfeld Girl* (1941); Carole Lombard's live-wire feet action against John Barrymore in *Twentieth Century* (1934).

In the film Lamarr's character leaves show business for marriage, Garland's graduates from the chorus line to the star spot on the musical program, and Turner's, with neither Garland's talent nor Lamarr's exotic beauty, dies. It's not quite clear why her career girl falls ill, but she crawls out of her deathbed to attend the opening night of Garland's new Broadway show, only to leave before the finale. Enacting an inebriated version of a Ziegfeld girl's staircase descent, Turner walks down grand marbled stairs wobbling woozily while struggling to maintain her dignity. The scene elevated Turner to M-G-M stardom.

Before she appeared in *Twentieth Century* (1934) Carole Lombard had made a number of films without having established a niche for herself. And while she's not as distinctive in *Twentieth Century* as she was to be in later thirties screwball comedies like *My Man Godfrey*, *Nothing Sacred* (1937), and *True Confession* (1937), she has terrific energy— and, as with Turner, a star was born in one movement. Seated in her railroad berth as Oscar Jaffe (John Barrymore), her erstwhile mentor-producer-lover, towers over her and gives her a verbal lashing, Lily Garland (Lombard) retaliates with her legs, kicking and shaking them and then kneeing her opponent in the groin. A feisty woman offscreen, famous for her blue language, Lombard improvised some of these moves without warning either her costar or her director, Howard Hawks. Those saucy legs waving in the air are exactly in character (Lombard is playing a dizzy, temperamental movie diva) and provide a preview of the kind of physical vitality the actress exuded in her prime.

Turner on that staircase and Lombard kicking in that train compartment epitomize for me two basic kinds of body talk that recur in Hollywood acting: the mannequin and the live wire. Turner's walk represents a self-conscious bodily display; Lombard's thrusting legs seem to be an instinctive, spontaneous response. Turner's movements are studied, she's aware of being looked at; Lombard is a natural upstart whose body language flows out of her character's feelings. On film Turner doesn't have a spontaneous bone; Lombard is wonderfully nimble. Turner poses for each shot; Lombard's movements are fluid and continuous. Though I prefer Lombard's kind of body language to Turner's, within the contexts of the two films both are effective.

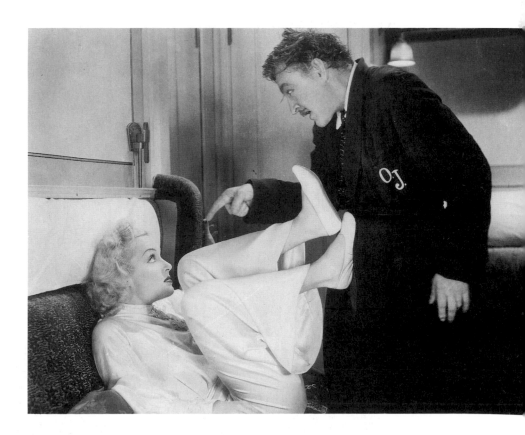

One further example of Turner's mannequin style and Lombard's live-wire loose-ness. In her first appearance in *The Postman Always Rings Twice* (1946), Turner is "an-nounced" by a tube of lipstick rolling on the floor, which catches the attention of the hero (John Garfield) and the camera. Following the direction from which the lipstick came, the camera travels across the floor until it reaches a pair of legs. Intercut shots of Garfield's transfixed gaze whet our own curiosity before the camera then completes its inspection by moving slowly up Turner's body. Clothed in a forties version of hot pants, the star stands in a doorway, framed in a frame within the frame, as she invites her costar's admiring look. A closeup on her face reveals a faint, taunting, come-hither smile. Having allowed the stranger to see just enough, she then closes the door, while on the griddle in the roadside diner where she lives and works, a burger sizzles.

With her platinum hair stiff as steel, her rigid beauty-queen posture (she places one leg behind the other, just so), and her breathy voice encrusted with "acting," Turner is all studio artifice: the model as movie star. She isn't really believable as a waitress in a highway hash house, yet within the conventions of Hollywood star acting her performance is acceptable.

FROM LEFT
Placed on staircases, actors become mannequins—spectacles to be looked at—whether they are performing in an extroverted musical like *There's No Business Like Show Business* (1954, with Johnnie Ray, Mitzi Gaynor, Dan Dailey, Ethel Merman, Donald O'Connor, and Marilyn Monroe) or an introverted drama like *Mr. Skeffington* (1944, with Bette Davis).

In her first scene in *Made for Each Other* (1939), Lombard comes bounding into her future mother-in-law's living room. The two women are natural antagonists: Lombard is a free spirit, her future husband's mother is a stiff blue blood. Unlike Turner, whose movements seem to start and stop just for the camera, Lombard flows on with an energy that suggests a continuing life beyond the limits of the frame. As Lombard enters talking fast and trailing a bright, quick energy, you can see why John Mason (James Stewart) falls for her at first sight. They are indeed "made for each other": her force and spine are bound to overcome his hesitation.

Mannequins and live wires describe the two dominant types of body language in Hollywood films. Although mannequins are often lush women, the style is not gender-restricted. Men can strike poses for the camera too. Actors who are either mannequins or live wires, however, use their bodies in ways a performer like Spencer Tracy, for example, does not. Watching Tracy, you are attentive to his eyes and to how he speaks; the way he moves is rarely a crucial part of his technique. Just as Tracy deplored makeup, so he didn't intrude his body into his acting: most of the time it is simply there. In this disembodied approach Tracy is certainly not alone. Does Bogart really use his body? Does Henry Fonda? Or James Stewart? Or Claudette Colbert? Or Jean Arthur? For these major players, as for many others, acting is concentrated in their faces and eyes and in their distinctive voices. The performing energy of actors like Turner and Lombard, Cagney, Jean Harlow, James Dean, Marilyn Monroe, and Marlon Brando, on the other hand, is fused to their body language.

Mannequins who act in an external style that is rarely more than skin deep follow an acting tradition codified by a nineteenth-century French teacher and acting theorist, François Delsarte (1811–1871). "Delsartean" has become a byword for acting that uses a series of conventionalized gestures in which arms, legs, and torso are placed in specific ways to indicate general emotions such as fear, despair, anxiety, and joy. Delsartean actors are untouched by the emotions they are presenting; miming a succession of codes, they are technicians who dissemble feeling. They are thus the kinds of actors Denis Diderot anticipated in his famous book *The Paradox of Acting* (1773), which inaugurated an enduring debate on whether or not actors should feel their characters' emotions. Diderot maintained they should not, that actors can best accomplish their goal of inciting responses in the audience by themselves remaining detached and by imitating rather than actually arousing in themselves their characters' emotional responses.

Live wires, in turn, are the true progeny of Constantin Stanislavski (1863–1938), the Russian director and teacher whose ideas about how to create truthful acting became the cornerstone of the American Method as developed by Lee Strasberg at the Group Theatre in the thirties and at the Actors Studio from the late forties until his death in 1982. Impatient with the external style that dominated stage acting at the turn of the century, Stanislavski encouraged in his Moscow Art Theatre ensemble a more intimate approach to creating characters. Countering Diderot's belief in actors' detachment, he developed a series of exercises, in improvisation, sensory work, and emotional recall, designed to bind actors to their roles.

If Delsartean mimes begin with the outer image, the message inherent in the gesture, and then may or may not move inward to deepen their physical codes, Stanislavskian actors begin closer to home, inside themselves, as they explore their own intuitions and then transfer what they discover directly into their characters. Stanislavskians light their work from within; Delsarteans remain actors of surfaces. Delsarteans display their bodies; Stanislavskians use them organically to express their characters' inner lives. Stanislavskian live wires aren't necessarily as active as Carole Lombard, but all their movements, whether expansive or restrained, are internally motivated.

The Stanislavski "Method"—there is no one method, and Stanislavski intended his research to be an ongoing process, to be added to and reinterpreted—provides a blueprint for helping actors to create an illusion of spontaneity. Emotional truth—which comes from within, generated by the actors' insight into and control over their own psychic resources, their storehouse of sensory and emotional memories—is the goal toward which Method actors aspire.

Delsartean actors come in two basic types: the Lana Turner mode of look-at-me performers, who remain basically static, and the Douglas Fairbanks mode of actors, who are physically agile but mime emotion in an external style that is usually quite deliberate. (Performers sometimes switch or blend styles, but for the most part Hollywood actors present themselves either as mannequins on display or as live wires with twitching inner lives.) Whether inert or active, Delsarteans play on the surface—strictly for show. And since they act in a style that is cleaner, more calculated and beautiful than real life could ever be, their work complements the many Hollywood scenarios in which reality has been reupholstered into a perfect-looking communal dream world, a realm in which emotional as well as physical truth has been more or less eliminated.

Movies, then, need Delsarteans, actors who show off their bodies, as well as actors whose bodies seem fused to their characters' inner lives—Douglas Fairbanks as well as Marlon Brando, Mae West as well as Meryl Streep. Sometimes actors surprise us by combining the two traditions: Buster Keaton and Charlie Chaplin are mannequins whose dumb shows vibrate with rumblings from an inner monologue. More often, Delsarteans like Fairbanks, Mae West, and Groucho Marx are entertaining puppets happily innocent of private lives.

Actors can of course work externally or internally by instinct rather than training. Carole Lombard never studied the Method; Lana Turner didn't train with a disciple of Delsarte. Nonetheless the kind of grooming Turner received at M-G-M certainly was in the Delsartean mode, whether or not her studio vocal coaches and body trainers had ever heard of Delsarte. And while Lombard's aliveness on screen may have been instinctual, she was exhibiting qualities Method-trained actors since the forties have consciously aimed for.

Lee Strasberg created an uproar when he told members of the Actors Studio that movie stars like Gary Cooper and Spencer Tracy were true, if unconscious, Method actors. Yet his comment was merited, since many of the best screen actors have always performed with the sense of being inside their roles, in a style of unforced simplicity, truthfulness, and inner conviction that are the Method's stated aims. The Actors Studio Method—an ideal technique for film—provides a systematic approach to representing convincing human behavior.

Here are some further mannequins and live wires.

When Joan Crawford as a factory worker in the aptly named *Mannequin* (1937) walks up tenement stairs striped with *noir* shadows, she converts "Hester Street" into a Hollywood sound stage. This is not a factory worker who lives in a crowded tenement with her family on the Lower East Side, it is Joan Crawford ascending a stairway, glamorously backlit, with every fiber of her body aware of the camera. When later she picturesquely wipes some straggling bits of hair from her eyes as she dries dishes in a hot kitchen, her gesture seems enclosed by quotation marks: the movie star is valorized at the expense of the character. But the film protects its star by moving her quickly out of the working-class setting and into the world of high-fashion modeling, where she can be what she has been all along, a mannequin.

As in *Mannequin* and *Ziegfeld Girl,* staircases in Hollywood movies are a recurrent site for the display of performers who have cultivated a camera-conscious style of movement. Stars on stairs occupy a privileged position from which to command our attention. Placed on stairs, as in *The Little Foxes* and *Mr. Skeffington* (1944), even a live wire like Bette Davis adopts the self-aware movements of a mannequin.

Stairs are also a good location to show off the star's wardrobe. And in mannequin acting, clothes like anatomy often define a character's destiny: changes in apparel signify a personality overhaul. Although Charlotte Vale in *Now, Voyager* (1942) is played by Bette Davis, her transition from spinster to knockout is announced externally, through the character's wardrobe. In *Working Girl* (1988) Melanie Griffith's ascent up the corporate ladder is indicated by her character's increasingly upscale wardrobe and hairdo. And in *Pretty Woman* (1990) a prostitute (Julia Roberts) is purified when she wears high-fashion clothes. Davis and Griffith create full-fledged characters, but even if they didn't, the way they are dressed in itself tells the story. When a performer either can't or isn't allowed to create an inner life for a character, dress codes shoulder much of the acting burden. In *Ruby Gentry* (1952), for example, Jennifer Jones' costumes do most of the work of projecting the strong-willed backwoods sexpot "from the wrong side of the tracks" she is supposed to be playing. Our first view of her is as a figure posed provocatively in a dramatically lit doorway: she's a mannequin displayed to elicit a lustful male gaze. To his companion's remark, "It's only anatomy," the new doctor in town rejoins, "I never saw anything like that on a dissecting table."

Dressed in tight-fitting jeans and blouse and swaying her hips in exaggerated rotation, Jones acts with a cosmetic sexiness, a result of what she wears and how her director, King Vidor, has told her to swivel, rather than a force that comes from within. Later in the story, when Ruby inherits her dead husband's money and seeks revenge on the town that scorned her, Jones is dressed to kill in a severe executive outfit and an outsized hat, which immediately define her as a dangerous black widow. Props like guns and dark glasses and agitated music, which supply an emotional kick the actress cannot, all collaborate with the wardrobe to help Jones put over her character.

Jennifer Jones' remote style, glazed and inert, thus turns her into a mannequin whose body is used as the neutral ground on and around which to drape signifying elements. Yet her hollow acting—like Lana Turner's and that of many other studio-trained divas, it is at once utterly sincere and utterly artificial—is oddly appropriate to a stylized melodrama like *Ruby Gentry.* In carrying out orders while allowing clothes, props, music, and mise-en-scène (the film ends in a studio swamp that oozes an aura of unleashed sexuality) to do most of the acting for her, Jones performs with a detachment from reality that precisely complements the film's.

The connection between costumes and mannequin acting dates back to the origins of the star tradition—to Theda Bara's overdressed vamps in the teens, and to Gloria Swanson, the first actress lifted to stardom primarily by her flair for wearing stylish clothes. In many of Swanson's vehicles wardrobe reveals character and class status, and fashion and feeling are intimately bound.

In *The Affairs of Anatol* (1921), one of a number of society comedies Swanson made with Cecil B. DeMille, she's a neglected wife swathed in chic clothes. When her character decides to paint the town, she orders her maid to bring "my lowest gown! my highest heels! If there's room for husbands on the Gay White Way—there's room for wives!" Typically, then, her character is concerned about sartorial messages: she dresses for success.

Clothes also preoccupy her character in *Manhandled* (1924), a shopgirl who yearns for money and the nice clothes money can buy. The plot requires her to wear borrowed clothes; she has to masquerade as an exotic dancer and as a Russian countess. When her boyfriend sees her all dressed up, he takes appearance for reality and lashes out at her, "You're like the goods you hated to sell in Thorndyke's basement—rumpled—soiled—

FROM LEFT
Clothes create character: Jennifer Jones' ensemble in this scene from *Ruby Gentry* (1952) bespeaks executive authority; in *Pretty Woman* (1990), a prostitute (Julia Roberts) is purified when she is dressed in expensive Rodeo Drive outfits.

pawed over—manhandled!" But she's a good kid underneath the sophisticated outfit. "Dear God, show him the truth!" she petitions—in other words, teach her beau how properly to read her fashion system, how to see through clothes and thereby separate her from her clothed image.

Swanson's strongest silent film, *Sadie Thompson*, also pivots on dress codes. In the first part of the film Sadie's trash-flash costumes proclaim her profession: she's a fun-loving prostitute whose expansive gestures (hands on hips, lascivious winks, a swaying walk) help fill out her clothes. When Sadie is temporarily transformed, born again through the influence of a hypocritical prude, she changes her style. Our first view of the new Sadie is from behind—her hair is down, hanging straight and lank, her shoulders slope (for the first time in the film her body is in repose), and she wears a plain dress. To see the star—and certainly this star—defrocked is shocking, and not right. We want the old gaudily dressed Sadie to be restored, because in movies the world of the flesh is more enticing than the spiritual realm. When Sadie reappears in full maquillage and sexy clothes, after the man who reformed her commits suicide, we're satisfied. Like most star vehicles *Sadie*

A live wire in perpetual motion: James Cagney on the move in *White Heat* (1949).

FROM LEFT
In dynamic movement (as in *East of Eden*) or being forcibly restrained (as in *Rebel Without a Cause*, 1955), James Dean's body language flows from his characters' turbulent inner lives.

Thompson vindicates the star's style: it rejects the image of her in sackcloth and without any makeup and applauds when she returns in full regalia.

It's only a passing gesture but it establishes at once the core of the character. In long shot James Cagney as Tom Powers, Public Enemy, enters the frame with a jaunty walk and, before going into a bar, passes his hand over his hat in a gesture that immediately reveals the character's cockiness. Brushing his fist lightly against his mother's face, smashing a grapefruit in the face of a whining moll, weaving when he's drunk, slapping a saloon owner and spitting beer into his face—Cagney gives his thug a vibrant physical life. Translating thought into instant movement, he turns the public enemy into a human pinwheel. Like Lombard's, his actions seem ripped from a momentum that endures beyond the frame. Audiences instinctively like actors who move with zip, and contemporary censors feared that Cagney had made his criminal too energetic and perhaps therefore too likable. And in fact it is part of the film's subversive strategy to present virtue as passionless and badly acted—Tom's good, law-abiding brother is played by an actor who doesn't seem to have a body at all.

The life force Cagney embodies is stilled only when at the end he is wrapped up like a mummy, encased in bandages from head to toe. As if sensing that nothing less than binding the character would make audiences believe that his body had stopped moving, the film literally turns a live wire into a mannequin.

Live wires like Cagney speak a fluent body English that seeps into the crevices between their words. For Method-trained actors the links between physical and spoken language are unbreakable. James Dean, for instance, uses his body the way he delivers dialogue—as a means of conveying his characters' ambivalent and often tortured feelings. Dean seldom walks straight into a scene or remains in an upright position throughout it. When in *East of Eden* Cal's father rejects his birthday gift, Dean reacts as if he has been struck hard in the stomach, doubling over in a pain that fuses the psychological with the physical. Huddling on top of a moving train, sprawling on the ground as he runs mounds of earth through his fingers, squatting on his haunches as oil gushes over him, collapsing onto a table in drunken exhaustion, curling upside down on a couch—this résumé of moments from *East of Eden, Rebel Without a Cause,* and *Giant* suggests the reactive quality of the actor's live-wire body. Like his stammering voice blurred with overflowing feelings, James Dean's body bent over in anguish or springing impulsively into action is a highly sensitized instrument.

In *Easy Rider* (1969) Jack Nicholson became a star playing a straight Southern lawyer who leaves his job to go on the road with hipsters Peter Fonda and Dennis Hopper. When his character is killed early in his breakaway odyssey, the film's energy dribbles away. Like the audience, the film misses Nicholson's physical vitality, the way his character decorates language with sounds and smiles and gestures. When he hears bullfrogs off in the distance, for example, he imitates their croak as he crouches over, as if trying to change himself into a bullfrog. The same live-wire agility ignites the otherwise stillborn *Batman* (1989), as Nicholson's Joker strides brazenly through the film.

The high points in Nicholson's performances are often the ones in which violent movements complete feelings his characters cannot express in words alone. In *Five Easy Pieces* (1970) Bobby Dupea (Nicholson) flares up manically in the middle of a traffic jam,

FROM LEFT
The high points of many
Jack Nicholson perfor-
mances are conveyed
through unleashed physical
energy: climbing a fence in
*One Flew over the Cuckoo's
Nest* (1975); capping a fight
with a waitress in *Five Easy
Pieces* (1970).

shaking his fists in the center of a freeway, then hopping onto the back of a pickup truck to play a beat-up piano. To cap a fight with a sullen waitress, the character clears a table in a roadside diner with one furious sweep of his hand. His performance in *One Flew over the Cuckoo's Nest* (1975) builds to the moment the audience has been set up to expect and to root for, when McMurphy leaps forward to strangle the sadistic Nurse Ratched. In *The Shining* (1980) his character gradually retreats into a wordless demonism until, ax in hand, he chases his wife and son.

Part of the tension—the danger—in Nicholson's work is that we can't predict where his physical energy will carry his characters. During McMurphy's first interview with a doctor in *One Flew over the Cuckoo's Nest*, Nicholson swats a fly on the desk, a sudden movement that catches the rigid doctor off guard. He tenses, as if preparing for an explosion. And, like the people who run the asylum, the audience too doesn't know what this live wire might be capable of doing.

Even when his characters are not in extremity, Nicholson gives them a marked physical life. In a quiet scene in *Five Easy Pieces,* for example, Bobby Dupea crouches down to talk to his father, a stroke victim paralyzed in a wheelchair. In the opening scene in *Ironweed* (1987) Nicholson as a terminal alcoholic talks on his knees at the grave of the infant son he accidentally killed when in a drunken stupor. Both actions could have been played with the actor in a standing position, but in bending and squatting Nicholson impels his body into the scenes, in both of which his guilt-ridden characters break momentarily into tears.

The bodies of Method actors like Dean and Nicholson are never simply in neutral. How they move and stand and the direction of their arms and legs fluently express their characters' feelings.

Bombshells

In the Golden Age each studio maintained a portrait gallery overseen by photographers like George Hurrell and Clarence Sinclair Bull who turned contract players into enameled objects of sheer physical perfection. In a typical studio portrait stars have no wrinkles, no smudges, and no signs of life; they're mythically gorgeous and totally inanimate, and their flesh looks as glazed as their deadpan eyes. The high mannequin acting style, usually associated with nubile women groomed for the camera, as if movies were an extension of a sitting for a formal portrait, naturally enough coincided with the heyday of the studio system.

The two trained-for-the-movies mannequins I want to look at here were both promoted by the same mogul, Harry Cohn of Columbia Pictures. In the forties Cohn made a star of Rita Hayworth; Kim Novak was his fifties discovery. Eerily, in 1957, when Hayworth was past her prime and Novak at the height of hers, Cohn cast his two protégées as romantic rivals for a heel (played by Frank Sinatra, a convincing surrogate for the crass studio czar himself) in *Pal Joey*, a loose adaptation of a caustic Broadway musical that became an unwitting showcase for the worst kind of mannequin acting.

Coiffed and costumed like cartoon characters—Hayworth's hair is a too vivid dyed red, Novak's is intense platinum—both stars play strippers. Hayworth is a society hostess with a past, a former star of burlesque; Novak is a reluctant ecdysiast, a nice girl in the wrong business. As characters who expose their bodies for a living, the two actresses never for a moment seem to be able to forget their own. Waists in, breasts extended, they parade before the camera like dutiful beauty contestants—commodities rather than characters.

In training the two women for stardom, Cohn and his studio coaches eradicated any idiosyncrasies or humor they might once have had, and *Pal Joey* offers ample proof of the stars' obedience. They perform by the numbers, moving for each shot exactly as they have been told to do. Their synthetic style is underscored by the not-quite-real voices they have been coerced into. Overenunciating in breathy tones from which any trace of regionalism has been extracted, they talk "Movie Speech," a common feature of star acting in the studio era. Rita Hayworth's real voice—how she talked before she was made over into a screen goddess—seems to be encased somewhere beneath the quiet, low, ladylike tones she has assumed. She has an unnerving, ventriloquial style, as if her speaking voice is dubbed (Hayworth's singing voice, in fact, always belonged to someone else). Novak also has a muted, low-pitched voice but her diction isn't as refined as Hayworth's. She sometimes slurs her words, and her own natural sultriness hasn't been entirely erased. Cohn obviously didn't want his stars to be brassy or hard-boiled, and both Hayworth and Novak sound like "dames" who have been trained to pass as well-spoken ladies. Their pleasant, suppressed tones are as fabricated as their dyed hair and somnambulistic movements; they speak in voices that come from a void.

In contrast to the elocution-school sound of his costars, Frank Sinatra—with his crude, untrained speaking voice, his deep Hobokenese—at least talks as if he belongs in the film's tawdry nightclub setting. But if he doesn't sound like visiting Hollywood royalty, his acting is as mechanical as that of the hapless actresses. All he contributes is his own charmless dissipation and his lounge-lizard crooning style: the mannequin as saloon singer.

The only time in *Pal Joey* when Hayworth is released from the bonds of Harry Cohn's star-packaging sweatshop is when she dances. At a charity bazaar, for old time's sake her character performs one last strip number. Her singing is dubbed but her dancing reminds us that she can still put the blame on Mame. In dance, here as throughout her career, Hayworth happily escapes from the demands of acting. And, dancing with Gene Kelly in *Cover Girl* (1944) or with Fred Astaire in *You Were Never Lovelier* (1942), she has a freedom and an enjoyment in performing otherwise kept under wraps.

Built into all Hayworth's roles are insistent tributes to her body. In *Cover Girl*, she's a model from Brooklyn who is touted within the film as a great beauty and a great dancer; in *Down to Earth* (1947), she is a goddess who comes to earth to correct a spoofing treat-

ment of goddesses in a Broadway show. Cast typically as a spectacular object, Hayworth acts in a suitably statuesque manner, which she sheds only when she dances.

In her famous movie *Gilda* (1946), she's a former dancer who runs away from a damaging marriage to return to her old life, performing in a club. To dance is to free herself of men, and to assert control over them; and when she dances "Put the Blame on Mame," tossing her cascading hair and removing one long black glove at a time in a teasing, elegant striptease, you can see why, despite everything, Hayworth was a star.

Besides dancing Hayworth had one other release from her object status in movies: Orson Welles, who, in *The Lady from Shanghai*, made her seem alert without dancing. As the eponymous heroine, an enigmatic beauty who lures the naive hero (Welles) into her web, Hayworth is a twisty *film noir* femme fatale. Welles shrewdly transforms her limitations into assets by shading her characteristic vagueness into mystery. Instead of simply being on screen to be looked at, she plays a character with a secret agenda, and along with the hero we are placed in the position of piercing her facade. What is she up to? What do her words and gestures really mean? What lies behind her masked face? The film engages us in a more challenging relationship to Hayworth than any of her other movies allowed.

Kim Novak plays her big scene at the end of *Of Human Bondage* (1964) in partial undress, draped in a peekaboo sheet, as if her body rather than her character's rage against the crippled lover who has rejected her is what the scene is supposed to expose. Even in this moment of bitter denunciation—it's the scene in the original 1934 version that proved Bette Davis was born to act in movies—when the character's venom overflows, Novak can't transcend the mannequin style Cohn's starmaking regime molded her for. Where the encounter demands an unprotected eruptiveness, Novak, with her low, breathy, androgynous voice and halting gestures, remains soft and opaque, fuzzy rather than fierce.

But like Hayworth, Novak was once released by a great director from her becalmed mannequin style. In *Vertigo* (1958), under Alfred Hitchcock's guidance, she gives what may be the finest mannequin performance in American movies. Novak plays a tricky dual role. She appears first as a well-spoken lady of mystery (Madeleine) who is enacting a charade for the benefit of a private detective, Scottie (James Stewart), but she's really a shopgirl (Judy) with thick eyebrows and a twangy, low-class accent. Like the lady from Shanghai, Madeleine is a mannequin with a secret the hero and the audience must unlock. "If I could just find the key," Scottie says, as he studies Madeleine's every gesture.

Something is missing in Madeleine, and yet she is magnetic. Scottie is drawn to her even as he is puzzled by her Mona Lisa smile, her otherworldly look and movements. As a lustrous, ethereal woman whose tranced demeanor doesn't seem quite real, Madeleine is

FROM LEFT
Before and after: relaxing on the set of *Pal Joey* (1957), Frank Sinatra, Kim Novak, and Rita Hayworth look like real people; once the camera rolls, they are dehumanized.

Rita Hayworth escaped from bondage to her movie-star object status only when she danced, as in this scene from *Cover Girl* (1944, with Phil Silvers and Gene Kelly), in which she is clearly enjoying herself.

the perfect showcase for Novak's own movie-goddess style. When Scottie finds out that Madeleine was only a masquerade, he says to Judy, "Did he [the man who hired him to follow her and who in fact killed the real Madeleine] train you? Did he rehearse you? . . . Those beautiful phony trances. You were an apt student." His comments might well describe Novak's relations with her own real-life Svengali, Harry Cohn.

"Couldn't you like me just the way I am?" Judy asks Scottie. The answer is no. Before he learns that Judy played Madeleine, Scottie wants to turn her into an imitation of the beauty he has become obsessed with. He wants to transform a forlorn working-class girl with sloppy speech and hunched shoulders into the regal woman whose "suicide" has devastated him. Scottie goes to work on Judy the way Columbia attacked Novak, changing her hair and voice and makeup and clothes so that she becomes a replica of the remote Madonna whose image haunts him. When her makeover is complete and Judy looks just like Madeleine, Scottie is thrilled. And so are we since, typically, Hitchcock has slyly implicated us in the behavior of one of his obsessive characters. The camera scrutinizes the remade woman with a heroic 360-degree spin as Scottie embraces the mummy he has created.

As both cool blonde Madeleine and saucy brunette Judy, Novak's dual characters play out scripts written by cracked men. The elegant Madeleine follows the instructions of a murderer, Judy is putty in the hands of the unhinged detective. Like Novak herself, the characters follow orders, subduing their own desires in order to fulfill a male scenario. The important points about them are revealed entirely through external means, through speech and carriage and demeanor, and in both parts Novak is appropriately and effectively cosmetic.

While all screen goddesses are celebrated for the way they look, not all of them are mannequins. Two of the most popular empresses of screen sex, Jean Harlow and Marilyn Monroe, transcend their status as objects we can't take our eyes off. How?

For a start both Harlow and Monroe have an energy and directness, and an enjoyment in being able to entertain us, missing in the stately Hayworth and Novak. And they have humor, often self-directed. Their beauty usually is not presented on a pedestal, but as the source of comedy: wit and gags defuse the way we look at their emphatic bodies. They are good sports, and their likable personas take the edge off any awe their physical presence is likely to induce.

But for all their humor and humanity, it wasn't inevitable that they would escape mannequin status. As contract stars (Harlow at M-G-M, Monroe at Fox) they were straitjacketed into reiterative blonde bombshell parts that they both periodically came to resent

Jean Harlow's natural exuberance (evident here in *Dinner at Eight*, 1933) helped her to transcend the mannequin-like rigidity impressed on most of Hollywood's boudoir beauties.

and from which they tried to escape. And in addition to being typecast they both, like Hayworth and Novak, have fake voices. Harlow speaks in a high, shrill, nasal, piping twang that sounds part-Brooklyn, part–high society, and 100 percent bogus. The Bowery tinctured with Park Avenue, her accent finally is unidentifiable: Harlow speaks Harlowese in a one-of-a-kind voice that's made for comedy and hard to accept anywhere else. Monroe rarely erased her little-girl breathiness and, like Harlow's built-to-trap-a-man voice, it limited the roles she could play. Yet Harlow and Monroe, unlike Hayworth and Novak, never sound dubbed.

Before *Dinner at Eight* (1933), the film in which "Harlow" emerged at full blast, she had several times been mercilessly miscast—as a British girl in *Hell's Angels* (1930) and as a society belle, a Katharine Hepburn part, in *Platinum Blonde* (1931). In these unsuitable roles, in which her own proletarian brassiness keeps breaking through, as indeed in virtually all her movies, Harlow is physically awkward, rather a klutz, and that's part of her appeal. She's a not-quite beauty who doesn't hold herself like a beauty queen. The very fact of her physical flaws shields her from the numbing adulation with which mannequins like Hayworth and Novak are treated. Wide-hipped and flat-chested for a goddess and with a round face notably deficient in strong planes and contours, Harlow has a figure and face that invite puffiness. She lacks a mannequin's icy, silken control of her body or her voice (or, for that matter, her eyebrows, which move up and down with a life of their own).

Beneath the platinum hair and the clinging satin, Harlow was hoi polloi, part of the crowd, a screen star for the Depression masses. Like Cagney and Joan Blondell and Edward G. Robinson she was an early talkie star who was not grander than the people in the audience. *Dinner at Eight* celebrates her populist appeal. She plays a parvenu married to a vulgarian (Wallace Beery) whom she two-times with a doctor. The part releases her from any obligation to be a movie queen: she's a dame who lounges in bed eating candy, a virago who in domestic spats screeches and kicks and sticks her tongue out. And her overripe sexiness is the butt of jokes, as in the classic comment that ends the film (delivered sublimely by Marie Dressler, who assures Harlow, whose character is worried about the increasing mechanization of modern life, that machines will never be able to replace her line of work). Dressed to the nines in silks and satins or reclining in partial dishabille in a white-on-white bedroom, Harlow offers sex as an irrepressible natural force. Like Carole Lombard she is a physical comedienne, a feisty good-time gal who also has a good heart: her character prevents her bull-like husband from wiping out their society hosts. In *Dinner at Eight* as throughout her short, high-speed career (she died from uremic poisoning in 1937 at the age of twenty-six) Harlow supplied a refreshing no-holds-barred comic relief. Her talent wasn't for depth, or for straight acting; at her best, as in *Dinner at Eight*, *Bombshell* (1933), and *Red Dust* (1932), in which she is paired with her ideal costar, Clark Gable, she's a vernacular Hollywood sexpot with an unbuttoned style.

Marilyn Monroe's negotiations with the mannequin mode are more complicated than Harlow's, but like Harlow she both teased and humanized anatomy. In *Niagara* (1952), released the year before she became a big star, "Marilyn Monroe," she plays a character who's too sexy to live. By 1953, in the two films in which Fox pushed her to stardom—*Gentlemen Prefer Blondes* and *How to Marry a Millionaire*—her sexuality was declawed. She's a sprite, childlike and refreshingly innocent and the sweetest of all the Hollywood bombshells. But in both these versions of Marilyn, as in her few serious roles, in *Bus Stop* (1956) and *The Misfits* (1961), Monroe rises above the coils of sexual stereotype. Her victories were hard won because—like Harlow and Hayworth and Novak, like Lana Turner and Jennifer Jones and Marlene Dietrich, all of whom remained in their screen personas the playthings of autocratic producers or directors or studios—Monroe never entirely escaped the traps that are always in place for the Body Beautiful. All her movies fixate on and fetishize her creamy voluptuousness.

"She's a tramp!" is the way her unhinged husband (Joseph Cotten) describes her in *Niagara;* and that's how the film presents her. In her first shot she wriggles naked under the sheets, smoking a cigarette in a room crisscrossed with *noir* shadows thrown by venetian blinds. Here is prestar Monroe, down and dirty, a lascivious, cheap blonde. She wears

a hot pink dress and, almost like a cartoon character, she's usually bathed in hot lighting that seems to emanate from her character's overheated sensuality. When she walks across a street in a tight skirt, she's the human Niagara, a force of nature with the power to destroy itself as well as those it grabs on its way down.

In film after film her body is treated as a prizewinning object which, as in *Niagara*, threatens to stop the show. In *How to Marry a Millionaire* Monroe and Betty Grable, her predecessor as Fox's top-banana blonde Venus, appear in parallel shots as images reflected in the multiple panels of a mirror. In *The Seven Year Itch* (1955) Monroe's white dress billows up provocatively when she stands over a subway grating. In *River of No Return* (1954) and *Bus Stop* she's a saloon singer in fetishistic black lace panties and fishnet stockings. In *The Prince and the Showgirl* she wears a clinging white dress that showcases all her bulges, while her costar Laurence Olivier is all but invisible behind a beard, a monocle, and a fancy-dress costume, the ceremonial regalia of a crown prince. "Look at that! Look how she moves, like Jell-o on springs," Jack Lemmon gasps in *Some Like It Hot* (1959) as he and the camera salivate when Monroe makes her entrance as Sugar Cane: as she struts down a railway platform the train emits a whistle and steam shoots out from between train wheels. A long scene of Monroe paddling a ball seems to have been included in *The Misfits* so we could see her breasts jiggling like "Jell-o on springs," just as later in the film the camera stares at her bouncing bottom when she's mounted on a horse.

Like her anatomy Monroe's whispery voice and her perpetually puckered lips are a come-on: a show voice to go with a show body. Yet from time to time, early in her career, and late, it's possible to catch a different timbre, a voice behind the "voice." In *Niagara* she adopts the "Marilyn" voice only when she is putting on an act for other characters, enacting a show of wifely concern. In scenes with her husband and her lover, where her character isn't pretending, Monroe's voice is lower and tougher. In *The Misfits*, in a role that both at the time and in retrospect seems like a valedictory to the troubled offscreen Marilyn, a woman shadowed by sorrow, her voice is also deeper, with most of the vocal "makeup" scraped away.

Displaying her body and pitching her voice as she was directed to do, Monroe knowingly colluded in constructing her movie persona, and like most superstars she had the knack of immediately winning us over. In *How to Marry a Millionaire* and *Gentlemen*

ABOVE AND FOLLOWING PAGES Twentieth Century Fox presented Marilyn Monroe as a natural splendor, as in the poster for *Niagara* (1952) and a scene from *How to Marry a Millionaire* (with Cameron Mitchell casting a lascivious glance at her).

Prefer Blondes she succeeds in making her determined golddiggers appealing and thereby defuses the queasy equation in both pictures between sex and money. In her first appearance in *The Seven Year Itch* she is silhouetted behind a frosted-glass door; when she unlocks it and enters the room she's so fresh-looking that the audience I saw the film with at a recent revival-house screening let out a collective sigh. Documentary footage of Monroe facing a horde of photographers as she is leaving a hospital (after a suicide attempt) provides a glimpse of how she could turn on "MM" even offstage. She looks drained, yet even here, in real life, at a vulnerable moment, she plays to the camera as she smiles shyly, coyly moving her eyes from side to side and rotating, lowering, and raising her head so that the paparazzi surrounding her can get a few choice shots.

But though she did what her bosses asked, and played for them as she played for the photographers when walking out of the hospital, though she participated in turning herself into a spectacular object (and surely in some ways enjoyed doing it), she was never merely a studio-made blonde. She was never for a moment a replica of the utterly vacant Betty Grable. In the occasional dramas as well as the frothy comedies that were the backbone of her career she frequently rose above the mannequin packaging. Though she was often cast as the Girl from Nowhere, as in *The Seven Year Itch* and *There's No Business Like Show Business* (1954), Monroe filled in the gaps and created characters the audience could believe in and care about.

Unlike somnambulists such as Grable and Hayworth and Novak, Monroe quivers with feelings, and even in her fluffiest vehicles she supplies an emotional reality for her characters. Her acting, engrained with pieces of her real self, is both generous and intimate; indeed it is precisely her availability that has continued to provoke psychoanalytic speculation. Monroe is the one star almost every moviegoer feels entitled to talk about, to try to explain, to protect and feel sorry for. In an effort to satisfy the great public desire to find out all about Monroe, books on every aspect of her life and work continue to be published. A mannequin could never induce the kind of personal response from viewers Monroe still does three decades after her death.

Tantalizingly, her performances sometimes contain the promise of other, darker Marilyns: traces of the role of a psychotic baby-sitter she played, unforgettably, in *Don't Bother to Knock* (1952) remain throughout her career. This light-and-shadow quality takes center stage in *Bus Stop*, her finest performance. Here the two basic Monroe types, the

ABOVE AND OPPOSITE
Despite her carefully crafted sexpot persona, Marilyn Monroe had ways of outwitting a lustful male gaze, as in an early dramatic role in *Don't Bother to Knock* (1952), in which a neurotic Marilyn is unnervingly revealed, and in *The Prince and the Showgirl* (1957), as a dazed Marilyn invites a protective rather than a prurient response.

dizzy dame of *How to Marry a Millionaire* and the bereft heroines of *Don't Bother to Knock* and *The Misfits*, merge in perfect balance. As Cherie, another Girl from Nowhere, a floozy chanteuse who longs to be "somebody," Monroe layers her performance with the kind of sensory work and emotional recall she studied at the Actors Studio. When Bo (Don Murray), a rodeo Romeo, apologizes to her after he has lassoed her, she says, "I guess I been treated worse in my life." Monroe makes this bare statement rumble with the memory of the sexual indignities her character has borne. When Bo kisses her seriously for the first time and Cherie sees that his feelings for her are genuine, she shudders as she closes her eyes in a moment of private ecstasy. And when Bo gives her his coat, to protect her against the desert chill, Monroe treats the moment like a sensual rush. In these scenes, as throughout the film, she transforms Actors Studio exercises into reverberant acting quick with an overflow of truthful feelings.

In *The Prince and the Showgirl* Monroe again dusts comedy with poignant touches. As the prince talks on the phone, ignoring his guest, Maizie (Monroe), an American showgirl, picks at food on a buffet table and talks to herself as she reacts to his peevish and insensitive behavior (the prince speaks negatively about Americans) with a deft comic pantomime. She slaps food on her plate and makes faces in a running commentary on the bad manners of her host, yet another man who must be trained out of treating her like a mannequin. The film's coronation sequence—a series of closeups of Maizie in the cathedral looking in teary wonder at the pageantry and at the stained-glass windows that surround her—is an homage to the star. The closeups reveal the sparkle in Monroe's eyes, and the sensitivity. Here as throughout her brief career these qualities and her humor allowed her to triumph over the mannequin underpinnings of her roles—a battle the star herself was never really confident she had won.

Peacocks

In American culture it is traditional for women rather than men to be put on display as objects of desire, yet the kind of exhibition I've been considering is a factor of screen performing that transcends gender. From Douglas Fairbanks as the bare-chested title character in *The Thief of Bagdad* (1924) to Clark Gable modestly disrobing in *It Happened One Night* to Marlon Brando in a ripped, stained T-shirt in *A Streetcar Named Desire* to Sylvester Stallone as *Rambo* (1985) and Arnold Schwarzenegger in *The Terminator* (1984) showing off their glistening, oiled, thickly veined torsos, the male body has frequently been the object of the camera's gaze, sometimes covertly, just as often openly and with appreciation.

Peacocks and action heroes are two general categories for actors prized for their bodies or for what they can do with them. Peacocks are the romantic heroes, the actors women on screen and in the audience are expected to go limp over; action heroes are athletes (swashbucklers and cowboys and cops) rather than aesthetes, men on the move rarely caught in repose or in a reclining position. Hitching a horse, tying a rope, stalking prey on Western main streets or on the mean streets of the big city, guns at the ready, they often carry America's manifest destiny on their broad backs.

The peacocks are more problematic than the action stars, whose masculinity is never in doubt. Let's look at ways in which five improbably handsome actors, peacocks all—Rudolph Valentino, Robert Redford, Clark Gable, Paul Newman, and Cary Grant—have confronted their inescapable attractiveness; how, variously, they have embraced, undermined, and challenged the blessing and the burden of their good looks.

In the history of American movies Valentino remains a unique phenomenon, a male who gave himself to the camera to be looked at and sighed over in ways culturally encoded as "feminine." In an archetypal Valentino moment (in *Son of the Sheik*, 1926)—a moment virtually no other male star would undertake—the actor poses on a balcony like a female icon. Paying tribute to him from the street below, the heroine throws him a rose, but since the son of the sheik thinks (incorrectly) that she is an enemy, he tosses his head in the air in a gesture of contemptuous dismissal.

The male body as spectacle: Sylvester Stallone's physique, amply on display in *Rambo: First Blood Part II* (1985), has helped to make him one of the highest paid actors in Hollywood history.

This image, of Valentino igniting female desire, provides the essential spectacle of his movies. Like female mannequins the actor typically makes his conquests enticingly dressed, usually in exotic noncontemporary gear—the turbans and capes of *The Sheik* (1921) and *The Son of the Sheik;* the flounces and wigs of an eighteenth-century dandy in *Monsieur Beaucaire* (1924); the outfit of a toreador in *Blood and Sand* (1922). Most of his roles highlight costume and the rituals of getting dressed. In *Monsieur Beaucaire,* for example, we are first offered a glimpse of his bare chest before we watch as with the aid of servants Beaucaire dons his elaborate princely costume and makeup. Once they're all dressed up, Valentino's characters are typically performers who exult in being looked at. Valentino became a star dancing a sultry tango in *Four Horsemen of the Apocalypse* (1921). He's a court entertainer in *Monsieur Beaucaire,* a toreador with a flare for disporting himself in the arena in *Blood and Sand.* Sometimes his costumes are disguises: he's a masked outlaw in *The Eagle* (1925), in *Monsieur Beaucaire* he's a prince who masquerades as a lowly barber and as a woman, and in *Son of the Sheik* he plays both the son and his father.

Often, then, Valentino is literally on stage, as audiences within the films devour his spectacular presence. Sometimes the decor turns us into voyeurs with privileged access to the star; in *The Sheik* drapes and arches, behind which we observe him conduct his courtships, create a peephole effect.

Watching his characters perform, or receiving one of their loaded looks (also a kind of performance), women within the films are enflamed. The actor's studied slow-motion vocabulary of smoldering glances, flaring nostrils, and quivering, wettened, half-parted lips proves overpowering. When he makes his entrance on a stage in *Monsieur Beaucaire,* a prince who is an entertainer at the court of Louis XV (where "pleasure was the business of state"), only one woman in the on-screen audience remains unmoved, thereby giving him "the shock of his life: a woman is not looking at him." When the toreador in *Blood and Sand* favors Dona Sol with a hooded, acquisitive gaze, she nearly faints from the heat generated by his eyes.

Sometimes Valentino's seductions are exposed as a performance. In the early scenes of *The Sheik* the actor's eyes flash as we watch him monitoring the gestures of courtship. When he orders Lady Diana into his tent, he thrusts one arm out, spreads his legs imperiously, and glares fiercely when she hesitates. (It's in this scene that Valentino "speaks" his most famous line: "Are you not woman enough to know?" he says, when Lady Diana asks the sheik why he has brought her here.) But the sheik leaves his quarry unsullied: in the film's racist regime his restraint on the edge of committing rape is explained by the fact that he is not the real thing—his father was an Englishman, his mother was a Spaniard, he is an Arab only by adoption. Once he is revealed as a white man, the sheik becomes notably subdued; it's only when he's posing as an Arab that he's in full drag as an exotic lover. By the end he has dropped his role as a devastating romancer, and is rewarded by being united with a woman who is as true as he is.

In *Monsieur Beaucaire* his character must also relinquish playacting in order to earn true love. To win the acceptance of a deserving woman (and also probably of the men in the audience), Valentino then often had to renounce "Valentino." If the Valentino style is an anomaly in screen acting, and if his sexual strategies may baffle latter-day tastes, there is compelling evidence within the films that his florid manner aroused contemporary anxieties: his characters typically end up subdued or dead.

Like Marlene Dietrich, his closest female counterpart, Valentino carries unabashed, look-at-me mannequinism to often delirious heights. And like Dietrich, he's an original, a skilled miniaturist who makes love to the camera. For all its antique trimmings Valentino's seduction of the camera is the ancestor to erotic campaigns waged by actors of the moment like Tom Selleck, Tom Cruise, Mel Gibson, Bruce Willis, and Don Johnson, whose fame is based on their megawatt sex appeal. The current fellows are hip and loose, quick where Valentino is methodical, and a feigned modesty underlies their personas, as if with their "aw, shucks" grins they're apologizing for being so damned attractive. But scratch the contemporary surface and they're brothers to Valentino, linked by their own and their medium's hypnotized fascination with their physical appeal.

Among modern Hollywood matinee idols the actor closest in spirit as well as pac-

ing to Valentino is Robert Redford. Like Valentino, and in a less self-deprecating manner than most other heartthrobs, Redford welcomes the camera's caress. But where Valentino's erotic display is often encoded precisely as a performance, an act, Redford's is often played straight. In *Out of Africa* (1985), faced with the challenge of a rich role as a British adventurer who liberates the heroine, he simply brings on "Robert Redford," glamorous American movie star. While, with suitable accent and for the prologue aging her voice and face, Meryl Streep is submerged in her character, the Danish writer who took the pen name of Isak Dinesen, Redford as a character the heroine and the audience are supposed to fall in love with remains without an accent or a soul. Coasting on "Redford" even into advanced middle age, he plays the role by making what in effect is a series of personal appearances.

ABOVE AND OPPOSITE
Valentino, Hollywood's first male mannequin, in partial undress in *Monsieur Beaucaire* (1924) and in full toreador regalia, displaying himself on stairs, in *Blood and Sand* (1922).

In parts with built-in damage control—*Butch Cassidy and the Sundance Kid* (1969), *The Sting* (1973), and *The Candidate* (1972)—in which his calculating self-consciousness is either kidded or accounted for, "Robert Redford" can be appealing. His roles in *Butch Cassidy* and *The Sting* poke fun at his movie-star looks, and wisecracking with Paul Newman in these buddy movies noticeably relaxes him. As it charts the making of a political mannequin, *The Candidate* exposes the contrivance, the studied casualness and "naturalism," of Redford's persona. Redford as a senatorial candidate is coached into cultivating a slick style. "You're selling your face, that's what we have to sell first," his advisers tell him. Before a TV debate he is warned, "You can't say too much," and as makeup is applied he's told, "Keep your eyes steady, keep your fingers interlaced, don't look up." Gradually the candidate learns to reserve truthfulness for private moments out of the limelight, but at the end, after he wins and wants to talk frankly with his chief adviser, he can no longer find the words to express what he feels. "What do we do now?" he asks, an actor requesting lines from the prompter. As a sexy superstar politician with an Ipana smile who is coached to check his every word and movement, Robert Redford is eerily appropriate.

When *Gone With the Wind* was screened to a packed house at Radio City Music Hall to mark the film's fiftieth anniversary, Clark Gable's entrance as Rhett Butler elicited eruptive applause: the camera swoops down to Rhett at the bottom of the stairs as he looks up at Scarlett and grins like a Cheshire cat, with a smile so wide it extends to his ears and a look so piercing it seems to undress the startled heroine. The audience was welcoming an old friend, "Clark Gable," whose charm was clearly as devastating as ever.

The hitchhiking scene in *It Happened One Night* is another quintessential moment in the Gable iconography. As a snappy newspaper reporter on the road with a runaway heiress, Gable demonstrates his hitching technique, standing by the side of the road as he raises his thumb and smiles in a variety of inflections, in a montage of shots filled with the actor's vitality. The drivers who whiz by him must have been blind.

Both scenes are a pure display of movie-star charisma. And, as intended, the dazzlement is entirely on the surface. Gable reputedly never took himself seriously as an actor—never thought he really was an actor—and the studio system in which he was trained had no reason to disabuse him or his audience of his self-estimate. By popular demand and by his own real limitations, Gable always played "Clark Gable" even when his roles called for embellishments. Playing British men of the sea in *Mutiny on the Bounty* (1935) and *China Seas* (1935) or a Southern gentleman in *Gone With the Wind*, Gable speaks pure Gable-ese in a broad accent that retains remnants of his boyhood on an Ohio farm. What he could do, the role he could play, that of the confident lady-killer, he did without any actorly fuss.

Like Valentino Gable often plays the love object, but unlike Valentino he remains active, exerting masculine control and dominance. Gable never poses, and he wears his good looks lightly, in a way that never offended male viewers. Written into his roles is

FROM LEFT
Unlike a number of other handsome actors, Clark Gable did far more looking than being looked at. Notice the hot glance he has for Jean Harlow, preparing for a scene in *Red Dust* (1932). Often, of course, he did more than merely look; even Garbo couldn't stop him, as this scene of erotic conquest in *Susan Lenox: Her Fall and Rise* (1931) demonstrates.

something of a running manifesto on how to (mis)treat women (if you're Clark Gable). The master of the sexual put-down as come-on, Gable never changes his attack, treating both ladies and "dames" in the same rough way. He's the only leading man who knocked Garbo from her pedestal; his character's insults (in *Susan Lenox: Her Fall and Rise*, 1931) only incite Garbo's desire to possess him. "Do you want me to slap you out of this room?" he greets new arrival Jean Harlow in *Red Dust.* Of course she falls for him. To the demure Mary Astor in the same film, who also falls for him, Gable explains, after she has slapped him, "Out here we all slap each other sooner or later."

Like most movies *Red Dust* is about why the hero and the heroine are made for each other, and Harlow's ripe and unapologetic sexiness makes her Gable's ideal screenmate. In this case, like attracts like. And both also play sexy characters with a good heart, a prerequisite for stardom in the thirties. Even when, perhaps especially when, Gable is cast as a rogue or a scoundrel, he maintains his affable surface. His ingratiating grin, his dimples, his eager jug ears, his sly, appropriating look, his assurance that women respond to his harsh treatment, the humor that softens the underlying misogyny, and his ability to wear costumes—he looks great in a white suit in *China Seas* and in ripped, stained safari gear in *Red Dust*—are his unvarying stock-in-trade. He remains "Clark Gable" even in extreme circumstances, as in the finale of *Manhattan Melodrama* (1934), when his character is on Death Row. Insouciant in the face of death—Gable might be playing a scene from *It Happened One Night*—the actor delivers what in effect is the manifesto of a Hollywood buccaneer, maintaining that unless he can live as he wants to he doesn't want to live at all. Speaking with brio, in his characteristic clip, and grinning, Gable snaps out his character's declaration of independence before strutting off to death.

Unlike Gable and Redford, Paul Newman has tried from the beginning of his

career to beat the potentially dead weight of his chiseled face and form by doing a lot of acting. Newman was a serious drama student, first at Yale and then as a member of the Actors Studio, and his knowledge of Method techniques like emotional and sense memory helps to deepen his work, to divert our attention from how he looks to what his character is feeling. When as Eddie Felson in *The Hustler* (1961) he describes how his thumbs were broken, Newman looks offscreen as he summons sensory memories of the pain. In *Hud* (1963) his character's confession of having killed his brother in a drunk-driving accident fifteen years before is filled with pauses, stony silences, and a gaze transfixed by the past.

In his strongest roles Newman added further insurance against pretty-boy typecasting by playing amoral antiheroes. When he plays louts like Hud, a man who wants to disinherit his own father, Newman doesn't soften the character or court audience approval: his ice-blue eyes and his dry voice are chilling.

For all his integrity, however, his attempts to play against and beneath his appearance, Newman doesn't entirely escape mannequinism, and built into his most characteristic parts is an insistence on the way he looks. In *Cat on a Hot Tin Roof* (1958) and *Sweet Bird of Youth* (1962) he's a Tennessee Williams stud, an object of desire pawed over by women with voracious appetites. In both films the actor's taut chest is unbared, as it also is with far less thematic justification in potboilers like *The Prize* (1964). In *Hud* Newman often strikes picturesque poses, standing in a contrapposto position on the dry Texas land—the character becomes a figure in a landscape, dramatically placed on the Panavision screen.

As he stands a little to the side watching us watching him, Newman is a calculating rather than an intuitive actor. He's a proficient but cool technician, and the preening quality of many of his characters merges with the actor's self-regarding technique. To loosen his image, and to undercut the mannequin aura that trails his serious roles, Newman like Redford really needed the good-natured self-mockery of *Butch Cassidy* and *The Sting*. Embodying the late-sixties zeitgeist of the outlaw as culture hero, Butch and Sun-

ABOVE
Paul Newman strikes a classical contrapposto stance in a publicity shot for *Hud* (1963).

OPPOSITE
Even offscreen, resting between takes of *Butch Cassidy and the Sundance Kid* (1969), Newman and Redford pose picturesquely, while their less image-conscious costar, Katharine Ross, collapses.

dance are living legends, just like the actors who play them: cool, gorgeous, and forever wisecracking, even at the end when they're trapped by the militia. "I got a great idea where we should go next . . . Australia," Butch quips shortly before he and his partner run out to meet death from a volley of bullets.

Tall, lean, dark, and imperially handsome, Cary Grant looks as if he could be a stiff. But once he hit his stride, in *Sylvia Scarlett* (1935), after a few years of waxworks performances, he was never caught posing. Grant has a wonderfully limber gait and a loose-jointedness that counteract his movie-star sleekness. Many of his most memorable roles either celebrate his kinetic dash or, through slapstick, upend the privilege to which his looks entitle him.

In *Topper* (1937) and *Holiday,* two pictures that consolidated his image, Grant is cast as a free spirit. Although in both movies he dresses in tuxedo and black tie, he breaks the rules about how people in formal dress are expected to behave. *Topper* opens with Grant driving his car sitting on top of the front seat, then (with his wife, played by Constance Bennett) curling up to sleep in front of the bank where he's the largest stockholder.

Arriving late at the annual stockholders' meeting, he slides into a chair with a movement that recalls his early work as a stilt walker in a traveling circus.

In *Holiday* Grant's character somersaults (Grant performed most of the stunts himself). "When I feel a worry coming on, I somersault," Johnny explains to friends, winking before vaulting. When Johnny enters the mausoleum-like home of his absurdly wealthy fiancée, Julia, he performs another handspring, this time while yodeling. When he meets Julia's sister (Katharine Hepburn), he joins her in performing acrobatics in the upstairs playroom—"a room for fun," Linda calls it, in which she seeks shelter from her stodgy family. When Johnny breaks off with Julia, he announces his code: "I love feeling free inside even better than I love you." *Holiday* ends with the match that seems predestined—Hepburn's straight-ahead, take-charge energy merging with Grant's physical expansiveness.

Twenty-one years later, in *North by Northwest* (1959), Grant exudes the same dynamism. Here he's a top ad executive on the run, a man of affairs whose pace and command are announced in the opening sequence, in which he charges through doors, then barrels his way through Manhattan lunchtime crowds as he hails and enters a taxi like a man who expects the world to jump at his orders, speaking all the while in a staccato clip

OPPOSITE AND BELOW
Cary Grant's flair for physical comedy played against his leading-man good looks. Here he is in drag in *I Was a Male War Bride* (1949, with Ann Sheridan) and sprawled on the floor in *Holiday* (1938, with Katharine Hepburn).

that keeps up with his surging movements. Hitchcock's sly conceit is to humble this confident man on the go, making him a victim of mistaken identity. But even with the tables turned on him, Roger Thornhill proves inviolate as he successfully decodes the Byzantine narrative in which he has been miscast as the wrong man. Stuffed in a closed upper berth on a train, attacked by a plane on an open field, dangling from Mount Rushmore, leaping from cliffs and trains, falling "dead" in a fake shoot-out—the character's ingenuity is cut to the measure of the actor's own physical quick-wittedness. As "Kaplan," Grant's as on the move and resourceful as when he's brisk Roger Thornhill in the film's opening. His movements have such authority that when a lady in a hospital bed rises up in excitement when "Kaplan" races through her room (the film is deliciously ambiguous about whether she is responding to the character or to Cary Grant himself), his raised hand immediately silences her. Nothing is too much for him, as we see him wriggle out of one precipitous circumstance after another. His powers are hieratic: the great-looking movie star as magus.

In two films directed by Howard Hawks, *Bringing Up Baby* and *I Was a Male War Bride* (1949), Grant plays buffoons who are physically as well as emotionally clumsy. In the former he's a bespectacled fuddy-duddy anthropologist more interested in the intercostal clavicle of a brontosaurus than in his pious fiancée or in the dizzy, fearless, aggressive young woman (Katharine Hepburn, who else?) who pursues him. "I'm afraid of you," he tells this woman, who among other things has stolen his golf ball and his car, smashed his glasses, and caused him to fall on his hat, rip his coat, and wear her nightgown. To escape her ("our relationship has been a series of misadventures"), he climbs to the top of his beloved brontosaurus, but as we have known all along, avoiding her is not possible. Like the characters played by the same performers in *Holiday* and *The Philadelphia Story*, these two live wires are a matched pair.

In the not as congenial *War Bride* Grant plays a victim of another aggressive female. He's a French officer (though he sounds just like Cary Grant) who's continually humiliated by the American woman officer (Ann Sheridan) he's destined to marry. The woman "wears the pants" as Henri Rochard (Grant) is the fall guy, riding sidesaddle as she drives a motorcycle, breaking a door handle as he exits her bedroom, rowing a boat into a waterfall, being thrown into jail, having trouble finding a place to sleep on his wedding night and ending up in a bathtub, and dressing up as his wife's spouse in order to be allowed to enter the United States ("According to the American army, I *am* my wife"). These Hawksian farces of sex reversal and cross-dressing showcase Grant's willingness to rib his matinee-idol looks and his natural grace, a strategy that insured his victory over physical typecasting.

Walking Tall: Action Heroes

Early in *The Three Musketeers* (1921), in the scene in which the hero, D'Artagnan, bids his father farewell, Douglas Fairbanks puts his arm over his eyes, covering his face from his father and from us in order to conceal any expression of intimate feeling. Fairbanks' audaciously Delsartean gesture is both ironic and self-protective, as if the actor is signaling us that the portrayal of private emotion is not after all what his audience expects of him nor what as a performer he is capable of providing. Similarly, at the end of *The Mark of Zorro*, when the hero is alone at last with the heroine, Fairbanks also closes us out of an intimate moment, waving a handkerchief to conceal a kiss.

When in *The Thief of Bagdad* his character smells food, Fairbanks pats his stomach in a large, circular movement. In *The Three Musketeers*, when D'Artagnan gets an idea—that it is Lady de Winter who stole the queen's diamond buckle—his eyes first narrow, then widen, as he taps a finger on his forehead. Fairbanks thus translates inner thought into explicit outward gesture: violating Stanislavski, he "indicates." Acting with his full body, he creates his characters entirely through external means: details of costume, use of props, stance, gesture, style of movement. Closeups intruded on his acting space and unnerved him. They also revealed his double chin and the fact that when he was at the height of his fame in the late teens and early twenties he was already middle-aged.

Early in the development of screen acting, Fairbanks demonstrated the potential eloquence of Delsartean performance. He's the American screen's first self-delighted exhibitionist, a mime who harnessed his prizewinning physique and gymnastic skills to create characters whose body language tells us all we need to know. As if he's acting under the influence of Walt Whitman, Fairbanks sings the body electric.

Fairbanks certainly knew his limits, yet within the range of what he could do he was decidedly an actor rather than simply an engaging personality. Often, to prove his acting prowess he creates two bodies for the same role, one a comic fall guy and the other a superhero. Sometimes the split is a matter of disguise—Fairbanks pretending to be incompetent—and sometimes his character is gradually transformed from a dandy or a boob into a hero with a vaulting physical dexterity.

The star's first appearance in *Robin Hood* (1922) is as a bumbling knight, Huntingdon, who struggles with a helmet that seems to have a will of its own, cowers when court ladies crowd around him after he wins a joust, and collapses when he's thrown into jail. When, in part two, Fairbanks finally comes on in his Robin Hood costume, he seems almost magically released. Now, as the fabled leader in Sherwood Forest, the character as well as the actor becomes his own master. Swinging from ramparts, climbing a drawbridge, scaling a wall to save Lady Marian from suicide, catching her as she falls while also taking on a group of Prince John's henchmen, he's in rapturous perpetual motion. In the

Douglas Fairbanks, Sr., exulting in sheer physical well-being, in *The Thief of Bagdad* (1924).

scenes of merrymaking among his men in the forest, Fairbanks leaps high into the air, waving and extending his arms, stretching his entire body outward and upward. His jubilant acrobatics are dancelike.

The Mark of Zorro is Fairbanks' most spectacular body-double performance: he is both Don Diego, a bloodless aristocrat, and Zorro, a crackerjack, black-masked freedom fighter in early California. Our first view of Don Diego is behind a "feminine" object, a huge, twirling umbrella. He yawns and droops, wears a hangdog expression, takes snuff (which he gags on), offers a limp handshake, flutters a handkerchief, plucks girlishly at a long string attached to a sombrero. "He isn't a man, he's a fish," a disdainful young woman says about him. When no one is looking Fairbanks favors us with sly sidelong looks, smiling secretly at the success of his charade.

While Don Diego always seems to yawn, Zorro enters laughing, with a wide, toothy grin and a toss of the head that instantly identifies the character as a swaggering hero. The woman who called Don Diego a fish swoons at Zorro's presence. Once he puts on Zorro's mask, Fairbanks becomes an unstoppable force. Even in rare moments of repose—when, for instance, he sits on a high windowsill holding a flower and smoking a cigar and laughing, or when he takes a break during a chase to bite into a hefty sandwich—he oozes physical well-being.

To show his body in expressive movement Fairbanks required long shots, and to validate the fact that he performed his own stunts in real time he needed to act in long takes as well. But in *The Thief of Bagdad,* despite moments of splendid plastique, he breaks his covenant with his audience and for the first time depends on filmmaking tricks. Special effects accomplish most of the work, with the star usually doing little more than throwing his arms out wide as, a Siegfried in a land of marvels, he encounters or makes use of agents of the supernatural: giant spiders, undersea sirens, a dinosaur, a wizard, a flying carpet, a winged horse. Even in realistic actions, jumping from one urn to another and vaulting over a wall by swinging on the branches of a tree, the film undercuts him: it takes three shots for him to clear the wall.

Fairbanks in action, in *The Mark of Zorro* (1920).

Vigorous and external, Fairbanks' performances are ideally suited to moving pictures. And to portray his active heroes the star didn't need a voice—talk would only have confined him, as it did his most popular swashbuckling successor, Errol Flynn, whose thin, reedy voice doesn't command a throne room or a field of battle. The addition of speech seems to mute Flynn's body language, and his gestural codes—of burnished smiles, upraised arms, hands on hips, feet planted widely apart—evoke Fairbanks but without Fairbanks' panache. Silence released Fairbanks' athleticism; speech inhibits Flynn's.

Often as blank of face as of voice and body (at the end of *The Adventures of Robin Hood* [1938] his expression remains unchanged in the recognition scene, when King Richard reveals himself, and later when Robin Hood learns Lady Marian is to be executed), Flynn is a stolid buccaneer, a mannequin whose body doesn't enact "hero" with the brio that Fairbanks incarnates. To minimize Flynn's inertness quick cuts are often used. A key sword fight in *Captain Blood* (1935), for example, is filmed entirely in closeups and short takes, and in the sea battle finale Flynn merely stands in place (no swinging from the masts) while cannons and guns do the fighting. At the end, almost as an afterthought, Flynn takes one modest swing on a rope to get him from his own ship onto a French one nearby—no match for the wide, unedited leaps Fairbanks performed.

But if in action shots Flynn doesn't seize space the way Fairbanks does, and if his heroic gestures lack fluency, the actor does have an engaging light touch, a lusty laugh, and bedroom eyes. His popularity is solid evidence that in the movies youth and vivid good looks can sometimes catapult a performer into the winner's circle. If enacting heroism is a chore for Flynn, eating or drinking or making love are actions he performs with relish. His eating scene in *The Adventures of Robin Hood*, in which he takes big, greedy bites out of the deer he has carried into the mess hall on his shoulder and thrown down with bravado on wicked Prince John's dining table, bristles with Fairbanksian *jouissance*. And in his romantic scenes with Olivia de Havilland in their many costarring vehicles—he's the rogue to her lady, the Fred and Ginger contrast with the sexes reversed—his hushed, conversational style is irresistible.

THIS PAGE
Compare Fairbanks' vital hero in *Robin Hood* (1922) with Errol Flynn's less animated swashbuckler in *The Adventures of Robin Hood* (1938). Not entirely at ease with bow and arrow, Flynn speaks a less fluent body language than Fairbanks.

OPPOSITE
The Man of the West as American legend: Gary Cooper looking embalmed in *The Westerner* (1940; a color publicity still from a black-and-white film).

The original Hollywood Western hero, William S. Hart started out as a stage actor (he was Messala in the 1903 theatre production of *Ben-Hur*). Although he performed in a style that may now seem overembellished, he used his body more animatedly and probably suggested a more vibrant inner life than any later Westerners.

Hart's fervor was reinforced by florid intertitles. "This is a story of the Santa Fe Trail, where marched the pioneers, building a new Empire in the sand-rimmed wilderness," claim the opening titles in Thomas Ince's production of *Wagon Tracks* (1919), in which a wagon train is called "the white-sailed armada of an unconquerable race," and in which Hart as the wagon leader claims about the land that "it's like one of them old hymns, soft but mighty-like an' bringin' God right close." The setting of *The Silent Man* (1917) is introduced as "the region that God cursed and left unfinished; a vast mysterious sea of wind and sage. Primordial desolation, a huge waste shunned by beast and bird, fostering only a poisonous life of hiss and fang. A trackless solitude braved only by the superman, combating the eternal dryness in search of gold."

The first Western hero: William S. Hart, rugged-looking and more intense than any of his successors. Here he confronts some bad guys in *Hell's Hinges* (1916).

Framed by words like these, Hart cannot perform in the bare-bones minimalism that later became customary for Westerns, and the style he developed was more extreme gesturally and emotionally than that used by any talking cowboy. The core of many Hart performances is in the struggle between the stoicism expected of his Man of the West and the surplus of feelings that overtakes him. In the representative *Wagon Tracks*, Hart is Buckskin Hamilton, "desert guide and true son of the New Empire," who returns alone across the trail to meet his brother from the East. When he discovers that his brother has been killed on board ship in an argument over a card game, Hart doesn't constrict his reaction to the mere blink or twitch a later cowboy might eke out. He is struck dumb at first, then tears come and his shoulders heave as he bends over the figure of his slain brother, vowing to seek vengeance. The scene is capped by a slow iris out, as if the film itself is paying tribute to Hart's hard work. When he discovers that the woman he has grown to love was involved in his brother's murder, he has another seizure—jumping back, he jerks his head and holds onto a wagon post for support as the veins in his neck twitch. After learning that the woman's brother was the one who pulled the trigger, he denounces the culprit as though filled with the wrath of Jehovah, his fists alternately clenching and opening as he raises his arms.

Buckskin has another moment of reckoning as the villain's sister pleads for mercy; looking offscreen, his eyes alight to signal his character's inner debate. At the end, glancing away from the woman he is drawn to, Buckskin hits the trail alone—"the Empire Builder, riding alone through the frontiers of the Morning to meet the future and bid it welcome."

With his prominent hawk nose, close-set eyes, strong jaw, sunken cheeks, and Lincolnesque stature, Hart looks like a weathered pioneer, the real thing rather than a movie star pretending to be a Westerner. But talking pictures would have revealed the charade, for Hart spoke in a rich, resonant voice that made him sound like a cultivated Shakespearean actor, or like the voice of God in *The Ten Commandments*.

Another early Western actor, Tom Mix, was in fact a real-life cowboy who performed his own stunts and toured with Wild West shows. His unadorned style was closer than Hart's to the dry understatement of such later Western icons as John Wayne, Gary Cooper, and Clint Eastwood. In his most popular film, *Riders of the Purple Sage* (1925), Mix plays a distant forerunner of John Wayne's searcher, a man who vows, "I'll find Milly and Bess [his sister and her daughter, abducted by outlaws] if it takes a lifetime." Settling disputes with guns rather than words and, unlike Hart's heroes, never for a moment pausing to reflect or to debate with himself, Mix is a straightforward action hero who does most of his acting in long shot. He falters only when the camera moves in for closeups. When he learns that his sister and her child have been killed (the report turns out to be untrue), he simply averts his eyes from the camera. And in his big scene, when he finally confronts the villain, he stares blankly straight ahead, expressing emotion by opening and closing his eyes twice.

Like Tom Mix, the most popular of all Western stars is an actor with a frozen face and a body nowhere near as swift as Fairbanks' who nonetheless has a strong screen presence. John Wayne is a sagebrush mannequin who, probably more than any screen actor, embodies American notions of rugged manliness.

Although he had been a leading actor in films since 1930, when he starred in *The Big Trail*, John Wayne became a star playing the Ringo Kid in John Ford's *Stagecoach* in 1939. Seemingly out of nowhere, in the middle of Monument Valley (Ford's sacred place), the Ringo Kid appears, his gun raised high in the air. As if delighted by its discovery, the camera moves in toward the tall, lone figure. Sixteen years later, in Ford's *The Searchers*, Wayne appears on horseback in the distance, a traveler emerging out of the desert vastness. His heroic entry into the film is framed by the open door of a house. At the end, after the character's search has been completed, Wayne hovers on the stoop of another house, then turns away to head back into the wilderness as a woman closes the door on his retreating figure.

The films thus visually identify the actor as a man of myth, a character at home only in the Great Western Nowhere. And with his large frame, loping stride, grizzled face,

ungiving eyes, and husky drawl, it's a role Wayne seemed born to play: anatomy is destiny for actors as well as actresses. As an icon of the West Wayne has undeniable force—he's convincing on a horse, or tying a rope, or walking into a saloon, or reading the landscape for signs of Indians.

Playing a generic role in *Stagecoach*—Ford uses the actor for his hulking, monolithic presence, a guy who walks tall in a ten-gallon hat—Wayne fits the bill. But Ford also gives him plenty of protection. When Ringo early on bows his head as he sits squeezed into the stagecoach, his hat nearly takes up the entire frame; it represents, even in a sense "speaks" for, the character. When Ringo lifts his head to look up at Dallas (Claire Trevor), the Good-Hearted Whore, the two actors are supposed to exchange dewy-eyed looks that signal Love at First Sight—except Wayne doesn't seem to see anything, it's only Trevor's expressiveness that gives the scene a charge. After they have helped deliver the baby of a fellow passenger, Ringo and Dallas in a beautifully lighted scene stand in a long hallway in which shadows are broken by light streaming in from an open door. For the showdown, when Ringo finally faces his enemies, a heroic low-angle shot of Wayne stalking Main Street, and Ford's chiaroscuro lighting, supply the needed sense of urgency.

Adding no resonance or inner compulsion to the standard Western hero for whom taking revenge is a measure of honor, Wayne simply and cleanly plays the role of a man who does what he has to do. But Ford later cast his favorite actor in parts that demand complexity, and here Wayne's granitic presence is insufficient. In *Fort Apache* and *The Searchers* he has to perform difficult passages that his external technique cannot fulfill.

At the end of *Fort Apache* Wayne as Captain York, a stolid cavalry officer, meets the press after the death of his commanding officer, Thursday (Henry Fonda), who foolishly led the soldiers of Fort Apache into a disastrous fight against a tribe led by Cochise. To honor the military tradition to which he has devoted his life, and to preserve the illusion of Thursday's military greatness, York tells the reporters what they want to hear. On the wall behind him is a heroic portrait of Thursday, and the retreating cavalry is reflected through a window as York speaks about the importance of tradition and assures the reporters that

ABOVE AND OPPOSITE
John Wayne, Hollywood's most celebrated Westerner. Out on the open range, as in *The Searchers* (1956), he has iconic impact; indoors, in a scene like the climactic one in *Fort Apache* (1948), in which he has a complex acting challenge, he is less persuasive.

the slain troops did not sacrifice their lives in vain. He then puts on a military hat with feathers (the one Thursday always wore) as he departs to join the regiment. His Mount Rushmore face turned to look at the cavalry, his ceremonial gesture of putting on Thursday's hat—externally Wayne plays the scene well. But its manifold ironies are beyond him. His placid mask and erect body betray no trace of the character's rage at the memory of the pompous martinet whose reputation he is forced to protect. He conveys no sense of the private feelings roiling beneath the character's public performance.

In *The Searchers* Wayne plays an unheroic role, the part of a racist ("he's a man who can go wild; I seen the look in his eye at the mention of Comanche") who spends five years searching for his niece, stolen by Indians, only to discover when he finds her that she now thinks of the Comanche as her people. Ethan (Wayne) has two charged encounters with the girl. The first time, he prepares to shoot her—until his co-searcher, who's one-eighth Cherokee, stops him: "What kind of man are you?" The second time, his partner fears he will kill her, but no, when he finally meets up with her Ethan takes her in his arms and says, "Let's go home." That moment should vibrate with conflicting feelings the character cannot articulate; the actor's subtext should leap from the screen as he shares Ethan's inner turmoil with us. But Wayne's brusque, straightforward, mannequin style cannot embody the depth the confrontation demands.

Like Wayne in *Stagecoach,* Clint Eastwood is granted an enigmatic entrance in *The Good, the Bad, and the Ugly* (1968), Sergio Leone's delirious spaghetti Western. First, he is simply an offscreen voice; then we see his back, his hat, a gun crawling out of his jacket, a shoe, and finally, popping out of the shadow cast by the inevitable ten-gallon hat, his ruddy, handsome, creased face, his narrow eyes squinting against the sun as an ironic smile plays around the corners of his mouth. Like the Ringo Kid, all of a sudden he is there, a strangely magisterial presence who rides in from the plains. In his second scene, we first see smoke, followed by a shot of him lighting a thin cigar. The gesture is to be repeated throughout the film: he is a character wrapped in rituals, a man of mystery about whom we know no more than that he is intent on finding buried treasure. Eastwood, "the Good," is cooler and more assured than "the Bad" (Lee Van Cleef) and "the Ugly" (Eli Wallach)—the three are bound together because each of them has one piece of crucial information about where the money is located.

Difficult to read, Eastwood remains a masked presence who is as stingy with expressiveness as he is with words. Part of the tension the film generates is the burden we are handed of trying to crack the actor's opaque surface. Is he a sadist, or are we to take at face value this ironic film's designation of his character as "the Good"? What lurks behind the masked face and body, the cool, light voice, the bemused eyes?

Eastwood maintains the same pose in his other Westerns and in his urban crime pictures. In *Dirty Harry* (1971) he enters wearing shades and spouting a pithy police poetics—"When a man is chasing a woman with intent to kill, I shoot the bastard, that's my policy." He shoots bank robbers while eating a hot dog and grumbles to a pedestrian, "Get the hell out of the way, hammerhead." "Harry hates everyone; he doesn't play favorites," we're told.

The screenplay supplies a sketchy motive for Harry's meanness ("My wife's dead . . . a drunk driver, there was no reason for it") but is really as little interested in psychoanalysis as its laconic hero. Harry acts, he doesn't pause for introspection. When he is asked, "Why do you stay in police work?" he says, "I don't know, I really don't." And at the end, after he guns down the psycho whose trail he's been on for the whole movie, he throws his badge into the water. A Method actor would have turned the moment into an

acting aria, but Eastwood is a die-hard minimalist who gives the badge a brief once-over before tossing it away.

Like Wayne, Eastwood is a macho mannequin for whom feelings never retard actions and thinking never interferes with doing. Eastwood's acting is as lean as his physique. Because he's taken fewer chances than Wayne—he has remained self-protectively within his narrow patented range—he rarely comes up short the way Wayne sometimes does. (In *White Hunter, Black Heart* [1990], playing a character based closely on John Huston, Eastwood tries bravely to break out of his persona. But although he conscientiously imitates Huston's voice and rhythm, his performance is thin, an external impersonation.) His slick mannequin style, cryptic and gilded with irony, is a kind of high-tech male modeling that, under circumstances Eastwood himself closely monitors, has a decided iconic impact.

With his ritualistic boots, Levi's, serape, hat, and beard, Clint Eastwood is dressed for success: he's the generic Westerner, the strong, silent type, in Sergio Leone's delirious homage to an American genre, *The Good, the Bad, and the Ugly* (1968).

Spectacles

The performers discussed above are Hollywood versions of the Body Beautiful. Others—dancers, the silent comics, stars of melodrama and horror, and children—have bodies that are in some way unusual or extreme or that they use in stylized departures from reality. These actors comprise a pantheon of Hollywood spectacles who speak a variety of body-language dialects.

Dancing

Having difficulty proposing to a woman (Leslie Caron) almost scandalously younger than he is, Fred Astaire in *Daddy Long Legs* (1955) falters. He begins to sputter, grows silent, then starts to speak again before relapsing into another embarrassed silence. Since speech fails him, he starts to sing ("Something's Gotta Give") and then, at last, to dance, a language in which of course he is supremely fluent. Dancing, he not only completes his proposal, he seems to banish the difference in age between the girl he wants to marry and himself. Knowing exactly what his dancing says, she accepts his offer.

"[Dancing] is a way to tell what a man is going to do before he does it," says Ginger Rogers in *Kitty Foyle* (1940), responding to a partner who asks, "You like to dance, don't you?" The lines might well be spoken by Rogers herself, commenting retrospectively on her thirties movies with Astaire.

Astaire dancing is a privileged form of movie speech that no one else has ever spoken with such ease. Moving in ways that seem to defy gravity and the possibilities of the merely human body, Astaire seems weightless, a faerie spirit. His dancing is a special kind of screen acting, airy and frothy and pitched in the key of sparkling romantic comedy that is one of the specialties of American movies of the thirties and forties. In dance Astaire embodies a world of smart, big-city glamor; he dances the way such debonair denizens of Hollywood drawing rooms as Claudette Colbert, Myrna Loy, William Powell, Melvyn Douglas, Irene Dunne, Cary Grant, and Robert Montgomery act—with an entirely unforced charm.

Fred Astaire defying gravity in *You'll Never Get Rich* (1941).

When Astaire was doing the kind of dancing he wanted to do—dance enfolded within the film's story rather than dance as mere display or diversion, as pure production number—he used movement to release pressures that had built up within his character or even, as in the proposal scene from *Daddy Long Legs*, to complete a line of broken dialogue. His danced acting comes in three basic forms, all on display in *The Gay Divorcee*. As Guy Holden, Astaire plays an American musical-comedy performer dancing for his supper in Paris and resenting having to do just the kind of virtuoso show dancing Astaire himself disliked. After he meets and loses a girl who's come to Paris for a divorce (Ginger Rogers in a typically disdainful mode), he expresses his agitated feelings by dancing on the gleaming parquet floor of his apartment: the solo dance as an extension of the character's inner monologue. Pining for Mimi and vowing to find her again, Guy dances.

When by chance he encounters his Mimi at a seaside resort (in the scene previously discussed in Previews), Guy begins to declare his love as he dances to "Night and Day." Resistant at first, her back arched, her arms hanging stiffly at her side, her shoulders hunched with tension and uncertainty, Mimi slips into his rhythm, imitating his flowing movements as, gradually, she molds her body to his: dance as courtship and the birth of romance.

But since the story is not yet over, a misunderstanding occurs, and the new lovers are once again divided before they are ultimately and inevitably joined. In "The Continental," the final dance, they are partners from the beginning. And unlike their dance to "Night and Day," in which they speak only to each other, here their style is overtly presentational, a performance for an applauding audience within the film: dance as a public celebration of their romantic as well as terpsichorean partnership.

When he's not dancing, Astaire is a modest and casual actor. He has no range whatever, and when he tries to "act," as in the role of a heavy-drinking scientist in *On the Beach* (1959), he's a blank. Similarly, the few times he danced a character not "Fred Astaire," as in "Bojangles of Harlem" in *Swing Time* (1936), in which he appears in

blackface and is backed up by a geometric Busby Berkeley–like chorus line and three large shadows, or in the "Limehouse Blues" segment in *Ziegfeld Follies* (1946), in which he is cast as a Chinese tramp in a mise-en-scène that evokes Griffith's *Broken Blossoms* (1919), his energy is curtailed and his craft becomes visible. Like an actor caught "acting" in a part in which he is uncomfortable, in these numbers we catch Astaire dancing.

He is at his best when he remains genial "Fred Astaire" whose nonchalant delivery of dialogue is no better than it needs to be. (He's a superb and often underrated singer with a gift for phrasing particularly admired by lyricists.) His deepest acting moments are all contained in his dancing which, while it evokes high romance, is nonetheless oddly desexualized, almost disembodied. That's why he needed Ginger Rogers.

While Astaire was relaxed about acting, Rogers was not. She wanted to play roles rather than to rely on a persona as Astaire did. She thrived on accents (like the one she created for a fake Russian countess in *Roberta*, 1935), acting stunts (like playing a fifteen-year-old in a flashback in *Kitty Foyle*, in which her eyes, gestures, and voice are convincingly "fifteen"), and stylized comic characters like raffish Anytime Annie in *42nd Street* (1932), who sports a monocle and a British accent. As "herself," without any acting props, she was often dry or sour or simply flat, and she wasn't always able to conceal the fact that she was a tough woman only pretending to be sweet. As an average working-class girl, as in *Kitty Foyle* and in *Stage Door* (1937), where she's the sharp-tongued populist to Katharine Hepburn's hoity-toity aristocrat, she served as an ego ideal for millions of American young women who could readily identify with her vernacular speech and manner. It is in fact her distinctly common touch that made her an ideal partner for Astaire. As Katharine Hepburn memorably remarked about them, "He gave her class and she gave him sex appeal."

When she began to put on airs in the forties—her own, not a character's—in misguided projects like *Lady in the Dark* (1944) and *Weekend at the Waldorf* (1945), she lost her popularity. At the end of the decade *The Barkleys of Broadway* (1949) returned her to her proper place, singing and dancing with Fred Astaire. The film is about how, after a detour into Serious Theatre, Mrs. Barkley returns to the musical-comedy fold. "No more plays," she assures Mr. Barkley; "We'll have fun," he promises. In the next scene they are singing and dancing "Manhattan Downbeat," first in their apartment and then on a stage against a backdrop of a stylized Manhattan: Mrs. Barkley of Broadway and Ginger Rogers of Hollywood are back where they belong.

That Rogers' persona is less stable than Astaire's provides the dramatic fulcrum on which the plots of their movies turn. Rogers has to be prodded into the magic circle of the dance, and her characters' resistance helps to integrate dancing with dialogue and situation. Led into the dance by Astaire, who is already perfect, the imperfect Rogers then undergoes an intoxicating transformation, from commonness to elegance, from stiffness to grace. And as she begins to merge the line and contour of her body to Astaire's, becoming over and over again before our eyes the best dance partner in movie history, she can be forgiven anything.

Significantly, Gene Kelly's most enduring moment is a solo as he sings and dances in the rain to celebrate a budding romance. Like Astaire, working closely with his choreographer Hermes Pan, Kelly choreographed dance for film, and he begins the number (in *Singin' in the Rain,* 1952) with the camera close in, confining him to full-figure shots that allow no extra space. Then, keeping pace with the character's surge of feeling, the camera moves back to give the dancer more room in which to express his exhilaration. For the high point of his danced bliss, as he spins and kicks in ever-widening spirals, the camera sweeps up into a sudden, mimicking lift and turn. Kelly's energy gives a universal resonance to a simple theme, the joy of a man newly in love.

In *The Pirate* (1948) Kelly plays a womanizing troubadour who lures female patrons to his show by performing a virtuoso dance in a public square. Strutting on a platform, vaulting onto and off balustrades like a musical Douglas Fairbanks, and ending up posed narcissistically against a poster of his character, Serafin the Great, Kelly imbues his dance with a hard-driving athleticism. Unlike Astaire, Kelly is a dancer who clearly takes pleasure in showing off his physique.

Kelly of course also performed duets—in *Singin' in the Rain* he serenades Debbie Reynolds on a sound stage, where through lighting he creates the proper mood for dancing and romancing, and in "Broadway Rhythm" in the same film he partners Cyd Charisse in a steamy pas de deux. But Kelly is most persuasive when he dances for and to himself (as in the mirror dance, in which his image is reflected in a window, in *Cover Girl*), or when competition underlies the dance, as in the "Babbitt and Bromide" number in *Ziegfeld Follies,* the only time, except for their few moments hoofing together as co-hosts in *That's Entertainment II* (1976), that Kelly and Astaire share a dance on film. While Astaire was no stranger to challenge dances, with Rogers especially, the dance as contest is primarily a Kelly pattern, and in entering it Astaire is dancing on Kelly's terms.

The two top bananas of dance in American film are refreshingly unlike: Kelly, in tight pants and form-fitting T-shirt, is a roué whose muscular body is decidedly earthbound, where Astaire's seems poised to take flight. Kelly turns dance into a gymnastic workout—he makes hard work look like hard work—where Astaire makes dancing look as effortless as breathing. Where Astaire is in his element in top hat and black tie in an art deco penthouse, and sets his dances in enchanted places removed from the real world, Kelly is a plebeian who dances in streets and back alleys, amid garbage cans and urban debris (see *Cover Girl* and *It's Always Fair Weather,* 1956). Where Astaire is cool, Kelly is hot-blooded black Irish, a guy with a wide grin who throws sultry looks at the women he

With Ginger Rogers in *The Gay Divorcee* (1934), Astaire typically uses dance as a rite of courtship.

wants, and at the camera. Where Astaire through dance conducts classy courtships, Kelly is louche. He became a star on stage in 1940 playing John O'Hara's heel *Pal Joey*, and a touch of Joey remained with him. Where Astaire's films are almost always about partnering, Kelly's closest partnering was with Frank Sinatra in a series of utterly mediocre musicals based on the premise that Sinatra needed Kelly to instruct him in courtship technique. "If she's a dame she wants romance" is Kelly's typical advice to his lovelorn compatriot in *Take Me Out to the Ball Game* (1949).

Like Astaire, though, Kelly at his best dances what his characters cannot say. His purest acting moment is when he's kicking and sloshing in the rain, declaiming his love through song and dance. Even more than Astaire, Kelly is a severely limited actor; where Astaire's voice matches his dancing style, Kelly has a flat, strangely pitched voice scarred with Brooklynese, and he often sounds insincere, as if he's speaking with quotation marks around his dialogue. It's not by chance that his strongest performances are in *The Pirate* and *Singin' in the Rain,* in which he plays ham actors.

Although they are not known primarily as dancers, Mickey Rooney, Elvis Presley, and John Travolta are galvanized whenever music's in the air. Like Cagney they are actors whose best acting has dancelike undercurrents.

The lyric energy Rooney displays as Puck in *A Midsummer Night's Dream* (1935) became the backbone of his career. His elastic body, rather than Shakespeare's language, impels him into the play's spirit. Emerging out of a bank of leaves, he seems raw and elemental, a force of nature. As he jumps (sometimes with the help of movie magic) up hill and down, sprinkling fairy dust in the air, Rooney breaks up his lines with raucous, splitting laughter, with grunts and gasps and wheezes. With wild gesticulations and in a harsh,

OPPOSITE
Unlike Astaire, Gene Kelly places his body on public display, as in this scene from *The Pirate* (1948) in which he performs a gymnastic high-wire strut to solicit the approval of the crowd.

LEFT AND FOLLOWING PAGE
Whether or not he is actually dancing, Mickey Rooney imbues his work with a choreographic energy: here, he leaps in a dancelike movement as Puck in *A Midsummer Night's Dream* (1935).

guttural voice, he veers from declamation to song—he seems indeed a supernatural sprite, a being from a different order.

Rooney's body is musical even when he isn't performing in a musical; and when he's in song and dance shows, he's cast typically (as in *Babes in Arms,* 1939; *Strike Up the Band,* 1940; *Girl Crazy,* 1943) as someone who will explode unless he performs. (During breaks while filming, Rooney often performed for the crew.) Whenever there's a stage, Rooney's characters leap onto it to entertain. When in *Girl Crazy* he visits the office of the governor, where there is no stage, he nonetheless converts an anteroom into a performing arena. By chance a microphone is placed in front of him and he spins spontaneously into a vaudeville riff, parodying sports announcers. Like other unintegrated numbers in Rooney musicals, the scene is a throwaway, an entertainer's privileged way of killing time.

Rooney's musical compulsiveness often comes wrapped in a moral imperative, as when in *Strike Up the Band* he explains why he can't take up his dead father's career in medicine. "It's just not there . . . the way he loved medicine is the way I love music. When the music's happy, it makes the people happy. Isn't that sort of life-healing too?"

Where Rooney remained a live wire in and out of musical routines, Elvis Presley ignited only within a performance framework. As an actor communicating in dialogue rather than song and dance, he is dense. His muteness really had nothing to do with his

Rooney in a vigorous conga with Judy Garland in *Strike Up the Band* (1940).

inferior, formulaic scripts; he simply didn't have the instincts of an actor except in his music. *Jailhouse Rock* (1957), often cited as his best movie, is deadly, but when Presley performs the title song, swiveling his hips and gyrating in orgiastic release, his status as the king of rock 'n' roll is palpably evident. Presley projects an aura of fugitive danger that he is unable to carry over into the "book" scenes. In dialogue his curled lip remains inexpressive, almost a deformity; in song, it begins to twitch with erotic promise.

When John Travolta walks down the street at the opening of *Saturday Night Fever* (1977), he exudes animal magnetism. His peacock strut and his smiling eyes proclaim him a winner, and his entire performance maintains the buoyancy promised in his entrance. Unlike Presley, the way his body responds to music (in the disco dancing scenes) is of a piece with his kinetic acting style in nondancing moments.

But up to now Travolta hasn't had the kind of career that *Saturday Night Fever* seemed to insure, and that may be because in the film's misbegotten sequel, *Staying Alive* (1983), the actor surrenders his live-wire body to become a pumped-up mannequin. Where in the earlier movie his body fit his character, in the sequel Travolta acquired a body builder's torso, which he displays narcissistically. Turning his body into a spectacle, an end in itself, Travolta may have engendered doubts from which his career has yet to recover fully.

Dancing, Elvis Presley's a star, as this scene from *Jailhouse Rock* (1957) suggests; delivering dialogue, he's not.

Clowning

Comedians need some physical trait that sets them apart from civilians. Typically the comedian has an exaggerated body, either small and wiry like Chaplin's, Keaton's, Stan Laurel's, and Woody Allen's, or oversized like Fatty Arbuckle's, W. C. Fields', and Oliver Hardy's. Either way, big or little, fat or reedlike, their bodies invite stumbles, pratfalls, and humiliation. Comics with no distinctive bodily characteristics, the Marx Brothers, for instance, or Harold Lloyd, add an inflection or a twist—Groucho's painted eyebrows and slanted walk, Lloyd's glasses—that announces a comic presence.

While even in talking pictures body language has continued to be a part of the film comedian's arsenal, it is of course in the work of the three major silent clowns, Chaplin, Keaton, and Lloyd, that comic mime reached its most sustained movie eloquence. Despite differences of physique, all three are acrobats whose bodies endure repeated poundings while exhibiting a luminous grace.

Because of their seemingly unheroic size, Chaplin and Keaton face daunting odds: they are lone figures challenged by a world of hostile and often oversized people and objects. Chaplin is a diminutive wanderer in a vast, snow-filled landscape in *The Gold Rush* (1925); is entangled in the coils of a mechanized factory in *Modern Times;* confronts a big bruiser in a boxing ring in *City Lights,* a big cop in *Easy Street* (1917), a big wife in *Pay Day* (1922); wrestles with a houseful of menacing collapsible objects in *One A.M.* (1916). Keaton is stranded in the desert in *Go West* (1925); swings over a raging cataract in *Our Hospitality* (1923); is battered by a storm in *Steamboat Bill, Jr.* (1928); tries to control a runaway train in *The General* (1927); is abandoned on a huge, empty ship in *The Navigator* (1924).

Lloyd's nemeses, an average man's average frustrations—a suit that falls apart, as in *The Freshman* (1925), a collapsible car, aggressive drivers, mischievous kids, a jammed streetcar, as in *Hot Water* (1924)—are typically smaller and more familiar than Chaplin's or Keaton's. The movies' first comic Everyman, Lloyd developed his persona in conscious opposition to Chaplin's Tramp, who he felt was an oddball who lived in a world of his own. Nonetheless, like many of Chaplin's and Keaton's, Lloyd's most renowned stunt, climbing up a building in *Safety Last* (1923), has epic scale.

Regardless of the challenge to their bodies or the number of spills both physical and spiritual that beset them, the silent clowns persevere. Knocked out, driven over, punched, pummeled, winded, thrown, they pick themselves up and with a few shakes they're restored and ready for more. They are untrounceable optimists. If their bodies seem to invite catastrophe, it is through the quick, resourceful way they use their bodies that we witness them transformed from losers to heroes.

Sometimes they are saved by what they don't know. Blindfolded and unaware of the gaping hole behind him, the Tramp (in *Modern Times*) pirouettes close to its edge on roller skates. In *The Gold Rush* he walks jauntily on a narrow mountain ledge, followed by a

FROM LEFT
For the silent clowns the world is a precarious place. Whether beset by obstinate objects (Harold Lloyd perched on a scaffold in *Never Weaken,* 1921, and on a topsy-turvy bus in *For Heaven's Sake,* 1926; Chaplin confronting a collapsible bed in *One A.M.,* 1916) or an oversized adversary (Chaplin and his frequent nemesis, bearlike Eric Campbell, in *Easy Street,* 1917), they are forced to use their wits and their physical ingenuity in order to survive.

bear he doesn't see. In *Sherlock, Jr.* (1924) Keaton rides on the handlebars of a motorcycle that, unknown to him, has lost its driver. The most patient and scientific of these put-upon comics, Keaton lives and thinks in closeups and so is often spared by concentrating only on the task at hand. In *The General* he is so concerned with chopping wood to make the fuel that will run his train that he doesn't notice the battle that's raging behind him.

At times the silent clowns seem divinely favored. Walking into the cyclone at the end of *Steamboat Bill, Jr.*, Keaton is hurled over by the force of the wind and sinks into mud—surely he's a goner, but Lady Luck, as always, is ultimately on his side. Houses collapse on him, but there he is, standing upright, his head poking up through a window frame.

Most of the time, however, they achieve victory not through chance but by the way their bodies skillfully react to challenges. Thrown into a boxing ring in *City Lights,* the Tramp performs a dexterous pas de deux that outsmarts his opponent. When in *Sherlock, Jr.* Keaton is trapped on a roof with no visible means of escape, he converts a flagpole that stands next to the roof into a huge pogo stick that catapults him into a car waiting for him on the street below. (Like most of his stunts, that flying leap is filmed in a one-take long shot that shows that Keaton is really flying through the air.)

Their movies are often about how the comedians gain command over bodies that initially seem unpromising. Throughout *College* (1927) Keaton has been a failed would-be athlete, a klutz; for the finale, he becomes the athlete of his dreams as he leaps and vaults over obstacles in a dash to rescue his girl from a passel of villains. In *Grandma's Boy* (1922) Lloyd appears first as a rube who is "meek, modest, and retiring—the boldest thing he ever did was to sing out loud in church," a character entirely unequal to the task he's given of capturing a tramp who is terrorizing the entire town. When the sheriff hands him a badge and a gun, Harold looks wide-eyed with fear into the camera. But then his grand-mother gives him a talisman which, she claims (she's bluffing), transformed his grandfa-ther from a coward and a weakling into a Civil War hero, and Lloyd is empowered. He now takes big strides and closes in on the tramp's shack in virtuoso zigzagging movements so the culprit can't keep him in his line of fire.

In a famous essay on comedy Henri Bergson defined the comic as the spectacle of man turned into a machine. In their movement and in the way they repeat the same kinds of movements, the silent clowns for all their extraordinary agility are often machine-like. How they walk, the way they move their heads and necks and arms, is often jerky, oddly discontinuous—not quite real. Their bodies not only collide with objects, they themselves sometimes become object-like, and the mise-en-scène often links them to machines, dummies, the world of the nonhuman. Sometimes Chaplin takes on the mechanical ges-tures of a windup doll as a disguise, as when hiding from the police, the Tramp pretends to be a funhouse dummy (*The Circus,* 1928). More often "dumminess" is thrust upon him, as in *Modern Times,* where working in a factory among machines turns him into a robot, an

automaton who performs the same reflex action of tightening a bolt over and over, even when there are no bolts to be tightened. At the end of *The General* Keaton salutes a series of passing soldiers in a repeated mechanical gesture that prevents him from completing a human action, kissing his girl, though finally he positions himself to do both at once and successfully. The silent clowns' staccato rhythms, emphasized by the accelerated rate at which their films were projected, appropriately set them in a world apart, a movie dream world (despite the fact that most silent comedies were filmed on location).

    The bodies of the silent comics act and react in long shots that typically place them in the same frame as the people and things who oppose them. Closeups are reserved for glimpses of the play of thought, as the actors devise strategies for keeping their balance in a world filled with potholes. The alternation between body and face, between the acrobatics that fill the long shots and the looks of the closeups, contributes to the element of pathos

The silent clown as existential hero: Buster Keaton stranded in *Go West* (1925).

that distinguishes the comedy of Keaton and Lloyd as well as Chaplin. If in long shots arms and legs and torsos bend and sway, cave in and expand, swerve and dip and shimmy, closeups afford a peek into the minds that steer the dynamo bodies.

Along with Garbo, Chaplin has the most alert eyes in the history of movies. Not only in the last shot in *City Lights*, previously mentioned, but everywhere from his earliest appearance in shorts to his farewell in *Modern Times*, Chaplin's Tramp confronts the world with sentient, penetrating eyes, alight with the wounds of desire and hope. Most Chaplin movies contain at least one shot as poignant as that of the Tramp looking longingly through the window in *The Gold Rush*, a lone figure huddling in the cold as he gazes at a roomful of merrymakers. Like his body Chaplin's face registers the Tramp's responses to a topsy-turvy world. One of the most unmasked of all screen actors, he is unafraid of incorporating aspects of the childlike and the feminine into his persona—covering his mouth with his hands, he titters and then smiles coyly at the bloke who is to be his opponent in the boxing match in *City Lights*.

Stubbornly unmoving, as if frozen against the thousand natural shocks that flesh is heir to, Keaton's Great Stone Face is a seemingly fixed mask. Nothing in that wizened visage moves—except the eyes, which shift sideways as they register almost subliminal soundings from his characters' depths. Chaplin's face, always in motion, is as twitchy and kinetic as his body; Keaton's mask fits his slower, more deliberate movements. Keaton's closeups are rare but potent. While he never tries for Chaplin's moist sentiment, Keaton nonetheless lets traces of an active inner life pierce his stony demeanor. In a card game in *Go West* Keaton's offscreen looks reveal that beneath the trademark impassivity of his face his character is busy calculating his next move.

In the opening scenes of *Steamboat Bill, Jr.*, Keaton is a schoolboy reunited with a father he hasn't seen in years and cannot recognize. When he loses the white carnation that was to identify him to his father, he walks up to several potential "fathers" and is rudely rejected. Though his face remains embalmed, his flickering, downcast eyes are alive with humiliation.

Lloyd's eyes also "tell." Typically he plays characters who try to make an impression, and in closeups he often drops his mask as he measures the distance between how he would like to be perceived and how he suspects he may be perceived. In these private moments between Lloyd and the camera, the actor exposes the uncertainty behind the bluster of his characters' show-off facades. At the end of *The Freshman*, Harold is crestfallen when his romantic rival informs him, "You think you're a regular fellow—why you're nothing but the college boob." His face and body droop.

In closeup Lloyd, like Valentino and Fairbanks, often acts in a double space, keeping up appearances for the other characters and in fleeting asides to the camera revealing how he really feels. In *Grandma's Boy* Harold visits his girl and wants very much to behave properly. When he eats mothballs, mistaking them for candy, publicly he pretends to be enjoying the "candy," then when Mildred's back is turned he hurriedly spits it out. And like Chaplin and Keaton, Lloyd occasionally uses direct address when he seeks our collusion or agreement. When he's taunted by a bully in *Grandma's Boy*, he looks out at us as if appealing for help.

Like their trademark costumes, gestures, and props, the eyes of the silent clowns locate the individual beneath a comic type. Their closeup reaction shots do not contradict their physical comedy; they deepen it. The acting they do with their eyes only reinforces what they do with their bodies when, in their mature work in the twenties, they lace slapstick with poetry.

Chaplin charted the way for the kind of movie comedy in which knockabout routines expressing character and theme are intercut with poignant closeups. Though there was a great deal of vitality, there wasn't much poetry in his early work. Hitting and shoving, giving and receiving swift kicks and bops on the head, the early Chaplin is a sneaky street fighter who lives in a world of instant antagonisms. His characters are driven by basic needs, for food and shelter and money and often for drink. In *Tillie's Punctured Romance* (1914), which might well surprise viewers familiar only with the later Chaplin, he's a city slicker who lives by his wits and his ability to make quick getaways. A scoundrel,

The eyes have it. In close-ups the eyes of the silent clowns reveal an inner world beating beneath their elastic, resilient bodies: Buster Keaton intently listening and thinking in *The General* (1927); Chaplin gazing into infinity in *The Gold Rush* (1925); Harold Lloyd reacting to being crushed in *The Freshman* (1925).

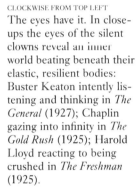

he marries a hulking farmer's daughter (Marie Dressler) because she has money. In the end he is dragged away to face punishment for his multiple crimes. In this world of social Darwinism, Chaplin is an acrobat of violence who mugs and feints in the kind of proletarian ballet that was Mack Sennett's specialty. This is frenetic slapstick, nonstop and low-class: profane pantomime that the instinctive artist in Chaplin rebelled against yet never entirely abandoned. What Chaplin did was to harness the mayhem of slapstick to the depiction of character and social statement, so that while his body retains the projectile elasticity the Sennett farces demanded, it becomes capable of speaking a "higher" language as well.

Here are two images from Chaplin's work, early and late, which suggest the distance he made his body art travel. In *The Immigrant* (1917) our first view of the Tramp is from the back as he leans over the deck of a ship, his body convulsed in spasms. Surely he's

seasick, but no, the joke's on us: those hitched shoulders and the jerking movements of his torso are revealed to be the exertions of fishing. In *The Great Dictator* Chaplin as the German tyrant Hynkel, having been seduced by his assistant into imagining himself Emperor of the World, performs a dance in which he balances a balloon globe on his feet.

The first scene is a slapstick gag, low humor that has its source in a bodily function. The second is a ballet of incomparable grace which expresses, gives body to, a sophisticated concept as it satirizes a madman's desire to conquer the world. From concocting sight gags to creating metaphors—a measure of how Chaplin over the course of his career deepened his body language.

OPPOSITE AND ABOVE
Dressed to enflame: Barbara Stanwyck's gaudy getup in *Stella Dallas* (1937) and Brando's snakeskin jacket in *The Fugitive Kind* (1960) ignite melodramatic misfortunes.

Melodrama and Horror Shows

Once they begin their turns, dancers and silent clowns depart from the realm of the everyday. Although the bodies of players in melodrama and tales of terror are not so clearly marked as performing instruments, they also enact stylized physical rituals.

Tragedy's poor relation, melodrama often carries misfortune to the limits of the preposterous, and in most melodramas bodies undergo a punishing regime. In a memorable scene in *White Heat* (1949), for example, James Cagney playing a gangster with an Oedipal complex throws a fit in the prison refectory when he learns that his mother has died. He hurls plates, overturns tables, flails his arms, twists and contorts his body as he emits cries of primordial pain—an aria of "the melodramatic body" reacting to a catastrophe.

If bodies in melodrama most often suffer the consequences of disaster, sometimes they also invite it, as in two popular melodramas, *Jezebel* (1938) and *Stella Dallas* (1937). The red dress the willful heroine (Bette Davis, of course) flaunts at the ball in *Jezebel* (the patriarchal code decrees that unmarried women must dress in white) and the gaudy getup Stella Dallas (Barbara Stanwyck) wears at a genteel resort incite retaliations: both heroines pay dearly for making spectacles of themselves. In melodrama overactive bodies that violate bourgeois repression spell calamity: Rosa Moline (Bette Davis again) in *Beyond the Forest*, strutting down the main street of a reactionary small town, and Val Xavier (Marlon Brando), entering another repressive backwater (in *The Fugitive Kind*, 1960), wearing a snakeskin jacket and tight jeans, are both too sexy to live. To allow the communities they have invaded to survive, their body language must be stilled.

127

Performers sometimes temper melodrama rather than simply surrender to it. Garbo and Irene Dunne, for example, who are so utterly unlike in such obvious ways, nonetheless approach the genre by strictly limiting their physical and vocal responses. For the most part Garbo plays melodrama intimately and subtly, with her face rather than her entire body. In occasional long shots, however, she slips into Delsartean clichés. In *Woman of Affairs* (1928), a silent melodrama, she paces in an upstairs room while below her men are deciding her fate; moving back and forth in a confined space, she "indicates" anxiety by putting her hands to her head. For Garbo, the large gesture is off-key, and she doesn't fill it the way a physically exuberant performer like Cagney or Davis would. She repeats the gesture in *The Kiss* and in *Anna Christie*, where again it seems to be a quotation from an acting tradition—nineteenth-century stage melodrama—that mars her modern realism.

Irene Dunne's body language in *Back Street* (1932) and *Magnificent Obsession* (1935) is as tucked in as her refined voice. She never lets us catch her acting, and while you can admire her taste and good manners you can't be thrilled by her choices as you can with Bette Davis' flamboyant attack.

Like the actor in farce, who must believe absolutely in the circumstances the plot has thrust upon him, the actor in melodrama must also play for real. As in Cagney's mad scene in *White Heat*—and unlike Garbo's head-holding—the boisterous external responses demanded of most melodramatic acting should be bound to a character's disordered inner life.

The answer to the problem of how to justify melodramatic excess on screen may be found in the silent film performances of Lillian Gish, working in creative partnership with her director, D. W. Griffith. Beaten and abused by men and nature, Gish's characters face stupendous physical as well as emotional turmoil. Despite all the regressive elements of Griffith's aesthetic—the preservation of virginity as a sacred rite, the sacrifices Gish's characters make to patriarchy, the sentimental Victorian pieties out of sync with the Roaring Twenties—Gish's acting retains a strength that outwits changes in morality or taste.

Before considering her mature work, I want to look at an early performance, in *The Birth of a Nation* (1915), in which her inventiveness is suppressed. As he dramatizes the events that hurl the South into War and Reconstruction, Griffith tells his story quickly; his characters are swept up into a spinning historical vortex, and there is no time to dwell on their inner lives. Gish is introduced as a photographic image—she's Elsie Stoneman, the Yankee girl the Southern hero, Ben Cameron, moons over after he's fallen in love with her picture, and it is as an icon that, once she appears in person, the film continues to view her. She's a vision of chaste Victorian maidenhood whose mere presence arouses male desire, from the lovesick sighs of the hero and of a sentry standing guard at the hospital where Elsie is a volunteer nurse to the rape fantasy of a black renegade, Silas Lynch, enflamed by a single look at her.

In her most intense scene, cornered by Silas Lynch in one of those inner rooms in which Griffith virgins are often trapped, Gish throws her arms in the air to indicate fright. The gesture is merely external; her body registers nothing of the atavistic terror that is to become her specialty, and Griffith's avoidance of closeups and of intercutting does not enable her to build her character's reactions.

Except for her cameo appearance as the woman who rocks the cradle in *Intolerance*, Gish is never again in her work with Griffith to be merely ornamental. In all their later films it is her frail yet powerful body buffeted by the mischances of melodrama that drives the narratives. Gish approaches the high points—the moments in each film in which her character is in extremis—with a combination of technical virtuosity and emotional plenitude that remains unsurpassed in the performance of melodrama in American movies. Gish is certainly not a modern minimalist, yet in context her bravura physical acting never seems silly or exaggerated. Her work, which in fact often attains a spiritual aura, is lit by her absolute conviction.

Here is a Gish sampler. In *Hearts of the World* (1918), set in France during World War I, when the Girl (Gish) learns of her mother's death, Gish begins to scream as she rotates her head and eyes, then suddenly her face goes blank and her body becomes rigid. Slowly her eyes widen in horror, as if she is experiencing the news of the death for a second

Lillian Gish, the silent screen's premier melodramatic actress, locked in a closet in *Broken Blossoms* (1919).

time. Later, on what was to have been her bridal night, the Girl sits on an open field, her head on the chest of her wounded fiancé. When morning comes she is frantic, nearly out of her mind as she wanders distractedly away from the Boy (Bobby Harron) she presumes dead, her body twisted as she cries out for help. When later she is reunited with the Boy, she shifts from initial disbelief to bliss. At first sight of him, her body goes limp, her eyes dim, she caves in on herself; then as if emerging from a dream, sensations of touch and sight seem to return to her as she is restored to ecstatic life. For the climax, the Girl is locked outside a room in which she imagines the Boy is being beaten to death by a German. She pounds wildly on the door, and finally in her extremity summoning superhuman powers, she begins to hurl the full force of her body against it.

In *Broken Blossoms,* the abused girl Lucy (Gish) hunches over as she takes small, mincing steps and creeps around corners. A child "with tear-aged face," she has fear in her eyes but forces a smile, lifting her hands to raise up her lips when she pleads to her brutal father, Battling Burrows (Donald Crisp), "a gorilla of the jungles of East London," not to hit her. She cringes when she spills food on his hand, cowers when she wipes off his boots. When the kind Yellow Man (Richard Barthelmess) looks at her with romantic feeling, she instinctively bends away from him, yet her chaste and terrified gaze holds him close to her. The line of Gish's body—resisting yet beckoning—suggests both Lucy's otherworldliness and her blossoming sensuality ("Her beauty so long hidden shines out like a poem"). When she locks herself in a closet to hide from a whipping and Battling Burrows begins to break in—the ultimate scene of Griffith claustrophobia—Gish incarnates fear at the outer limits. Her eyes widen, her head twists, her hands define the space of her entrapment, as if the walls are beginning to close in on her, and her entire body shakes in a premonitory death rattle.

In *Way Down East* (1920) once again a man is her mortal enemy. When the man who has seduced Anna (Gish) and pretends to have married her tells her the truth, that the marriage was a sham, Gish constructs one of her set pieces, a mixture of terror, hysterical laughter, and wild disbelief. Tears well up uncontrollably, she jumps up, and as if unable to absorb what she has been told, she begins to run in circles. Stopping abruptly in her mad pirouette, she raises up her arms, calls out for her mother, and then falls to the floor.

OPPOSITE AND ABOVE
Gish in two classical moments of physical and emotional extremity: caught on the ice in *Way Down East* (1920) and recognizing her long-lost sister (Dorothy Gish) in *Orphans of the Storm* (1922).

In the accusation scene, in which Anna names her betrayer, Gish stretches her arms in both directions and her eyes flash with anger as she summons a strength her character has not yet exhibited: the victim strikes back with an elemental fury. But Anna is banished nonetheless, thrown out into the storm for her alleged crime against bourgeois propriety. The snow lashing her face, the wind causing her body to sway and topple, she is a small figure smashed by "the barque of Fate." Again portraying physical suffering *in extremis*, Gish makes Anna seem to be transformed by her torment, to go beyond the pain her body endures to attain a kind of serenity.

The recognition scene in *Orphans of the Storm* (1922) is Gish's last great aria under Griffith's baton. Henriette (Gish) has been separated from her sister Louise (Dorothy Gish), who is blind. (The sisters have come to Paris during the French Revolution to find a doctor who can cure Louise and, like the Northern and Southern families in *Birth of a Nation*, are caught up in a historical tempest.) Henriette hears a voice faintly singing in the street outside her window; her head cocks, as if in response to a subliminal message, a call from the past. Gradually, as she begins to realize that it is her sister's voice she hears, her eyes brim with tears and she runs to her balcony, arms outstretched and crying out her sister's name. Gish's ecstatic cries pierce the film's silence. Griffith, who by this time in their work together had released Gish to build her scenes on her own, according to her own judgment, gasped in astonishment after the first take. "Why didn't you tell me you were going to do that?" he asked.

When Bette Davis adopted the mask of a sadistic hag to conduct a reign of Grand Guignol terror against her crippled sister (Joan Crawford) in *What Ever Happened to Baby Jane?* (1962), she tilted melodrama into the realm of the horror film, eliding two genres which, at their outer limits, often overlap. Even more decisively than in melodrama, in the tale of horror the body invariably occupies a central place. It is the site of grisly experiments, excursions to and from the zone of the supernatural. The horrific body—the ghoul, the vampire, the anthropomorphic monster brought to uncertain life in the laboratory—cheats death, terrorizes, defiles, and seduces vulnerable humans. Transcending mortal limits, its very existence is often a kind of blasphemy, a challenge to the Christian cosmos.

The two most famous supernatural bodies in American films, those of Frankenstein's monster (Boris Karloff) in *Frankenstein* (1931) and Count Dracula (Bela Lugosi) in *Dracula* (1931), were incarnated by non-Americans who seemed otherworldly. Larger than and not quite like life, their performances depend on a kind of mime rare in Hollywood movies.

Karloff felt it was a mistake to give the monster a voice in *The Bride of Frankenstein* (1935). His actor's intuition was correct, for in the original he created a character whose body alone fully "speaks" the drama of the monster's struggle upward out of a primordial sludge toward human consciousness. Emphasizing his inherent cragginess, his crater-like, deepset eyes, his hawklike nose and lantern jaw, Karloff's makeup deforms his face, while the actor himself, through his imagination, transforms his body. To mark the monster's ineffable Otherness, his status as a stranger among humans, he invests him with robotic movements, with hands and arms and legs that seem newly made and therefore unaccustomed to human purpose and time. His gestures seem like translations from some other dimly remembered language system. Karloff's shoulders stoop, his feet drag, his powerful hands seem as unused to the sensation of touch as his eyes, striped with intermittent glimmerings of awareness, are pained by light and terrified by fire.

Through grunts and measured movements, Karloff suggests the monster's primal feelings, the lust and rage that erupt from his body. Yet Karloff's mime also subtly imbues the monster with a will to decency, most vividly expressed in the famous scene between the monster and an angelic-looking little girl who is the first human who doesn't recoil in his presence. Not yet a part of the mistrusting adult world, the child offers him a flower, which the monster receives with a delight he doesn't have the language to express. The trace of a smile creases Karloff's face and eyes as his movements take on a surprising gentleness. He stretches out his hand to touch the little girl, an ambiguously motivated gesture that is both an attempt to convey affection and a sinister foreshadowing. (A cut blocks our sight of the monster killing his ministering angel—this shot has been recently restored.)

However reluctantly, in *The Bride of Frankenstein* Karloff gives the monster a voice that fits his body. He speaks in muffled, gravelly tones and in staccato phrases pitted with gasps and pauses. As it makes its way gropingly out of a deep darkness, Karloff's voice mimics the monster's physical travail, his attempts to communicate across the chasm of his own irreversible strangeness. Like his gestures, his voice struggles toward the creation of meaning. When the monster first hears a violin, he makes purring noises, and when he discovers the source of the beautiful sounds, produced by a blind violinist who befriends him, he holds out his hands and tries to give utterance to a feeling for which he does not yet have the vocabulary.

"Come . . . here!" Dracula snarls to Van Helsing, his nemesis, in their final encounter, curling his hands and thrusting out his arm. But when Van Helsing doesn't follow orders and instead holds up a cross, Dracula steps back in a broad pirouette and swirls his cape to protect himself from the object that can kill him. Lugosi's bold, theatrical gestures here, as throughout the film, invest the vampire with regal authority. His Dracula is quite literally a Prince of Darkness, an imperious aristocrat whose gestures and eyes demand obedience. "Renfield hears Dracula even when Dracula says nothing" is a tribute we can believe.

Lugosi's body language separates the character from the world of the fully human. As he moves with dancelike grace through the oversized Gothic sets and up the gigantic

Embodying horror: the eloquent mime of Boris Karloff in Frankenstein *(1931).*

curved staircase at Carfax Abbey, he's like an apparition responding to a secret code. His thick, fluted Middle European accent, which sets him apart from the flat-voiced B-movie American actors who surround him, completes his ghostly aura.

"I am . . . Dracula." "I never drink . . . wine." Lugosi's performance is honey-combed with this sly verbal tic, a measured caesura during which the actor seems to be enjoying a private joke with us. When he speaks, then, as when he seizes possession of another character with his eyes or when he makes a commanding gesture, this Dracula carefully orchestrates his effects. Lugosi turns the monumental sets into a stage on which we see him conducting his own witty performance.

For Karloff and Lugosi, as much as for the bombshells and the dreamboats, anato-my determined professional fate. The two actors were confined to horror movies for the rest of their careers, and working in increasingly disreputable projects, they slipped into a style of burlesque and self-mockery that does not, however, diminish the powerful body language of their original performances.

He was called the Man of a Thousand Faces, but Lon Chaney, like Karloff and Lugosi, acted with his entire body. "What's that got to do with acting?" Chaney (played by James Cagney in *Man of a Thousand Faces*, 1957) asks when his agent suggests movies. "For you, it's got everything: pantomime." When he applies for a job, a tough producer tells him, "You're not any type. You're a plain, ordinary guy with a plain, ordinary face: try it as an extra." But Chaney escaped from the anonymity of the extras' casting pool by transforming his ordinariness, hiding his own craggy, strangely unfinished face under an array of grotesque masks. He bucked the Hollywood norm to achieve an unusual kind of stardom. Where most film actors display their own faces and bodies, Chaney created a rogues' gallery that disguised his. And in an industry that deifies good looks and in which actors typically replay the qualities that earned them their fame, Chaney was an always-ugly chameleon.

Like Karloff and Lugosi, Chaney acts primarily in long shot, the torment of his deformed characters typically registered in full-figure shots rather than facial closeups. Quasimodo in *The Hunchback of Notre Dame* (1923) is Chaney's most punishing disguise. By limiting his facial expressiveness (one eye and his mouth are the only mobile parts of the character's mask), it places the primary interpretive burden on his body. When Quasimo-do discovers that Esmeralda, the gypsy woman he loves, is to be executed, the actor rears back in amazement, as if struck by some unseen hand. His mouth drops open, his one eye bulges, his hands stretch out as if to erase the scene of horror that affronts him. Then he shifts from shock to rage: his fists curl into tight balls, his tongue darts serpent-like in and out, and he springs into action. Climbing down a rope from his eyrie atop Notre Dame and swinging into the square below, he gathers Esmeralda up into his arms as, in his hunkering Neanderthal walk, he hobbles into the cathedral crying out "Sanctuary! Sanctuary!"

At the climax Chaney typically goes for broke as he tosses comedy, Delsartean convention, and sheer bravura overstatement into a wild mix that approaches sublimity. Protecting Esmeralda from the rabble, he jumps up and down and throws stones at the mob below—he's a proto–King Kong in the grip of an overflow of unstoppable feelings. After his enemy, Esmeralda's seducer, hurls him from a high wall onto the square below, Quasimodo staggers up to his bells one last time and rings them in a final farewell. ("The bells were the only voice of his groping soul," an intertitle announces, gratuitously, for the actor has made clear what it is that the bells represent.) Quasimodo sees a vision of Esme-ralda, and his body stretches to its limit as he calls out her name before he folds over in mortal collapse.

Chaney plays the hunchback with a physicality braided with emotional truth. By contrast his *Phantom of the Opera* (1925) seems merely external. Even at the time his performance was old-fashioned, a deliberate throwback to a theatrical style outmoded in the postwar era. The actor uses one large, ornate gesture—lifting a hand, or pointing a finger with his arm thrust forward, or swirling a cape—per shot. For his final gesture Chaney offers a sly send-up of his rococo performance. After leading an angry mob on a chase to the edge of the Seine, the Phantom turns, and pretending to have a dangerous

The vampire as aristocrat: Bela Lugosi in *Dracula* (1931).

weapon clutched in his hand, he raises his arm in a threatening pose. His larger-than-life movement stops the mob dead in its tracks. Having demonstrated the power of his sign language, he opens his palm to reveal that there is nothing in it, then gloating in his semiological victory, he throws his head back and begins to laugh.

At their best Chaney, Karloff, and Lugosi imbue their characters with resonating inner lives. While their movements are by design mannequin-like—not fully human—in films like *Frankenstein, Dracula,* and *The Hunchback of Notre Dame* the actors create images of horror in which disfigurement is emotional as well as physical.

CLOCKWISE FROM LEFT
The virtuoso physical transformations of the Man of a Thousand Faces: Lon Chaney in *The Hunchback of Notre Dame* (1923), *Oliver Twist* (1922), and *The Phantom of the Opera* (1925).

Children

In a reunion scene with her son Sergei (Freddie Bartholomew) in *Anna Karenina* (1935), in one of those subversive actions that illuminate her career, Garbo treats the boy like a lover. She looks at him with moist eyes and runs her hand along his face, tracing its contours as if in remembrance of a passionate liaison. Romantic underscoring and sensuous closeups abet the actress's interpretation. Cast out by a husband (played by the ever-chilling Basil Rathbone) and a lover (played by the hollow-voiced, dead-faced Fredric March, a perennial stiff), it's no wonder her character ignites with her son (played by a child actor with an astonishingly grown-up presence). Bartholomew's performance bristles with hints that, in his child's mind and body, he understands the Freudian scenario in which his frustrated mother is including him.

In a more casual key, consider a typical moment in a typical Shirley Temple vehicle, *The Little Colonel* (1935), when Gramps (Lionel Barrymore) cuddles the star, lifting her up onto his lap and squeezing her. Though set in the South, *The Little Colonel* is decidedly not Southern Gothic and Gramps technically is innocent, but in reaching out to touch her he's reacting the way the audience wants to. Under the titles of *Curly Top* (1935) Shirley lifts up her head, tosses her curls with a few vigorous shakes, and, as only she can, smiles at the camera. Our first view of her once the story starts is from the back of her head.

BELOW
Is there an Oedipal subtext in the mother-son embrace between Garbo and Freddie Bartholomew in *Anna Karenina* (1935)?

OPPOSITE
Touching Shirley Temple: in this scene from *The Little Colonel* (1935), Evelyn Venable does what most of the audience would like to do, as Hattie McDaniel looks on approvingly.

The film thus fetishizes a part of the child's body, and in this display Temple as always is a willing accomplice.

In a notorious contemporary review of *Wee Willie Winkie*, a 1937 Temple vehicle, Graham Greene suggested that the star's phenomenal popularity had sexual roots. At the time his assertion seemed blasphemous: Greene, a foreigner, had dared to assault a national treasure, an immaculate pop icon who was the top box-office attraction in the country. But was his perception completely off the mark? Temple's cute, cuddly, diminutive body, like those of all child stars, becomes a center of attention in each of her movies, provoking physical responses from characters like Gramps and, vicariously, from the audience.

Child stars are spectacles, moppet mannequins as chained to their bodies as bombshells, dancers, the silent clowns, action heroes, and the misshapen figures of the Other in horror stories. Occupying frames usually filled by the fully grown, their tiny bodies together with their adult composure are the source of their appeal. Temple's movies continually call attention to her small size: in *Curly Top* her reaching up for a doorknob or sitting on a chair that's too big for her constitutes a dramatic event. Her films are variations on the phenomenon of a child behaving like, and being given the narrative burdens of, a grown-up. She's usually cast in a reconciliatory role—in *The Little Colonel* she effects peace between her Southern grandfather and her mother, who violated patriarchal authority by marrying a Northerner. Healing a family wound, little Shirley thus enacts her own resourceful version of Reconstruction; and her ambassadorial skills are further underlined by the fact that she plays happily with black children, attends a black baptism, and elicits the devotion of black servants played by Bill Robinson and Hattie McDaniel. In film after film she's handed similarly enormous responsibilities, as through her uncommon savvy she sutures rifts in the adult world.

On the set, between takes of *The Little Colonel*, Shirley Temple shoots a remarkably mature glance at Lionel Barrymore.

A recurrent feature in her movies is the way her mimicry of adult movement mirrors her desire to transcend the limitations of her child's body. When she's inducted as an honorable little colonel, she walks like a soldier, mimes touching whiskers, and places her hands on her hips in a parody of military etiquette. In *Curly Top*, for a benefit show at her orphanage, she sings "When I Grow Up," in which she appears as sweet sixteen, as a young woman in her bridal gown, and as an old lady in a rocking chair with a quavering voice; and then, as if to dispel her transgressions, she performs as herself a tap dance and a number in which she jumps rope.

Temple's formidable self-assurance is so potent that at times she seems more like an adult midget playacting at being a child than a real child. Children, in fact, often thought she was a fake—that she was America's favorite child represented an adult rather than a child consensus. Her primary appeal was to parents who saw in her the ideal child they themselves wished (or thought they wished) to possess. For the most part, children felt oppressed by the standard to which her exalted image held them hostage.

Once her child's body began to take on the contours of a maturing figure, Temple's stellar career was doomed. As an almost-grown-up the qualities of leadership and spunk that marked her child persona began to curdle. *The Blue Bird* (1940), a legendary disaster, reveals Shirley in awkward transition, at a point where she was getting noticeably unchildlike. While the film is about her spoiled character's search for the blue bird, it can also be read as the star's search for the old (that is, the young) Shirley Temple, radiant child star. When the blue bird flies away at the end, Temple says, "We can find it again because" (and here, flashing a patented smile, she turns directly to the camera) "now we know where to look for it." But Temple didn't in fact know where to look, and eight years later, in an adult body in *Fort Apache*, the remnants of her childish charm have descended to a simpering sexlessness that makes her virtually unusable.

The child stars, from Temple and Bartholomew to Mickey Rooney, Judy Garland, Margaret O'Brien, Jane Withers, Elizabeth Taylor, and George "Foghorn" Winslow, have voices and eyes and an intuition, poise, and focus that defy their children's physiques. Garland, Rooney, and Taylor of course graduated to major careers as adults, but the three most popular and persuasive of all child performers—Temple, Bartholomew, and O'Brien—did not. Their radiance dimmed as they dwindled into adulthood.

Bodies as Burdens

The body language we've been watching is the kind that is overt, the kind "spoken" by actors in conscious command of their bodies as performing instruments. There is, however, another kind of body language to consider—one that is covert, vibrating with subtextual reverberations.

Of all the Hollywood goddesses Garbo may be the most reluctant to show us her body. Her seductions are conducted for the most part through her eyes and her voice, and indeed part of her allure is in the way she withholds herself, shielding her body from the gaze of the characters she entraps as well as from the eye of the camera. Because she doesn't give herself easily, a scene like the one in _Queen Christina_ where, disclosing that she is a woman in male disguise, she lets her hair fall onto her shoulders and then turns away from her soon-to-be lover with a shy smile has a special impact. We have the illusion that we're seeing the star almost naked.

As the diva of the divan, Garbo is a femme fatale seen most often as an inert, reclining figure, and in roles where full figure movement is mandated, as in _Susan Lenox: Her Fall and Rise, Mata Hari_ (1932), and _Grand Hotel_ (1932), in all of which she plays dancers, she is noticeably ill at ease. In _Susan Lenox_ as a hooch dancer in a circus sideshow she isn't remotely convincing. The one scene in which the character is shown at her trade is filmed in extreme long shot with Garbo (or, more likely, a body double) glimpsed in the distance on a stage festooned with baubles and hanging crêpe paper. Dense as a nightclub scene in a von Sternberg movie, the shot underlines while attempting to conceal the fact that the star is not really able to do what her character is supposed to. A dance in _Mata Hari_ is filmed more intimately, but Garbo (with the probable help of a double in some shots) again performs it without joy. Her movements are perfunctory, and the frequent intercutting is an attempt to cover over the star's inadequacy. Although her prima ballerina in _Grand Hotel_ is never seen dancing, Garbo does not carry herself the way a famed dancer would. However rich it is, her performance is not centered in her character's body.

Her last film, _Two-Faced Woman_ (1941), contains the most revealing glimpse of the star's physical reticence. Garbo plays a double role—she's a cool ski instructor and the earthy, good-sport "sister" she invents—that was intended to democratize her image the way _Destry_ had enlivened Dietrich's. At a party the made-up sister dances the latest craze,

FROM LEFT
Defrosting Garbo in _Two-Faced Woman_ (1941), the film that ended her career. A reluctant Venus about to rise from her shell, Garbo plainly conveys her disapproval as the cameraman takes his measurements; dancing, she moves with somewhat greater ease than in earlier roles. (A color still from a black-and-white film.)

and while the scene may be an obvious attempt to cut La Divine down to mortal size, Garbo dancing looks, for once, as if she is enjoying herself moving in front of a camera. In *Two-Faced Woman* it isn't dancing that Garbo resists but another myth-leveling scene in a swimming pool. In a two-piece bathing suit, chaste but inescapably revealing, Garbo swims across the pool as the camera waits for her, to record her ascent from the water. Instead, however, of photographing the star in unbroken movement—Venus rising from her shell—the scene is nervously edited into separate shots designed expressly to prevent a full view of her. In the first shot she is just coming out of the pool, with our view cut off at waist level; in the second she is again bisected, visible only from midtorso up. We never get the full body shot that would seem to be precisely the point of a merely punctuational scene like this. Emerging from the pool, Garbo looks as if she is trying to hide out *behind* her body. It's this scene, I think, rather than the dance at the party that signals the end of Garbo. If this is what Hollywood wants, has reduced her to, a body to be looked at in a wet swim suit, it's time to be alone.

If at moments Garbo's body seemed to turn against her, Charles Laughton's was a calamity from which the actor seemed never to recover. Some of his most celebrated performances—as Nero in *The Sign of the Cross* (1932), as the monarch in *The Private Life of Henry VIII* (1933), as Javert in *Les Misérables* (1935), as Captain Bligh in *Mutiny on the Bounty*, and as Quasimodo in *The Hunchback of Notre Dame* (1939)—are intensely masochistic. They constitute panels in a continuing psychodrama in which the actor punishes himself and others for the body he has been chained to. Consider this moment in *The Epic That Never Was* (1965), a documentary about the uncompleted *I, Claudius* (abandoned in 1936). Playing someone who's laughed at for his swollen body and his limping walk, Laughton demands a number of retakes of a scene in which his character runs the gauntlet of a jeering mob. With each retake he exaggerates his limp as his face and eyes move toward beatitude; playing the scene becomes exorcism and exaltation.

In both *Les Misérables* and *Mutiny on the Bounty* Laughton plays outsiders in twisted pursuit of handsome heroes—Fredric March as Jean Valjean and Clark Gable as Fletcher Christian. The young Laughton had the face of a misbehaving and perhaps even demented overgrown child, and in *Les Misérables* he suggests a perverse hidden life for his character. Before Javert commits suicide, Laughton, unforgettably, has a look of sexual ecstasy—contemplating the pain Javert is to inflict on himself, the actor looks radiant.

Thirsting for control over his crew, his Captain Bligh behaves with a malignity which, as Laughton plays it, is entwined with sexual envy. Bligh's adversary, the man he wants to punish for having led the mutiny, is played by Clark Gable, an actor who projects a joyful male lust from every pore of his being. Laughton performs the early scenes with Gable like a would-be lover. "I like having a gentleman as a subordinate, being a self-made man," he announces, with a hint of sexual conquest. "I expect you to carry out my

FROM LEFT
Sexual envy and masochism as performance subtexts: Charles Laughton as Captain Bligh glares at an American hunk, Clark Gable, in *Mutiny on the Bounty* (1935); crouching among gargoyles, Laughton in *The Hunchback of Notre Dame* (1939) is intensely self-punishing.

orders!" he rasps, once he begins to sense his quarry's disaffection. A rejected lover now, Bligh is enraged when he sees Fletcher at ease in Tahiti cavorting bare-chested with a native girl and wearing a peekaboo loincloth. The perennial sexual outcast, Bligh scowls at the display of heterosexual pleasure. (Earlier, to a sailor who asks clemency because he has a wife and baby, Bligh snaps, "I asked your name, not a history of your misfortunes.") Raging against the well-formed, topless crew disporting themselves in an island paradise, he bellows, "So you're all against me, officers and men: before I'm done I'll have you eat grass."

Laughton's most intensely masochistic performance is as the hunchback Quasimodo. When she first sees the hunchback (before we do), Esmeralda recoils; then we see the sight she is shocked by. A misshapen monster with one mobile eye and a hunched-over, loping walk, he is a beast literally bent over by the terrible burden of his physical deformity. At first the ugliness seems excessive, greater even than Chaney's, but it is Laughton's intention to reveal human layers beneath the inhuman surface, reversing his arc in roles like Bligh and Javert in which he uncovers monsters lurking within.

In both mime and dialogue his performance has personal overtones. His hunchback is a nightmarish distortion of his own self-flagellation. When Quasimodo is publicly whipped and his bloated body is exposed, Laughton does not cry out or scream, but accepts the punishment stoically, as if it is a confirmation of the destiny his body has prescribed. When he brings Esmeralda to his sanctuary at the top of Notre Dame, he tells her, "I'm going away so you don't have to see my ugly face when you eat." "I am neither man nor beast but as shapeless as the man in the moon," he tells Esmeralda, and to protect her he often covers the most deformed parts of his face so that only his one seeing eye is visible. At the end he asks a gargoyle, "Why was I not made of stone like thee?" as the camera retreats to a high overhead long shot that links the human to his nonhuman Other, the beast made of stone.

Playing the hunchback was a culmination for Laughton, who never again immersed himself so deeply in the enactment of ugliness. It's as if after the challenge of embodying one of nature's misbegotten figures, he could retreat into the merely human unhandsomeness of his own being. After Quasimodo he became almost exclusively a lovable character actor who played crusty eccentrics.

In repose or in movement, bodies on screen are often presented as spectacles that arouse desire, stimulate fantasy, express heightened feelings, and perform with a grace and control and heroism people in the real world can seldom manage. The array of different languages that bodies can be made to speak, from the calculated gestures of mannequins to the emotionally expressive movements of live wires, helps to fulfill the visual and narrative requirements of moving pictures.

The Landscape of the Face

Enigmas

GARBO LOOKING OFFSCREEN IN THE LAST SHOT OF *QUEEN CHRISTINA* and Chaplin smiling at the end of *City Lights*—portraits in motion of two of the most famous faces of the century—are images that pinpoint one of the pleasurable challenges of moviegoing: reading into the open-ended play of thought and feeling on the human countenance. With the intimacy afforded by closeups, movies provide us greater access to faces than ever before in the history of acting. Moving close in, we're expected to interpret facial maps, to decipher possible meanings in the movements of an actor's eyes and mouth, and to grade levels of tension, defensiveness, or ease in the set of facial features.

Like bodies, faces on screen range from blankness (deliberate or inadvertent) to quicksilver vivacity. Some movie faces are porous, receptive, saturated with feeling, others trap or suppress emotion beneath a surface we have to work to interpret, while yet others seem scrubbed clean of any trace of an inner life whatever. Some faces look real; blemished and rumpled, they are striped with experience. Others, without a single wrinkle or sag, are so splendidly proportioned that the only possible place for them is within the confines of a movie screen.

Whether true-to-life or idealized, alive or frozen, exposed or hidden, bursting with information or tight with repression, the faces of stars are the ones audiences not only want to see more of but also have at least the illusion of seeing *into*. The actor's face is a text, and the players who have proven most enduring are the ones whose faces invite response, arouse desire, identification, curiosity, appreciation, envy, or intimidation—anything but indifference or neutrality.

Just as actors' bodies are deconstructed by the very nature of the filmed image, dismembered by closeups and the fragmentation of editing, so are their faces scanned and parsed by the camera as well as the spectator. Watching movies, we're drawn to a distinctive nose or mouth, an emphatic chin or jaw or cheekbones, lustrous or protruding eyes. Many stars possess one outstanding trait. William S. Hart has a large, hawklike nose. W. C. Fields' nose is bulbous. John Barrymore was celebrated for his sculpted nose and

Elizabeth Taylor close up, with a melting gaze for Montgomery Clift and for the camera, in *A Place in the Sun.*

Is this young man (Montgomery Clift in *The Heiress*, 1949) a sincere suitor or a fortune hunter? Miriam Hopkins, Ralph Richardson, Olivia de Havilland—and the audience—have to decide. Clift's subtle performance entices us to examine his face for clues.

noble profile. Marlon Brando and Barbra Streisand have noses with notable bumps. Clark Gable has large, active ears which, when aroused, seem to send and receive signals to and from the object of his desire. Jeanette MacDonald has a thrusting, pugnacious lantern jaw. Jean Harlow and Kirk Douglas have cleft chins. Humphrey Bogart has thin, twitching, oddly sensuous lips. Burt Lancaster has prizewinning teeth. Katharine Hepburn has imperial cheekbones. Garbo, Bette Davis, Lillian Gish, Clara Bow, Elizabeth Taylor, Chaplin, and Valentino have large, liquid, often hauntingly beautiful eyes. Douglas Fairbanks and Bette Midler have incandescent smiles. Garbo, Joan Crawford, and Meryl Streep have faces that are ideally planed and angled—faces just waiting to be photographed.

In the movies, as often in life, the most compelling faces are enigmatic, brushed with emotion that is incompletely expressed. Meeting such faces, we know that a drama of some kind is taking place and we are drawn by what is not revealed, or revealed only partially. These ambiguous faces set us the task of discovering the look behind the "look," the face behind the mask. For example, Montgomery Clift in *The Heiress* (1949), Meryl Streep in *Sophie's Choice* (1982), Bette Davis in *The Letter* (1940), and Spencer Tracy in *Bad Day at Black Rock* (1954) play characters in hiding, and along with other characters within the films we are placed in the position of becoming an investigator, sifting clues and hints and peeling away layers of subterfuge in order to determine the truth.

In *The Heiress* Morris Townsend (Clift) makes his first appearance at a dance with his back turned to the camera. The placement heightens our curiosity; when he turns and so reveals his face to Catherine (Olivia de Havilland) and to us, he is startlingly handsome—the young Montgomery Clift at the height of his dark, Byronic glamor. When Catherine, a plain young woman living under the constant specter of her own imminent spinsterhood, gasps to her stern father (Ralph Richardson), "Oh, don't you think he's the most beautiful man you've ever seen?" her question reinforces the report of the camera. After Catherine leaves the dance where she first meets Morris, the camera moves in on him; the deliberate forward movement underscores our desire to find out about the character, but the actor shrewdly does not reveal him. As he looks off at the woman he has just met and charmed, Clift maintains a bland expression. When Morris later calls on Catherine in her drawing room, Clift leans into her, pinning her with his eyes and with his quiet voice. Awkward and insecure, and with a vulnerability she does not know how to disguise, she backs away from him. Her eyes search him for clues: does he really care for her, as he claims, or is he paying court because she is an heiress? Her father dismisses him as a cad, her heart tells her he is sincere.

The crucial moment occurs when Catherine announces that, if she marries him, she will receive no dowry. Surely Morris now will drop his guard. But no, Clift plays the scene quietly, casting his eyes downward as he receives her news. This inner monologue arouses our doubts, and Catherine's, but still we remain uncertain. The memory of his intense looks directly into Catherine's eyes and his beguiling voice are with us still, and we reserve the impression that he may be honorable after all.

In fact, as it turns out, Morris Townsend is a fortune hunter, a man who lives off and has been spoiled by his looks, but as Clift plays him he is more interesting and more complex—he's a man whose charming facade contains an element of truthfulness. Clift gives the role a double edge, enforcing the truism that appearances after all have their reality. When Morris returns to Catherine years after having jilted her, he expresses his regrets with apparent sincerity, and indeed to play him now as merely callow, a slick opportunist, would betray his earlier subtlety. Though Catherine no longer believes Morris, the special triumph of Clift's performance is that he makes her earlier uncertainty credible. He has given his character a face of enticing opacity on which charm and calculation wage a struggle provocatively hard to read.

"I can't talk about that . . ." Sophie (Meryl Streep) says, touching her hair and looking offscreen when Stingo (Peter MacNicol) asks her about her experience in a concentration camp. The power of the unspoken text, of what Sophie cannot talk about, resonates throughout the remainder of *Sophie's Choice*. We see Sophie mainly from Stingo's viewpoint: he is an outsider, a Southerner, who comes to New York to become a writer

What is the secret locked in the haunted eyes and face of this woman, played by Meryl Streep? Her lover (Kevin Kline) isn't looking, and he doesn't know; by the end of *Sophie's Choice* (1982), we do.

and by chance is thrown together in a Brooklyn rooming house with characters radically different from him, Sophie, a mysterious Polish survivor, and Nathan (Kevin Kline), her high-strung lover. Although Stingo hasn't the worldly wisdom to be able to understand these two characters, he is instinctively drawn to them. He doesn't realize the dangers his new friends present, however, nor how far he will have to go to find out who they really are. Nathan, he learns, is not a biologist as he claims to be but a paranoid schizophrenic with delusions of grandeur. Discovering the truth about Sophie becomes Stingo's as well as the film's goal.

The movie is punctuated with several long scenes in which Sophie reports to Stingo about what happened to her during the war. Streep gives Sophie the face of a medieval Madonna with a secret; her darting eyes and stammering speech are strategies to evade Stingo's probing questions. During Sophie's first remembrance, as the camera remains absolutely still, "hushed" as it waits for revelation, Streep's eyes and face seem veiled. When Stingo later finds out that she lied about her past, he tries again to penetrate her facade. "I'd like to understand," he says. "I'd like to know the truth." As he speaks his desire, the camera moves in toward Sophie for a closeup, as if to suggest that this time her mask will be removed. But no, although Streep seems to peel off another layer of her character's armor, this confession too is only partial.

Only at the end, after Stingo proposes to her, do the lids lift from the actress's face and voice. "You wouldn't want me to be the mother of your children," she says, this time speaking without her usual hesitation and keeping her gaze steady. As she confesses to the choice she was given and the reason she survived—in flashback we see the scene in which a Nazi officer asks her which one of her two children she is willing to sacrifice in order to save the other—Streep's eyes seem to be looking into an endless darkness.

Like Montgomery Clift in *The Heiress*, Streep plays, with virtuoso nuance, a veiled character whose face and eyes contain hints of a turbulent inner life. And like Clift's, Streep's face is a map that invites misreading as it provokes our interest.

At the beginning of *The Letter*, a woman stands on a porch with a gun blazing in her hand; the camera moves in to look at her face. Her expression is curiously muted for someone who's just committed a murder, and the rest of the film is devoted to uncovering what lies behind her rapt yet reserved gaze at the body of her victim. That this withheld woman is played by Bette Davis is a jolt, for Davis was not ordinarily stingy in her facial reactions. But like *The Heiress* (and *The Little Foxes*, which contains another tight-lipped Davis performance), *The Letter* was directed by William Wyler, a man who clearly did not suffer scenery-chewers gladly.

ABOVE
Not giving it away: in the opening scene of *The Letter* (1940) Bette Davis is un-characteristically masked. Her closed expression, and the gun in her hand, invite our inspection.

OPPOSITE
Who is the man in the dark suit, the stranger in a strange town? Spencer Tracy's taut, impassive performance in *Bad Day at Black Rock* (1954) doesn't make it easy to find out.

Maintaining her character's facade as an offended British matron forced to kill in order to defend her honor, Davis is surprisingly calm as she narrates her version of the events that led up to the murder. Where Davis usually uses words as weapons, to assault and to attack, here her character uses them to disguise her feelings. But while her voice remains even, her nervously twisting hands and shifting eyes—her asides to the camera—belie her tone. Davis thus cheats in a way that Streep and Clift do not: where they keep us guessing, Davis, the cagiest cheater in the business, enlists us as her conspirators as she shows us her character both on stage and off, engaged in putting on and taking off her mask. Even so, Davis does not portray Leslie as being obviously guilty, but more as a hidden character; she lets us see that Leslie is lying, but we aren't sure why. The role requires Davis to bury her character's true motives beneath a mask of British propriety: if she'd come on as "Bette Davis" in full tilt, she would have given the show away in the first closeup.

In her confrontation with the wife of the man she killed, Leslie covers her face with a lace mantilla. Frustrated by having her vision blocked—she wants to see the face of her husband's murderer—the woman (Gale Sondergaard) asks Leslie to lift her veil. When she complies it is another veil we see, for Leslie refuses to reveal herself to her adversary. Her expression is unyielding, stony: Bette Davis in uncharacteristic retreat.

Only at the end, after she has withstood the tension of a trial and been found innocent, does the character break. She admits the truth at last: that she had an affair and that her anger at being jilted enflamed her to shoot her lover. When she erupts, confessing to her husband (the perennially frostbitten Herbert Marshall) that with all her heart she still loves the man she killed, the patented Bette Davis is in full cry, released at last from the bondage of playing a masked character.

In *Bad Day at Black Rock* Spencer Tracy is a poker-faced stranger in a xenophobic small desert town. Who is this character? and why is he here? are questions that preoccupy the town's suspicious citizens as well as the audience. An actor who distrusted "acting" (when asked what Charles Laughton died of, Tracy is said to have quipped, "Overacting"), Tracy performs in a severely minimalist style. His technique is as much under wraps as his character's motives. Though he plays a one-armed character, his performance is

notably unphysicalized: he is not Lon Chaney putting on a pyrotechnic mime show. Despite the fact that the film is set in a sweltering place, Tracy remains dressed in a jacket and tie and never does any of the overt sensory work that a Method actor would do to register a character's reactions to the heat. His face remains set in a stoic mask, even when the town bullies taunt him with various strategies meant to unnerve him. Tracy constructs his performance on the apparent belief that to act is *not* to reveal anything about his character. He doesn't send us signals the way Davis does when she's cornered into playing a character with a hidden agenda, and unlike Streep and Clift he has no probing closeups but, in well-composed, wide-screen shots, shares the frame with his antagonists and the sinister town.

And yet, though his face maintains an impassiveness that seems to thwart interpretation, Tracy holds us. We know something is going on inside his character, and the actor keeps up our curiosity about what it might be. Tracy's iconography (long in place by 1954)—his stern, patriarchal veneer and strong sense of moral rectitude—helps to fill in the blanks of the deliberately cryptic narrative. We assume, as the other characters do, that he's an investigator, probably for the FBI, someone who represents Justice and the Law, who has come to exact retribution for the unnamed past crime that hovers over Black Rock. But no, that isn't it, we have misread the character, as indeed we were meant to: he is not a public defender but a burnt-out case (a character closer to Graham Greene than to Raymond Chandler) engaged in a purely private errand. He is a vet who has come to town simply to give a medal to the father of the dead Japanese boy who saved his life. He had thought he was washed up, not good for anything anymore, until he got to the town, where he not only solves the crime—a group of townsmen killed the Japanese farmer—but also inspires the sheriff and doctor to rise up against the racists who have polluted Black Rock.

Playing dumb: can you see Dustin Hoffman in this character's eyes, or has the actor succeeded in emptying his expression in order to portray the title character in *Rain Man* (1988), an idiot savant?

Retroactively, once we have been told who the character is and what he wants, Tracy's performance seems not only logical but evocative. Without any big scenes or set speeches, by his presence alone, the actor projects moral and physical force, power held in reserve. Tracy succeeds with his skeletal "score" not only on the strength of his stature as an American icon but also because he conveys the sense of a character who talks to himself, a character who is always thinking. And while that ongoing inner monologue remains indistinct, beyond our hearing, it provides a potent undertone. In the set of Tracy's features and behind his eyes is the imprint of a vigorous mind in action.

Although ultimately we discover what it is their characters are concealing, in their exemplary masked performances Tracy, Davis, Streep, and Clift provide models of how not to give it away. In *Rain Man* (1988) Dustin Hoffman plays an idiot savant whose mask always remains in place, and the actor's challenge is to stay hidden behind the face of a character incapable of a normal human responsiveness. To enact a person locked in a world of his own, Hoffman empties his face and eyes, and part of the tension in watching the movie is in seeing if we can detect the actor himself peering through his character's facade. If we ever catch him, if we can detect his own alertness seeping into his character's eyes, the performance is exposed. Since in all his roles Hoffman seems to be acting with one eye cast over his shoulder, as if watching us watching him (his usually showy choices place him at the opposite end of the acting spectrum from a minimalist like Tracy), the role was particularly risky. But in fact Hoffman's eyes remain dimmed, cut off, shrouded, as if some essential human spark is missing. Fleetingly, when expressing feeling for his brother (Tom Cruise), he seems to see more, to connect in a normal way, but he never quite makes it. Inevitably the rain man remains within his mask.

Masks and Faces

In the language of the face, as in the mannequins and live wires of body language, Hollywood acting has yielded two large categories: faces as masks and icons, and faces that reveal inner lives. But as in the preceding examples, in which entire performances pivot on the actors' skill in suggesting faces behind the masks their characters assume, the types often interact. "Mask" and "face" are indeed slippery concepts, and in a sense all faces in movies are masks within which actors assume fictional identities. Here are some basic distinctions. As I'm using the words, faces reveal emotion, even when (as above) a character's goal may be to disguise or withhold a display of feeling. Signaling messages from within, faces acquire depth and dimension as, to varying degrees, they are marked by reaction and are open or struggling toward openness. Masks, in contrast, are to varying degrees petrified, frozen into an expression without nuance or modulation. Where faces have both surface and depth, masks are mattelike, maps from which traces of a world within have been, often with great calculation, utterly erased. Where faces are ruffled, masks achieve a poise and equilibrium possible only in the movies. Masks, typically, are without physical or emotional blemish; they're molds from which the creases of normal aging have been banished. Mannequins have masks; live wires have faces. And while clearly I prefer the latter, in the stylized realm of Hollywood filmmaking masks are sometimes exactly what is required and sometimes in fact can be as resonant as faces.

In movies faces don't have to move a lot, or do much at all, to reveal truthful human behavior. The camera's intimate gaze prohibits extreme reactions from performers, and whether their technique is external or internal or even if they have no technique at all, actors usually reduce facial movements to a minimum. On the screen a blink, a pursed lip, a tightening of the jaws or cheeks, can read with absolute clarity. Here's a good, representative example of the facial minimalism that is one of the codes of the Hollywood style. At the end of a scene in *A Stolen Life* (1946) the camera moves in on Glenn Ford, playing a character who has become suspicious. Ford has been conversing with Bette Davis, who portrays an evil twin pretending to be her good sister; he is uneasy, for a reason he can't name. How does Ford, a fine movie performer who never overstates, express his character's doubts? He narrows his eyes as he looks offscreen—that's all he does and in the circumstances it's enough.

Before looking at some examples of typical Hollywood masks and faces, it would be profitable to consider the masks and faces of certain actors who break the rules—the inert masks of Buster Keaton and Marlene Dietrich, the hyperactive faces of Chaplin and Bette Davis.

Keaton and Chaplin are antitypes who nonetheless end up in the same place, and with a comparable impact: they each create a flat comic character who achieves a universal human vibration. Transgressing the limits of "realistic" movie acting, Keaton, the Great Stone Face, created the severest, most wooden, most reticent mask in the history of movies, a visage seemingly emptied of recognizable emotion and of movement, except crucially for the movement of his sentient eyes. Chaplin's face, on the other hand, is a movable feast of reactiveness. By doing either too little, like Keaton, or too much, like Chaplin, the actors transform their faces into comic masks, which nonetheless reflect their characters' thoughts. Keaton's dry mask and Chaplin's liquid one ripple with activity. By grafting quicksilver, subterranean feelings onto the flat surface of comic masks, these great and original film actors confound the usual distinction between masks and faces.

Like Keaton, Dietrich transforms her face into a slate apparently wiped clean of human expressiveness; like Chaplin, Davis uses her face more actively than screen acting convention decrees. And like the comics, their daring collapses the usual gulf between masks and faces.

The glazed perfection of Dietrich's face is a mask constructed for the camera. And

Noir sleepwalkers, Veronica Lake and Alan Ladd in *This Gun for Hire* (1942): Paramount's deadpan, deep-frozen forties twosome.

yet her sculpted face is stippled with enticing secrets, a promise of Krafft-Ebing erotics and an intermittent, potentially detonating irony. Uniquely, Dietrich's mask has a life of its own. "You're a mess, honey," Dietrich as a "gypsy" coolly evaluates a mountainous Orson Welles in *Touch of Evil* (1958). The same remark could never have applied to her at any time during her long career. While time and indulgence had treated Welles with brute indifference, Dietrich seemed immune from their erosions. She may not have been an authentic gypsy—she wasn't really meant to be—but she was still an authentic diva, as smooth-skinned and as icily erotic as she had ever been. Dietrich preserved her mask up through *Judgment at Nuremberg* in 1961, her last full-scale performance. Through will and discipline and repeated cosmetic surgery she prolonged the illusion of being an ageless thirty-five for well over three decades—a record. When she could no longer count on the protection of her mask, she disappeared from public view; in *Marlene* she is present only through her voice, the wobbly voice of a bitter old woman.

Quite unlike Dietrich, Bette Davis grew old on screen and off in full view. Where Dietrich had only one mask to protect, Davis in the course of her career donned many. Davis is not a Method actress. For the most part, she plays on top, on the surface—and what a surface it is. To project the rage and the strong will that drive most of her characters, she bats her eyes and contorts her face. Like Chaplin, she has one of the most mobile and transparent faces in movies. Her effects are full-blown, and except in *Dark Victory* and when William Wyler restrains her, she is a shameless, irresistible scene-stealer. But if Dietrich's frozen mask contains surprising depths, Davis' lively, reactive face is often masklike, a stagey caricature. Both actresses are bad models whose techniques are certain to be fatal if imitated. They are both one-of-a-kind code smashers.

From the somnambulistic masks of Keir Dullea and Gary Lockwood in *2001: A Space Odyssey* (1968) and of Alan Ladd and Veronica Lake in *film noir* to the reactive expressiveness of Marlon Brando in *On the Waterfront*, faces on the screen can usually be gauged in terms of their "give." For some kinds of films, like science fiction and like the thrillers Ladd and Lake starred in, the deadpan style is exactly what is needed; for dramas like *Waterfront*, which is about a character's moral growth, a lifelike responsiveness is called for. Most screen actors might thus be seen as falling along a curve that rises from the acting degree-zero of the *noir* antihero and the dazed astronauts in *2001* upward to Brando's Method spontaneity. What follows is a gallery of Hollywood portraits ranging from the tautest masks to the most porous faces.

At its best the American *film noir*—a crime thriller with a psychological twist—was a studio-made style that created a world apart, an "elsewhere" of chiaroscuro lighting, walls scarred with the artfully arranged shadows of venetian blinds, banisters, and barred windows, and rain-slicked studio streets that don't quite look like real streets. The characters in *noir* are victims, as marked by a capricious destiny as the figures in a German expressionist dream play. Trapped and hounded by a malevolent world out there as well as by demons within—the assortment of psychological and sexual perversities that sting them—they typically meet their fates in a daze.

Whether the characters are patsies of the fickle *noir* universe or insidious victimizers, faces in *noir* tend to be ominously still, frozen either in defense against misfortune or as the very embodiment of it. The *noir* mask isn't the blank look of actors who can't act, it is blankness à la mode, encoded with meaning and style. With glazed eyes and refrigerated face and voice, the *noir* actor is a World War II version of the mechanical man, a figure in a dreamscape propelled irreversibly toward nightmare.

Alan Ladd and Veronica Lake in *This Gun for Hire* (1942) and *The Blue Dahlia* (1946), Barbara Stanwyck and Fred MacMurray in *Double Indemnity*, Joan Crawford in *Mildred Pierce* and *Sudden Fear* (1952), and Humphrey Bogart in almost anything are prime specimens of *noir* somnambulism—performers who by emoting within a narrow range remain within *noir*'s zonal restrictions. Of these, Ladd and Lake, Paramount's deep-frozen forties twosome, are sleepwalkers nonpareil whose otherworldliness is enforced by their similarly chiseled features, porcelain skin, and blonde hair. Playing opposite each other, they provide an eerie mirror effect, an androgynous visual doubling. (In *This Gun for*

Hire, Lake actually becomes Ladd's body double when she puts on his hat and trenchcoat.)
An everyday human expressiveness never disturbs the perfection of their features, while
voices of steadfast monotonality issue from their masks. Hardly moving their lips and
mouths, they speak in husky voices that retain the aftereffects of too many stiff drinks; as
they move cautiously and self-protectively through a booby-trapped *noir* landscape, they
act as if they're on the wagon. One step up from pure zombie, their post-trauma, dead-end
style is ideally *noir,* and whether or not they can "act" in the usual sense is irrelevant. In
noir they have an aromatic presence.

In *This Gun for Hire* Ladd plays a lynx-eyed hit man who wears a regulation trenchcoat and a grey fedora that shades half his face and who "has a job to do." Without
flinching, he shoots two people, then tells his contact: "I don't trust anyone . . . I'm my own
police." The character is memorably established in the first scene, set in a grimy back
room in a Skid Row flophouse. Getting up from a rumpled bed, he takes out a gun, which
he touches fetishistically, is nice to a cat, then brutally slaps a maid who comes in to clean.

"You're trying to make me soft, I don't go soft for anyone," he warns Ellen Graham
(Lake), whom he meets on a train. They're both tracking the same man, the assistant to a
mad scientist who has developed a poison-gas formula to be sold to the Japanese. The B-
movie plot is serpentine, but the two stars are all straight lines and sharp angles. Though
Ladd's antihero is doubly wounded—he has a mauled left hand, and he's haunted by a
recurrent dream of having killed his stepmother—the actor remains encased in his own
icicles. And even though Lake here plays a softer version of her standard hard-boiled
dame, she too is entrenched in her glacial iconography. These golden zombies glaze the
film with a hard crust that actually strengthens the material. "Acting" would only expose
the script's deficiencies, while their taut, matte style gives it a *noir* shimmer.

Because his mask, like Lake's, has no "give," Ladd never broke out of the *noir*
mold. When he was mistakenly cast as *The Great Gatsby* (in 1949), he enacted the role in
the only way that he could, as a B-movie gangster, a little tough guy from the slums. Erased
were the yearning and the poetry of Fitzgerald's questing hero, and scaled down to accommodate the star, Gatsby is presented as a gigolo who turned con man. When Gatsby looks
across the water at Daisy's house, the image turns misty in order to cover the star's
blankness.

Unlike Lake, whose career ended when cracks began to appear in her armed-
fortress face and makeup could no longer conceal the blemishes of time and alcohol, Ladd
continued to find roles until his death in the early sixties—American culture can more
easily tolerate scars in Apollo than in Venus. And once, in his post-perfect phase, Ladd
had a part ideally suited to his style. As *Shane* (1953) he isn't expected to be anything more
than an icon, a Western hero as seen from the point of view of a kid. In how he moves, what
he wears and does and says, Shane is a ceremonial character, a lone ranger who comes
from out of the hills to help farmers win a fight against ranchers and then returns to the
hills at the end. A savior with a gun, an Arthurian knight in the Old West, Shane is a
generic hero rather than an individualized character. The role doesn't call for an actor who
could fill in the gaps—Shane becomes a universal figure by virtue of what Ladd *can't* act.
His deep, dry voice and poker face help to give the film its aura of bare-bones legend.

A spider woman who preys on corruptible men, the *noir* femme fatale is a monster
in human guise. With her air-conditioned face and voice and her hard eyes, she's a sultry
iceberg, the Circe of Hollywood and Vine. Though the men in *noir* are often fooled, the
audience is usually wise to her right from the start. Joan Bennett, Gene Tierney, Ava
Gardner, Yvonne de Carlo, Rita Hayworth, Jane Greer, and Joan Crawford are among the
actresses who emptied their faces and voices to an unnerving minimalism in order to play
noir temptresses. The sweepstakes winner, however, the most fatal femme in *noir,* is Barbara Stanwyck in *Double Indemnity.* Her cold-eyed killer, who arranges to murder her
husband to collect double indemnity and then two-times the man she has seduced into
becoming her conspirator, is the meanest woman in American movies. With her tense
shoulders and taut, mannish face, Stanwyck is always physically stiff. Her rigidity, though,
is usually offset by the way she "throws" her voice, filling it with an emotion that boils until
it explodes in a hysterical outburst that is often the climax to a Stanwyck melodrama (see

Hard core: the most fatal
femme in *noir,* Barbara
Stanwyck in *Double Indemnity* (1944).

the end of *Meet John Doe*, for a prime instance of the actress in vocal eruption). But in *Double Indemnity* she reins in her voice to match the severity of her face and gestures. Like her tight smile, her voice cuts like a surgeon's incision; razor-sharp and ready to strike, she's the human equivalent of a lethal weapon.

"There's a speeding law in this state," she hisses to the insurance salesman (Fred MacMurray) who responds to her siren call by making a quick play for her. But she's already two stop signs ahead of him. Narrowing her eyes, she sizes up her quarry and realizes he is hers for the taking. Stanwyck doesn't make the mistake either of softening her praying mantis or of suggesting inner complexity. Beneath her shield is another shield, layer upon layer. Stripping away the positive qualities of strong will and integrity that made audiences like her, Stanwyck gives her character an unflinching mask. In this one, she's strictly hard-core.

Joan Crawford, on the other hand, acts with a mask that leaks; in film after film her characters unravel with contradictions. Because she wants her audience to like her even when she plays hard-boiled characters, she doesn't stick to her potentially formidable guns but pours a gooey movie-star glossiness over all her tough cookies. To butter us up, she switches masks in midstream or for a treacly finale we can believe only if we forget the rest of the movie. Crawford is two-faced, the star as Janus. (The best Crawford performances—in *Grand Hotel*, *The Women* [1939], and *What Ever Happened to Baby Jane?*—are the ones in which she plays one note rather than two and so is not given the chance to take it back. Her Crystal Allen in *The Women* is an unreconstructed comic bitch, and a joy from first frame to last.)

Crawford's manufactured two-mask style is especially evident in *A Woman's Face* (1941). When she has a facial scar, Anna Helm (Crawford) is a criminal, the head of a gang of blackmailers; when a surgeon corrects her face (she emerges from the operation with Crawford's movie-perfect looks), Anna begins her trajectory toward secular sainthood. At first her remade criminal returns to her gang, announcing "I'm not on the side of the saints yet." Crawford fans would know just how much weight to give that "yet," confident that by film's end that is exactly where the star would be positioned. After she reforms, her surgeon assures her and us, "That cold-blooded creature wasn't you; it never was you." (Oh, no?) And Anna, throwing off what the doctor had earlier called a "ruthless, terrifying mask"—he says he has "created a monster, a beautiful face with no heart"—admits, "I always wanted to get married, to have a home and children." She looks up sweetly at her doctor as they walk off hand in hand into the sun.

Typically the film creates an alibi for Crawford's hard mask: it is dismissed merely as the outer shell of a melting alter ego who desires to "belong to the human race." The audience was expected to accept her surgeon's assessment that she is "not as tough as [she seems] to be," and as Crawford's lengthy stardom proves, millions of viewers did. In one of the most successful charades in American movies Crawford disguised her own toughness with a veneer of upbeat sentiment that convinced her fans that, at heart, beneath the increasingly taut face, she was just like them.

Despite Crawford's calculations, there are moments of undisguised ferocity in her performances, as in the famous confrontation scene between mother and daughter in *Mildred Pierce*. Mildred and Veda (Ann Blyth), the daughter she has spoiled into terminal rottenness, are dressed in black as they face each other on a staircase. "You'll always be a common frump," Veda says, as her mother tears up the check she was going to give her. Veda slaps her. Then, as the camera moves in close, Crawford puts on her hurt expression, her how-could-you-do-this-to-me? look. Her eyes fill with tears as she stares stricken at the daughter for whom she has sacrificed her life. Her face brims with emotion waiting to be expressed, and though often Crawford's mask suppresses the display of feelings, this time anger gushes out. "Get out before I kill you!" she rages at Veda. When Veda continues to walk up the stairs, Mildred cries out her name with a force that is momentarily terrifying: as if obeying a military command, Veda stops dead in her tracks. In this moment Crawford forgets her carefully constructed star mask to reveal a glimpse of the forbidding woman her real-life daughter claimed her to be. She makes a quick recovery, however, as her expression returns to its zombie mold, the star's "Mildred Pierce" mask. There's real

power in Crawford's explosion, but to pursue it would push her into playing a character the audience might not like.

Crawford's attempts to maintain a star image falsify much of her work. Though her appeal is quite different, Ingrid Bergman also suffered from star masking. Introduced to American films in 1939 in *Intermezzo,* Bergman was presented as the Swedish anti-Garbo, a natural, wholesome beauty who lives for love. Typically she was cast as a wishy-washy heroine utterly dependent on men. In *Gaslight* (1940) she plays a woman driven by a sadistic husband to think she is mad. In *Dr. Jekyll and Mr. Hyde* (1941) she's a terrorized

Examining one of the most hard-boiled masks in movies: Joan Crawford in *A Woman's Face* (1941).

Cockney barmaid. In *Casablanca* (1942) her character is prepared to go off with either her husband or her former lover Rick; in effect she asks Rick to decide her fate for her. In *Spellbound* (1945) she plays a professional woman, a frigid psychiatrist who wears glasses, smokes, and pulls her hair back in a severe bun but who needs help from a male colleague in order to solve the mystery of her patient's amnesia.

Where Crawford tries mistakenly to give depth to her mask and thereby only underscores its superficiality, Bergman suggests complexities that her Hollywood star packaging rarely allows her to develop. Star acting confines her to a surface—warm, sympathetic, "natural"—that she always seems capable of piercing but doesn't choose to. Her one great failure in Hollywood, *Joan of Arc* (1948), was in a role that demanded forsaking the star mask that had been imposed on her. But Bergman plays Joan like a gracious actress receiving her subjects: the movie star as saint. Where Falconetti's Joan (in Carl Dreyer's 1928 silent film) is performed from deep within, Bergman's is external. For a role requiring turbulent inwardness, she is pretty and charming, and instead of deconstructing her image to embrace the character, she brings on "Ingrid Bergman," which isn't enough. When, repeatedly, Joan looks up to heaven to commune with her voices, Bergman's eyes are hollow. And in the finale, the character's terrible moment of self-recognition—"I damned my soul to save my life"—Bergman poses for her picture, with her arms open wide and her eyes thrust upward, as a light beams on her face to denote spirituality and a "heavenly" choir provides substitute cues for passion.

Only at the end of her career, and working in Sweden in her native language (in Ingmar Bergman's *Autumn Sonata*, 1978), did she fully discard her starry iconography. As a neurotic, self-centered concert pianist, Bergman divests her work of its signature sentimentality—the star's need to please. For once she rips off the skillful, jeweled surface in which she had been trained and gives a performance as open and undisguised as her age.

OPPOSITE AND BELOW
Ingrid Bergman, masked, as a superficial, movie-star *Joan of Arc* (1948); unmasked at the end of her career, playing her age in *Autumn Sonata* (1978, with Liv Ullman).

Where Ingrid Bergman often seems to be suppressed by her star image, Claudette Colbert's is liberating. Unlike Bergman, who projected dark undercurrents she was not permitted to explore, Colbert presents a shimmering, uncomplicated surface: she's a winner who typically plays unflappable sophisticates. She ran into big trouble only once, when Cecil B. DeMille miscast her in the title role in *Cleopatra* (1934). Unlike Bergman—who might well consider, along with Cleopatra, that in the cause of romance the world is well lost—such obsession does not rest comfortably on Colbert's dry, ironic, modern style. She's too shrewd, too much in control, to lose all for love, or for anything else, for that matter.

Artifice, not nature, is Colbert's milieu, and in two of her most representative roles, in *Midnight* (1939) and *The Palm Beach Story* (1942), she plays an adept masquerader. In both parts appearances are everything, and an actress who brought on the aroma of a complicated inner life of secrets and repressions would only have dismantled the films. In *Midnight* she arrives penniless in Paris wearing a gold lamé evening gown. She's Eve Peabody, who's spent most of her life on a Bronx local and who has just lost her money in Monte Carlo. Now, in one of those Cinderella stories that tickled Depression audiences, she's about to become Queen for a Day. Immediately sizing up her potential, a baron (John Barrymore) hires her to seduce his wife's lover and installs her, as Baroness Czerny, in a suite at the Ritz. From this initial masquerade Eve and the baron, who are both master storytellers and brilliant liars and improvisers, keep the plot spinning. As an impostor Eve is utterly convincing, and so beguiling that even exposure cannot dim her lustre. Like the cat with nine lives she always lands on her feet.

In *The Palm Beach Story* Colbert plays a gold-digging adventuress who lives by exploiting her charm and who gets her cake and eats it too. She's a happily married woman who wants to help her penniless husband (Joel McCrea)—they can't pay the rent on their

BELOW
A mask that charms: Claudette Colbert in *The Palm Beach Story* (1942) as a skillful gold digger who captivates her audience on both sides of the screen.

OPPOSITE
Would this wry, modern sophisticate (Claudette Colbert, miscast as *Cleopatra*, 1934) give all for love?

Park Avenue duplex—by divorcing him in order to find a rich man. She nabs one in no time flat, of course, a millionaire who has a bachelor sister, and to win this double prize she and her estranged husband pass themselves off as brother and sister. "I hope you realize this is costing us millions," she observes, ever commonsensical, when they decide to tell the truth to the rich folks who have fallen for them. But again even the truth can't hurt Colbert. A deus ex machina tossed in by scriptwriter Preston Sturges—Colbert and McCrea are twins—assures a merry end: the film concludes with a triple wedding. Sturges' final sting, a title card that announces "And they lived happily ever after . . . or did they?" is dispelled by Colbert's presence. With her as the presiding spirit, of course they did. Her irony and effervescence convert a potentially sourish story into a ludic fairy tale for adults. In a way that a neurotic actress would never be able to, she defuses the film's sexism and materialism.

Where maintaining a star mask made Bergman less interesting than she was, wearing hers releases Colbert's sparkle. Her mask frees her, and playing concealed characters only intensifies her vivacity. Her best roles, like those in *Midnight* and *The Palm Beach Story*, constitute a sophisticated defense of the energy and skill it requires to sustain a masquerade.

Humphrey Bogart is the master of the deadpan style of the forties. Only a handful of his movies—*The Maltese Falcon* (1941), *The Big Sleep* (1943), *Dead Reckoning* (1947), *In a Lonely Place* (1950)—are authentically *noir*, yet Bogart's presence lends a *noir* ambiance to practically every film in which he appears. Like Alan Ladd's, his face is a form of theatrical maquillage, a made-up "look" that separates the actor from his audience. But unlike

ABOVE
The master of the deadpan style, Humphrey Bogart, in his star-making entrance as a killer in *The Petrified Forest*.

OPPOSITE
Cracks in the mask: Bogart brooding in *Casablanca* (1942).

Ladd, who remains hidden behind his hard-boiled mask, Bogart breaks through his. His mask can, and in fact demands to be, interpreted, and reading it is often the focus of his films. Like Ladd, Bogart typically plays men with a veiled past, but where Ladd's wounds are buried, Bogart's are at least partially exposed. His forbidding mask is a field criss-crossed with leers, snarls, grimaces, winces, as if in response to bad food, bad liquor, and bad memories; the actor always radiates ill health.

When Crawford's mask slips, another mask takes its place, whereas Bogart's leaks reveal a human face. For example, in *The Petrified Forest* (1936) the actor has a sensational entrance that momentarily exposes his character, killer Duke Mantee. After other characters have talked about how vicious he is, and just after his henchman comes into the Southwestern diner where the action is set to announce, "Duke's hungry," Bogart comes in looking mean, his features set in a scowl, his eyes moving once from left to right as Duke cases the joint. By his sour, dyspeptic presence, Bogart gives the character the allegorical heightening the story demands: one look and we know Duke represents the Force of Evil. Yet in that furtive movement of the eyes Bogart suggests a chink in the character's armor—this embodiment of evil seems as if he is himself chased by demons. A man on the run, he lives in fear as well as inspires it.

The action in a number of Bogart's most memorable roles centers on the actor's brooding face and the tension between his mattelike surface and his festering insides. In *Casablanca,* for instance, sitting at a table at Rick's Café smoking and staring moodily into offscreen space, he presents a mask waiting to be decoded. What is Rick thinking? What action is he going to take? are questions that drive the narrative. "Under that cynical shell you are at heart a sentimentalist," the police inspector (Claude Rains) tells him. It is not a point Rick is willing to admit.

As it uncovers a heroism that is stealthy and repressed but nonetheless genuine, *Casablanca* explodes the fiction of Bogart's mask. Like the police inspector, we learn to see across his character's facade. In *To Have and Have Not* (1944) as in *Casablanca*, Bogart's tough-guy mask cracks to reveal a reluctant humanitarian. In *The Maltese Falcon*, after a scene in which private eye Sam Spade challenges superthief Sydney Greenstreet, raising his voice and adopting a physically threatening posture, Bogart alone "offstage" grins in self-delight at his act. This private moment with Spade reveals him as a sly fox who creates a veneer and then drops it when he doesn't need it.

When Bogart, late in his career, plays characters who lose control—his neurotic screenwriter in *In a Lonely Place*, his mad tyrant Captain Queeg in *The Caine Mutiny* (1954)—we're seeing the flip side of his earlier deadpan style. In Queeg's courtroom testimony at the end of *The Caine Mutiny* Bogart begins as if he's still playing Sam Spade, a cool customer claiming command of his surroundings. His sentences have the familiar Bogart rhythm, measured and just a bit lulling. But as the character's confidence begins to erode, he takes marbles out of his pocket and rolls them nervously in his hands, while his verbal and facial coverups begin to come apart. He speaks with increasing rapidity, his eyes

dart around the room, his face twitches as he performs mouth and lip gymnastics, and then, at the height of his frenzy, Queeg stops himself, looking around the courtroom fearfully as he realizes in a moment of awful self-realization that he is utterly exposed. Read in the context of the actor's career, the scene has a special impact—for once Bogart plays a character who cannot claim or retreat back into the protections of a mask.

In *The Temptress* (1926), her first American film, Garbo is introduced in a party scene wearing a mask, and with only her eyes to speak with, she attracts the hero (Antonio Moreno). Once she takes off her disguise and begins to talk, her character remains veiled; her first statement, that she is a free woman, is a lie.

"Who are you?" a smitten John Gilbert in *Flesh and the Devil* asks of her soon after they have met in an exchange of sizzling looks. In extreme closeup and in a soft focus that emphasizes Garbo's "mystery," she responds, "What does it matter?"

Like the men she arouses with a single glance, we too want to know who she is behind the hooded eyes and face. And usually, in her richest performances, Garbo in her own way and at her own pace reveals her characters to us. Her acting, at its best, is like Salome's dance of the seven veils—a progressive uncovering. In her layered style secrecy and disclosure collide in enticing interplay. Garbo's hidden quality is never erased entirely from her countenance, and she engages us in a tug-of-war between her aloofness and the displays of emotion she subtly releases. Watching her, we have to be on the lookout for the activity taking place *behind* her eyes.

Directness is uncomfortable for her, as her performance in *Susan Lenox: Her Fall and Rise*, in which she plays a character in hot pursuit of a desirable male (Clark Gable), bears witness. Gable's bluntness, his no-nonsense assault on love and sex, and his plain-spoken American manner are not only impatient with her exoticism, they demolish it. To glitter, Garbo needs a fiery but puppy-like John Gilbert (*Flesh and the Devil, Queen Christina*) or a John Barrymore on the skids (*Grand Hotel*), a somnolent Fredric March (*Anna Karenina*), a callow Robert Taylor (*Camille*), or a lightweight Melvyn Douglas (*Ninotchka*, 1939). These are men she can control, whereas a self-assured stud like Gable keeps her from "speaking" her own kind of elusive and ambiguous Romance language.

OPPOSITE
Letting go: Garbo in *Camille* (1936), looking past her lover (Robert Taylor) into a world beyond.

ABOVE
Could John Gilbert possibly resist Garbo's incendiary look in *Flesh and the Devil* (1926)?

FOLLOWING PAGES
Enacting secret ceremonies: Garbo handles a phone (in *Grand Hotel*, 1932) with the same transforming sensual touch with which she fondles a flower in *Camille*.

The gaze she typically directs at her male victims sends a contradictory message. Emerging out of the fog at the beginning of *Anna Karenina*, she gives Vronsky (March) a look filled with the weight of destiny that seizes him at the same time that it pushes him away. Playing another mystery woman in *Flesh and the Devil*, a woman like Anna Karenina who enters the film en route from someplace else, she first gives John Gilbert an enigmatic Madonna-like half smile as he picks up a fallen bouquet and then, as she goes off in her barouche, she cruises him. In quick succession she has gilded religion with sex.

Climactic scenes in *Grand Hotel* and *Camille* highlight Garbo's ability to play two emotions at once. When Grushinskaya (Garbo) enters the lobby of the Grand Hotel in an excited state, the character does not yet know what the audience knows, that her new lover, the baron, has been killed. But she senses something is wrong. With a growing fear in her eyes she looks nervously about her, as if questioning the meaning of the silence that surrounds her. Yet at the same time—and this is the essence of Garbo's art—her eyes sparkle with the excitement of a woman in love about to elope with her lover.

In her deathbed scene in *Camille*, Garbo regards Armand with feverish longing and at the same time looks past him as if into the next world. As Armand speaks to her, assuring her of his love, Garbo "releases" her eyes, a change that seems to happen while we aren't watching, even though the camera focuses unblinkingly on her upturned face. When her eyes let go in this transcendent moment, Camille seems freed from her body.

In passing moments Garbo's face expresses a rapid succession of feelings. When in *Grand Hotel* the baron hands her pearls, she looks puzzled at first, then hurt, then angry, as we see her trying to interpret the meaning of his gift. Then, impulsively, she arrives at her conclusion. Her face lights up, she kisses him and then begins to waltz around the room. In *Camille*, in a similar scene of quicksilver shifts, another baron gives her money, then slaps her. She looks at first like a stricken animal, then, recovering, she becomes assertive, almost imperious—Camille is wonderfully resilient after all. But Garbo caps the brief sequence with a sly smile: her pragmatic capitalist is pleased to have the money.

In *Ninotchka* Melvyn Douglas tries to force a laugh out of Garbo, playing a frozen Russian. Ninotchka maintains her mask, looking down and away from him, and continuing to eat while he tries to loosen her up. She laughs only when he falls off his chair.

FROM LEFT
Garbo laughs, in a famous scene in *Ninotchka* (1939), but even better, in the following scene, her face is suffused with an imprint of the happy moment.

Because it issues from such arctic depths, her laughter is wonderfully healing. But the payoff to this famous scene really occurs in the following scene: in the middle of a stern meeting with fellow Russians, a private memory overtakes Ninotchka and she laughs to herself, a low, sexy laugh that excludes the other characters.

Garbo's acting is crisscrossed with scenes like this in which forceful memories invade her character's face. Evoking the past through a technique that is one of the cornerstones of Actors Studio naturalism, she endows objects with charged personal significance. At the end of *Ninotchka*, for instance, back in Russia and reminiscing about Paris, her character caresses a slip she's brought with her, and her eyes, gazing into offscreen space, fill with transporting memories. In *Queen Christina*, after she has had a night to remember with a Spanish ambassador (John Gilbert), Garbo in a trancelike state begins to touch walls, a spinning wheel, a pillow, a piece of hemp, a painting, a bedpost, as her eyes and face become suffused with a sensual inner music. "I have been memorizing this room," she explains, after we have seen her enact her secret ceremony. "In the future, in my memory, I shall spend a great deal of time in this room. This is how the Lord must have felt when He first beheld the living world."

In *A Woman of Affairs* her character emerges from a coma to bury her face in a bouquet of roses, clutching them to her as if they were the remembered body of her lover. As she caresses a slipper in *Grand Hotel*, her face is flooded with memories of a career that seems to be sliding away from her. "What will I do? Grow orchids? Die?" In *Flesh and the Devil* her character fondles a wine goblet during communion, brushing it against her lips while she looks sultrily offscreen. Garbo's work is laced with these private moments in which an object, a place, the weather ("What delicious air," Camille exults, looking out a window into a sylvan landscape), trigger a sensual flush.

In her apparent reticence, her resistance to lowering her guard, Garbo resembles Bogart. But ultimately she allows us to see beneath her mask at a far deeper level than Bogart—or for that matter almost any other Hollywood player—ever could. As she sheds her characters' masks, her Sphinx-like countenance contains flashes of extraordinary openness and sensuality.

In *The Heiress* Montgomery Clift's face remains provocatively closed, but in later roles it becomes increasingly porous. Clift remained a skillful actor despite the weight of his private demons—his alcoholism and his guilt-ridden homosexuality, the damage to his face in a serious car accident in 1956—but the gap between the actor and his roles steadily narrowed as he seemed to transfer his own torment directly to that of his characters.

Like *The Heiress*, *A Place in the Sun* is about reading Clift's countenance. In the earlier film he is disguised; here, playing a poor relation given a factory job by his rich uncle and caught between a fellow factory worker (Shelley Winters) and a rich girl (Elizabeth Taylor) who both desire him, he has a complicated inner life that leaves more ample, though not always easily interpretable, traces. "You seem so strange and deep and far away, as though you were holding something back," Angela Thornton (Taylor) comments to George Eastman (Clift) soon after meeting him. Packed with latent meanings, his look attracts other characters too—what he's holding back becomes the narrative fulcrum. And at key moments the camera, mimicking the curiosity of the characters, moves in toward George as if attempting to penetrate his thoughts.

Clift plays the character as if an unseen force is weighing on him. He stoops, his voice and face are cracked with indecision, the residue of an inner tempest over whether or not to kill his nagging girlfriend in order to be free for Angela. The turmoil within comes to a boil in a famous scene on a lake during which George debates with himself about drowning Alice. Clift plays the scene with, at first, a preoccupied cheer Alice doesn't know how to read. While his words are amiable, his eyes remain unsmiling as he judges himself and his potential quarry, but at least fleetingly they also contain compassion for the woman he may or may not kill. As he tries to suppress his mounting anxiety, he seems to be suffocating. "Stop it!" he erupts, his body and face quivering, when he can no longer tolerate Alice's litany of complaints.

After what happens on the lake—was it murder or a tragic accident?—Clift brings the character's inner struggle closer to the surface. His face begins to twitch, his eyes take on a haunted look, and his voice trembles. "You look tired," his rich relatives, still trying to read his face, tell him. "I don't believe I'm guilty," George says to Angela in his jail cell after he has been convicted. "I wish I knew . . . I want to know." Though George admits he contemplated murder, his defense has been that at the last moment he could not do it and that Alice drowned when the boat tipped over accidentally; and as Clift plays the role the defense is plausible. Steeped in self-analysis, Clift's brooding face furnishes a true moral dimension. As he plays him, George is not a young man on the make who "of course" would get rid of a dumpy girlfriend to pursue a rich beauty; there is no "of course" in Clift's exquisite performance. Rather, with his increasingly haunted face, he carries melodrama inward as he blurs distinctions between guilt and innocence. In his jail cell at

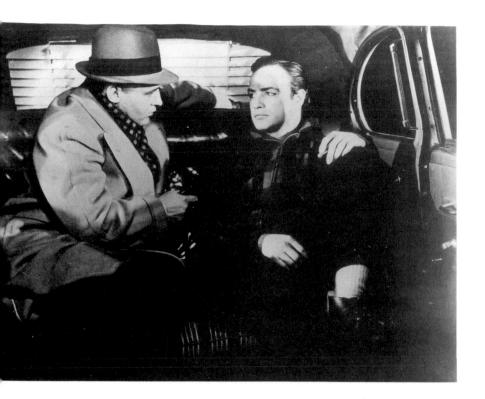

the end, as George searches for answers that elude him, Clift's face transforms a convicted murderer into an existential victim.

In early films like *The Heiress* and *A Place in the Sun* the contradiction between Clift's unblemished good looks and his characters' troubled inner lives supplies a dramatic tension no longer playable after 1956. The actor's ravaged postaccident face "speaks" with an unmediated directness, and by 1958 it was so absorbent, so coated with suffering, that he could only play victims and outsiders, as in *The Young Lions* and *Judgment at Nuremberg.*

As his face began to reveal the traces of a sorrow greater than that called for in his roles, Clift became incapable of creating a mask. As the doctor in *Suddenly Last Summer* (1959), a part in which he has to investigate someone else's trauma while maintaining the pose of a disinterested scientist, he is cruelly miscast. He seems far more fragile than his patient, a terminally sane Elizabeth Taylor. But in *Freud,* his hungry look, his groping, fazed expression, and his slurred voice enrich a reductive script. When Freud must speak with the voice of authority, Clift is colorless; his tone flattens and his face empties. But in most of the film he plays a questing, uncertain character rather than one who embodies the Law. In these scenes Clift, near the end of his life, with his nerves barely under control, turns the doctor himself into a prime candidate for Freudian therapy. Out of his own mortal emotional and physical illness, one of the most inward of all movie actors ends his career playing the great hermeneut of the inner world as a tormented spirit.

As a concluding word on masks and faces, consider two great contrasting performances, Brando's in *On the Waterfront* and Al Pacino's in *The Godfather I* and *II.* In *Waterfront* Brando plays a character who is gradually unmasked as he moves toward the self-recognition of the taxicab speech, "I coulda been a contender . . . instead of a bum, which is what I am." Pacino plays a character who undergoes an exactly opposite arc, as he assumes by degrees the hard, cold-eyed mask of a Mafia chieftain. As Terry Malloy evolves from the blankness of an unthinking thug into a man who grows to confront the truth about himself and the corrupt labor union he has been passively linked to, *Waterfront* dramatizes the birth of a face. As they follow their antihero's descent into the befouling Mafia underworld, the *Godfather* films dramatize the death of a face. (In *The Godfather III* [1990] Pacino's face is dead from the beginning—the film adds nothing to what we already know by the end of the second part.) Where Brando's face slowly opens, Pacino's irreversibly closes off into a mask of cruelty; where Brando's eyes acquire light, Pacino's eerily darken.

OPPOSITE
Life merges with art: a battered Montgomery Clift plays a Holocaust victim in *Judgment at Nuremberg* (1961).

ABOVE LEFT
A face is born: Terry Malloy (Marlon Brando) begins to see the light, in the acclaimed taxicab scene in *On the Waterfront* (with Rod Steiger).

ABOVE RIGHT
A mask in the making: in *The Godfather* (1972) the face of Michael Corleone (Al Pacino) gradually hardens.

CLOCKWISE FROM LEFT
A face made to be looked at: Elizabeth Taylor looking inhumanly lush as Maggie the Cat in *Cat on a Hot Tin Roof* (1958, with Paul Newman, also looking too good to be true) and on display in *Suddenly Last Summer* (1959, a color still from a black-and-white film). In *Cleopatra* (1963), although she is not playing Helen of Troy, her face might indeed launch a thousand ships.

Spectacles

Beauty and the Beast

In Hollywood, youth and beauty, beauty and youth, are an essential couplet. So strict is the code that, especially for women and especially during the studio era, careers were often over or severely curtailed after a performer reached the DMZ line of thirty-five or forty. Only character actors or stars with legendary personas like Bette Davis and Katharine Hepburn have been able to retain their stardom into middle age and beyond. Because the industry links physical ripeness with the profession of acting, film actors confront a race against the clock as pitiless as an athlete's or a dancer's.

Performers displayed on screen at the height of a perfectly maintained physical opulence are inevitably set up for comparisons with their images as they traverse time. In positing a "then," the pictures of actors in their prime are measured against a series of "nows" that mark a progress away from the moment of transient glory. As time passes, the

The greying of Elizabeth Taylor: shredding the beauty mask as Martha in *Who's Afraid of Virginia Woolf?* (1966, with George Segal).

filmed image becomes both a celebration and an indictment of what once was but is no longer—a document of paradise lost.

Some two decades after her last movie, the actress asked an interviewer, "Can you believe that I was once 'Hedy Lamarr'?" As Lamarr's rueful query suggests, the beauty mask is a trap that ultimately accuses its owner. What would have happened to Marilyn Monroe, had she lived to grow old? For how long could she have sustained the illusion of being MM? For how long would she have wanted to? Like Hedy Lamarr, would she have come in time to regard her celluloid self as a remote ancestor or a virtual stranger?

If beauty is in the eye of the beholder, then to my eye the most lustrous of all Hollywood stars is—was—Elizabeth Taylor. When she was most deeply and vividly "Elizabeth Taylor," her beauty mask was almost inhumanly splendid. Though a performer who looks like the young Taylor isn't expected to do much more than offer herself to be looked at, she often did do more. Despite the fact that, inevitably, her entire career has been conducted under the sign of her beauty, Taylor has sometimes acted well. Quite unlike her later Chaucerian persona, the young star of the forties and early fifties had a sweet and almost otherworldly quality. Her high, breathy, whispery, oddly accented voice (a mixture of British and Beverly Hills), which often throbbed with feeling, together with her violet eyes and chiseled features gave her a radiance unscarred by vulgarity. She had to be cast carefully, as either outsiders or as characters who could pass for "normal" only within the protected realm of studio-made imitations of life.

In *A Place in the Sun*, the exquisite young Taylor is used to represent a world of wealth and privilege that fatally entices the weak-willed protagonist. And in at least this one role Taylor's beauty is also morally idealized. Her character is neither a tease nor a tramp but charming, even soulful, the Girl who really does have Everything, and nobody, either in the film or in the audience, resents her for it. George Stevens celebrates Taylor's face in a series of famous sensuous closeups as she dances with Montgomery Clift. But he does more for his star than pay tribute to her physical perfection. He makes her seem what she has only occasionally seemed since, a natural actress unself-conscious about her fame or her looks, a performer in whom beauty and a modest but genuine acting talent are in comfortable alliance. In *Giant* five years later Stevens also erases the "acting" that often creeps into her voice. In both roles she is more real than her unavoidable movie-star face would seem to entitle her to be.

As a bride-to-be in *Father of the Bride* (1950) and as a young matron in *Father's Little Dividend* (1951), she is meant to be a typical bourgeoise, the daughter of Hollywood Everyman Spencer Tracy. Though Taylor could never be merely "typical," she was playing "typical" as conceived by M-G-M in the Golden Age, and she was protected as well by the fact that her director, Vincente Minnelli, like George Stevens, realized that with Taylor less is more and that too much decoration would only result in visual overload.

In movies like *A Place in the Sun* and *Father of the Bride* Taylor is wonderfully subdued, but once she ripened into full womanliness, her attack became more pronounced. In *Raintree County* (1957), *Cat on a Hot Tin Roof, Suddenly Last Summer,* and *Butterfield 8* (1960), she does much more acting, as if to prove that she could. Though she remains encased in her beauty, she enacts neurotic, unstable characters whose beauty is in fact problematic (a threat or a burden or, surprisingly enough, undesired by the men her characters desire). And she adds a wit and temper that indicate her eagerness to crack through her movie-star facade.

In *Who's Afraid of Virginia Woolf?* (1966) she dismantles "Elizabeth Taylor" to become a braying middle-aged housewife who is earthy, bitchy, and fat, and freed from her beauty mask, she acts up a storm. At the time, her willingness to shred her image in full public view seemed like the desecration of a national shrine. In her post–*Virginia Woolf* phase, she's gaudy and shrill but often good-hearted. She has escaped from bondage to physical perfection and from the manicured M-G-M house-style imposed on her in the forties. But she has never escaped from her identity as a movie icon, and on either side of *Virginia Woolf* the only reality she has ever truly represented is that of being an intensely famous Hollywood star. (Her health problems, her affairs, and her fluctuations in weight can still command headlines, some two decades after the peak of her film career.) A woman with a face like Taylor's was destined to be on the screen, but once there her beauty could refer only to itself, to its own photogenicity. Inescapably, her face speaks "movie star."

If Taylor looks like a film star and nothing else, Edward G. Robinson looks like anything but. His stardom, along with that of Lon Chaney and of Charles Laughton, is one of the anomalies of American movies. If with Taylor expectation of acting prowess is low, with Robinson it is high: if someone who looks like him is playing a leading role, doesn't the spectator assume that the actor must be dynamite? As with Taylor, and for exactly the same reason—his *extreme* face—Robinson was constrained by Hollywood codes. If Taylor's face condemned her characters to romance as a career, Robinson's rubber mask confined his characters to a life of crime. When Robinson changed his image, he simply moved to the other side of the law. Whether he played a hood or an investigator, crime was his beat.

Unlike Cagney, who also became a star playing a gangster, Robinson had no romance in his face or body. In the opening scene in a diner in *Little Caesar* (1930) his character holds a dinner knife like a weapon as in his distinctive snarl he says, "This game [the life of crime] ain't for guys that's soft." Robinson's growling staccato delivery together

Why was this man a movie star? Edward G. Robinson in *Key Largo* (1948), looking truculent and dyspeptic and surrounded with phallic images.

Where are the stars? Crossing a swamp in *Mississippi Burning* (1988), Willem Dafoe (second from right) looks like an actor—an outsider, which is what he plays—while Gene Hackman (fourth from right) looks like a regular fella, a good ol' boy.

with his chronically dyspeptic expression excluded him from conventional Hollywood heterosexuality. His most "romantic" moment is the one near the end of *Little Caesar* when he moves toward his former partner Joe to shoot him. With a murderous gleam in his eye, he says, "Nobody ever quit me" (Joe has left him to begin a dancing career with a female partner); as the camera moves in, his eyes get watery and he doesn't know quite what is happening to him except he knows that he can't shoot Joe because he loves him. "That's what you get for liking a guy too much." By breaking the gangster's code—the kingpin mobster never places heart above business—Enrico (Little Caesar) quickly falls. Love undoes him, makes him uglier than ever as, unshaven and drunk, he hides out in a flophouse.

Throughout *Little Caesar*, as indeed in most of his films, Robinson's appearance—like Taylor's in her films—is underlined and commented on, as if to remind the audience of what they could not at any rate forget. *Key Largo* (1948), his last major gangster role, seems designed to showcase an actor who not only lacks vanity but has no claim to it. In his first scene Johnny Rocco (Robinson) is taking a bath; a cigar dangles from his mouth and he's sweating as he bares a pendulous chest. When later he plants a sloppy kiss on the face of his tipsy mistress, the gesture is clearly intended to make her and us squirm.

In Hollywood an actor who looks like Robinson is doomed to romantic catastrophe. As a meek bank clerk in *Scarlet Street* (1945) and a fuddy-duddy professor in *The Woman in the Window* (1944), he plays characters phenomenally unlucky in love who are driven to commit crimes once they hear the siren song of a femme fatale (Joan Bennett in both films). In *Double Indemnity*, as in *Little Caesar,* Robinson plays a submerged homosexual. His character is a tireless insurance investigator married to his job who acts as a father surrogate for a young co-worker (Fred MacMurray) who is destroyed by just the kind of heterosexual desire from which Robinson is isolated.

Actors with extraordinary faces, Robinson and Taylor are condemned to the realm of the exceptional. In contrast to them is a player like Gene Hackman, who looks like the brother or son or uncle or friend each member of the audience could claim. In *Mississippi Burning* (1988) he is a good ol' boy Southern sheriff, and in a film shot on location and filled with extras who are the real thing, Hackman blends right in. He doesn't look like a celebrity but like an insider, a man who knows from a lifetime of experience how to read the behavior of the locals. By intended contrast, Willem Dafoe as a Northerner is clearly a stranger to the isolated redneck community in which (circa 1964) civil-rights workers have been killed by a local vigilante group.

Looking as they do, Taylor and Robinson belong in worlds that exist only within the borders of a film screen. Taylor's beauty places her at a distance, as an idealized figure of the Hollywood imagination, an icon who inspires awe and admiration. Robinson's craggy appearance destined him to portray characters who enact the audience's nightmares; his victims and losers play out fates the audience surely does not wish to share. Part of the skill of both performers is that they humanize the otherness their looks impose on them: at her best Taylor enlivens her beauties, as Robinson endows his unfortunates with a measure of his own dignity and intelligence. Watching Hackman, the audience looks neither up nor down but directly across—he is strictly on the level, a figure on the screen who offers the shock of immediate recognition.

Age

For an actor like Hackman, aging only burnishes the lived-in quality of the face, while for the Young and the Beautiful, cracks revealed in the mirror are signposts to oblivion. In Hollywood iconography the aging face is an antimask: a record of experience and vulnerability that cannot be disguised. Since "life is for the young" is a sacred Hollywood code, aging is hazardous even for performers willing to show their age. Hence the spectacle of no-longer-young stars playing marginal roles, or cast in horror shows in which age itself is linked to the grotesque, or disappearing from the screen entirely.

Films in which aging or aged actors are both central and allowed their dignity are rare. Here are two.

At the end of *The Whales of August* (1987), the camera pans across objects on the mantelpiece of the living room in which two elderly sisters (Bette Davis and Lillian Gish) have lived for decades until it stops at a photograph of the sisters taken at least a half century earlier. This glimpse of their younger selves is a tribute to the fact that Gish and Davis, whose careers span the entire history of narrative film in America, have generously shared with us the process of growing old.

The two stars draw on the personas they have built up over a lifetime in front of the cameras. Visibly recovering from the effects of a stroke, wracked by age and ill health and almost unrecognizably gaunt, Bette Davis is still capable of giving us "Bette Davis" as she plays a character who spoils for a fight and isn't necessarily good-hearted underneath her vinegary veneer. As her wise, life-affirming sister, Gish offers a reprise gilded by age of the soulful heroines she first delineated in silent movies. As Davis' astringency brushes against Gish's sentimentality, the film's slight story is elevated by the gift of their presence.

Roles for visibly aging men are not only more plentiful than ones for older women, they often downplay or even disregard the age factor. In *High Noon,* for example, Gary Cooper, noticeably aged, plays a character who has a decisive role in his community (unlike the sisters in *The Whales of August,* whose secluded lives are marginal) and who, moreover, has just married a woman (played by Grace Kelly) clearly young enough to be his daughter.

In *High Noon*, twenty-one years after he was pursued into the Moroccan desert by Marlene Dietrich, Cooper looks old, perhaps even prematurely so. Weathered and lined with concern, his face has deepened over time, his former movie-handsome good looks replaced by a rich patina of wisdom and integrity. As in *The Whales of August*, the memories audiences bring to a veteran actor's work charge the movie. While Cooper is assisted by the film's complex crosscutting, heroic angles, and haunting theme song, ultimately it is his face that drives the story and gives it its mythic force.

The actor's face is so filled with thought that his character needs only a few simple words with which to express himself. "I've got to go back to town [to confront the gang he sent to jail]. That's the whole thing," Will Kane (Cooper), just retired as sheriff, explains to his new bride, a Quaker. "I can't leave . . . I don't know why," he says later, to a former lover (the wonderfully worldly Katy Jurado) who understands him better than his inexperienced bride does. Whatever needs to be known and said is written on Cooper's careworn face and in his eyes, alight with his character's ongoing inner monologue—all his big moments are wordless. When Will is lied to and knows he is being lied to (no townspeople will come forward to help him face the gang) and when he comes to church to assemble a posse and is roundly rejected, Cooper's eyes and face express the hurt his tight-lipped character can't put into words. When he hears the whistle of the noon train, he looks up with an intensity that suggests he is about to meet his destiny. And in the showdown, as Will hunts his adversaries, he hears with his eyes. After he has stood up to the gang on his own, he looks accusingly at the townspeople, his former friends who now emerge from hiding, and then, without a word, in a silence loaded with disappointment, he throws his badge onto the ground.

Cooper's famously lean acting style, nowhere more effective than in *High Noon*, is cut to the demands of allegory. His every look and gesture acquires a ceremonial impact strengthened by the fact that the actor is no longer the romantic Westerner of his youth. His stern, creased face raises the stakes—his hero is fighting to maintain the honor he has spent a lifetime to earn.

The wisdom of age: a weathered, deeply thoughtful Gary Cooper in *High Noon* (1952, with Katy Jurado).

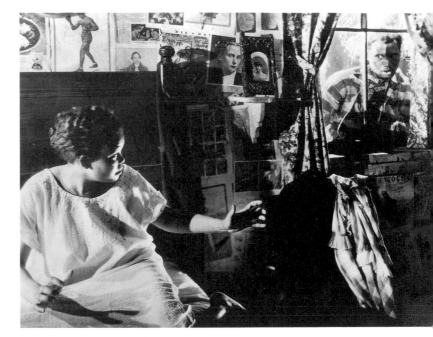

Color

OPPOSITE
Age as an anti-mask: Lillian Gish and Bette Davis act their age, truthfully and beautifully, in *The Whales of August* (1987).

ABOVE, FROM LEFT
Two views of Paul Robeson in *The Emperor Jones* (1933): before his fall (with Dudley Digges) and on the run (with Ruby Elzy). Significantly, in both stills Robeson is confined in frames within the frame.

One of the most adhesive masks in Hollywood acting, as in American culture, is that of color. Forced to perform from within a color barrier, black actors historically have occupied a marginal place on screen: as mammies, servants, attendants to privileged whites (the *Gone With the Wind* formula), or as the stars of race movies (the pioneer works of Oscar Michaux, on the one hand; the black action films on the order of *Shaft* (1971), on the other). Both kinds of films insist on the fact of their blackness. Though the blaxploitation pictures of the seventies, set almost invariably in an inner-city criminal underworld, provided more employment for black actors than ever before, the image of black life the films purveyed was possibly even more damaging than the Uncle Toms of yesteryear and certainly did more to foster white phobias.

Within the limits of what they were allowed to do, Golden Age performers like Butterfly McQueen and Hattie McDaniel were considerable artists, manifestly more talented than the Jim Browns and Pam Griers of the seventies cycle. While performers like McQueen and McDaniel can claim local victories—they performed with a sly wit that allowed them to comment on their parts, while at the same time remaining within narrative and social boundaries—American movies had no place for an actor like Paul Robeson, whose sheer force of personality threatened to explode the racial status quo.

The political blacklist that hounded Robeson out of America was a convenient way to exclude a black man who did not conform to expectations. He was so clearly larger than his roles and larger than the culture, either white or black, could conceive a dark man to be. When he is cast in demeaning parts, as in the silent black-made *Body and Soul* (1925), in which he plays a fiendish ex-con who masquerades as a preacher, it seems a crime against nature. With the promise of thunder in his voice and body, Robeson was majestic; yet only fleetingly, in the fragmented film of Eugene O'Neill's *The Emperor Jones* (1933), is there on screen an imprint of the size of his talent. While O'Neill's conception of his black antihero as a superstitious savage spooked by ghosts is racist, Robeson's performance has a galvanizing physicality. "I wants mirrors, plenty of 'em," he intones, and when the Emperor Jones in full sartorial glory strides before a wall lined with them, Robeson is imposing indeed.

The film is a showcase for Robeson's voice. To demonstrate his power over the natives, Jones barks orders in a tone that could shatter glass. Dubose Heyward's screenplay is so episodic that it doesn't allow Robeson to build a performing rhythm until the final fifteen minutes, when the character delivers a sustained monologue; Robeson rises to the challenge, "singing" it in a pulsing voice.

Except for his rendition of "Ol' Man River" in the 1936 version of *Showboat*— Robeson acts the song with such power that the character leaps out of his cameo status— the actor was all but erased from American pictures and had to seek film work in England. But even if he had not been blacklisted, it is unlikely that American movies of Robeson's era could have provided more than they did—a truncated *Emperor Jones*, which contained at least an echo of the actor's rumbling presence, and a show-stopping walk-on in a landmark operetta.

Before the advent in the eighties of comics like Eddie Murphy and Richard Pryor, whose personas as hip blacks outwitting white opponents give a spin to the theme of the outsider as insider, only Sidney Poitier had a major sustained career. (Before Whoopi Goldberg, no black actress has had a sustained career.) Poitier exercised a degree of control over his work that, in historical terms, is astonishing: he never accepted a racially unflattering role. Thinking of himself as who indeed he was—a representative of black people—he played characters who help to educate whites out of their racism, and who triumph over circumstances to achieve status in the dominant culture. His performances are bound inextricably to what he stood for—his unavoidable tokenism. And because of his color mask, his own self-imposed constraints, and the racial preconceptions of the white authors who wrote most of his roles and of the white industry in which he worked, Poitier's fire remained tamped.

Playing a good kid in *The Blackboard Jungle* (1955), Poitier is eerily restrained. And with his innate dignity, his strong screen presence, and his smooth, trained voice, he seems too mature and too assured for the character. Except for a moment in which he flares up before a classroom race fight erupts, in effect dropping his mask, he seems hidden. As his white opponent, a deep-dyed juvenile delinquent with a barrage of twitches, Vic Morrow does most of the acting.

In *The Defiant Ones* (1958), as an escaped con chained to a white man (Tony Curtis), Poitier with a Southern accent and fractured grammar seems again to be playing a character beneath him in class and education. Again the tumultuous feelings that his character surely harbors—he has a wife and a child he hasn't seen in five years; he's labored at back-breaking work for a miserly wage—are expressed only fleetingly. "Don't

ABOVE AND OPPOSITE
Marginalized: Sidney Poitier in *Blackboard Jungle* (1955, with Glenn Ford) and in *The Defiant Ones* (1958, with Tony Curtis) is not permitted to command the frame.

call me boy!" his character explodes in the opening scene; later he spits at the ringleader of a lynch mob. The film is really thrown to Poitier's white costar—Tony Curtis with his shirt off is made the object of the camera's desiring gaze, while Poitier remains fully clothed; Curtis' character has a sexual relationship with a hungry widow, while Poitier's remains a sexual outsider. At the end Poitier cradles his wounded white "brother," lights a cigarette for him, and serenades him with a folk song—a pietà in which the black man evinces traces of a Mammy.

Poitier's obduracy and imperturbability are underlined when he plays supercompetent characters, black men whose lives are removed from the world of the disadvantaged. In *Guess Who's Coming to Dinner* (1967) he is a physician of international repute, a man with such a colossal curriculum vitae that he brutally surpasses his upper-crust white fiancée. "He's so calm and sure of everything, he doesn't have any tensions in him," the young woman (Katharine Houghton) tells her liberal mother (Katharine Hepburn). In-

deed, Poitier's Buddha-like performance is so perfectly poised that his character is as beyond scrutiny as he is beyond reality. In two scenes, however, Poitier rips through the mask within which the risible screenplay binds him. When he exults to his mother, "These last few days with her I feel like I'm alive again," he lifts the lid off his imposing character to reveal a joyful person within. And when, with defiance mixed with love, he lashes out at his father, "You think of yourself as a colored man, I think of myself as a man," the strength and tenacity that have driven his overachiever are momentarily exposed.

"They call me *Mr.* Tibbs!" Poitier explains, tears of indignation welling in his eyes, to the redneck sheriff (Rod Steiger) he will of course win over by the end of the movie, *In the Heat of the Night* (1967). As a homicide expert from Philadelphia who helps to solve a crime in a sweltering Mississippi outpost, Poitier again is remarkably cool. As in *Guess Who's Coming to Dinner*, he plays a character who does not change; change, and showy acting, are reserved for the white antagonists who grow to appreciate the man behind the color mask. Where Steiger slouches, scratches, chews gum, wheezes, and chortles, filling each moment with a veritable *horror vacui*, Poitier retains his propriety, his quietude and measure, and dresses in a suit and tie even in the blistering heat. His Mr. Tibbs is so magisterial that when he touches characters it's like the laying on of hands.

After a self-imposed sabbatical in the early seventies—black liberationists for the most part rejected his screen persona—Poitier returned with race comedies like *Uptown Saturday Night* (1974) and *Let's Do It Again* (1975) in which he was clearly determined to demythicize his idealized image as the Saint Sidney of white cinema, and to play "black." Typically, however, Poitier did not merely follow the trend and turn himself into a copy of contemporary black action heroes; rather he mocked the stereotyped view in blaxploitation movies of urban blacks as a collection of hoods. *Let's Do It Again* is a clever, self-reflexive black comedy that sends up generic clichés. To raise money to save their lodge, marked for demolition, the straight guys played by Poitier and Bill Cosby turn crooked and concoct a scam in which they take lodge savings and parlay them into a mint. To work their con, the partners-in-mock-crime dress up as race stereotypes, Poitier in a white pimp outfit, Cosby in a red dude one, as they outwit real gangsters and gamblers.

Where Cosby is loose-limbed and overflowing with shtick as he gives the satiric material a nice spin, Poitier is noticeably straitlaced, an actor without comic instincts. When, in jest, his character acts "black," rolling his eyes, doing wide-eyed double takes, and gobbling corn, he seems stifled by his earlier persona, the stolid Sidney Poitier.

Savoring makeup: Laurence Olivier as Richard III *(1955).*

Makeup Artists

Because disguise is unpopular—audiences want stars to look like themselves—aging is often the only change the faces of most movie stars wear. "Makeup" is for the British: Alec Guinness playing eight different roles in *Kind Hearts and Coronets* (1949); Peter Sellers in a variety of disguises in *Lolita* (1962) and *Dr. Strangelove* (1964); Laurence Olivier blacking up for *Othello* (1966) and *Khartoum* (1966), bleaching his hair for *Hamlet* (1948), putting on a wig and false nose for *Richard III*, transforming himself into the dead-eyed music hall performer in clown makeup in *The Entertainer* (1960). Olivier's fabled attention to what his characters look like—finding the right nose or eyebrows, he built his roles from the outside in, using physiognomy to stimulate psychology—and his eagerness to rearrange his own features counter two strains in the American screen acting tradition: first, the star mode, which mandates that every character Clark Gable plays should look like . . . Clark Gable, and second, the influence of the Method, which emphasizes inner work and distrusts makeup as a merely external tool, a kind of cheating.

When he played a dual role in *Dr. Jekyll and Mr. Hyde*, Spencer Tracy wanted to suggest the transformation of the good doctor into his demonic alter ego without using any makeup at all. M-G-M insisted he darken his hair and thicken his eyebrows, but Tracy is still recognizably himself. Instead of the elaborate transformations of the two earlier Hollywood Hydes, John Barrymore and Fredric March, he suggests Jekyll's changeover primarily by widening his eyes and speaking in an aspirate voice as camera angles, lighting, music, and editing become increasingly intense. Tracy's reaction against disguise, like his refusal to change his homegrown accent in order to play a British doctor of 1887, is typical.

OPPOSITE
Spencer Tracy, in light makeup and recognizably himself, in one of the transformation scenes in *Dr. Jekyll and Mr. Hyde* (1941).

Only a few American film stars have embraced cosmetic makeover as an acting tool, most notably: Bette Davis; Dustin Hoffman in such films as *Dick Tracy* (1990), *Tootsie* (1982), *Papillon* (1973), and *Little Big Man* (1970); and Marlon Brando, who has an Olivier-like relish for false noses and for changing his body language as well as his face, in his performances as a Mexican revolutionary in *Viva Zapata!* (1952), a Japanese interpreter in *The Teahouse of the August Moon* (1956), and an aged prince of the underworld in *The Godfather.*

To play the neurotics who were her specialty, Davis often put on makeup that indicated disorder and disarray: the mask of Baby Jane is the one Davis seemed to want long before she herself looked anything like that refugee from Grand Guignol. In her first film in color, *The Private Lives of Elizabeth and Essex* (1939), Davis as the Virgin Queen wears a red fright wig and a ton of old-age makeup. She exults in growing old in *The Old Maid* (1939), and in *Now, Voyager*, before she's transformed into a swan, she's in spinster drag—mousy hair, librarian's glasses, sexless print dresses—as a pop-eyed ugly duckling. When she aged in *Mr. Skeffington*, she is reported to have told the makeup department to pour it on, to give her a mask of consummate decrepitude. "My audience likes to see me like that," she said. Surely she liked to see herself that way too, old and withered, gashed by the tolls of time—as if not looking like a movie star were an earnest of good acting.

By the sheer force of their inspiration, Brando and Davis transcend the Hollywood prejudice against disguise; on the other hand, John Barrymore and Paul Muni, who also frequently hide out, today have low reputations as actors who do entirely too much acting.

From the beginning of his film career Barrymore seemed determined to lose his looks. What drink accomplished for him by the start of the talkies, when his matinee idol days were already a memory, makeup achieved in the twenties before the sweet bird of youth had fled. In each of his major silent performances—*Dr. Jekyll and Mr. Hyde* (1920), *The Sea Beast* (1926), *Don Juan* (1926), and *Beau Brummel* (1924)—Barrymore plays characters who undergo spectacular physical transformations. As Dr. Jekyll, Barrymore is elegant, but it is as Hyde that he does most of his acting. When he first takes the potion that changes him, his body becomes contorted, his face wrinkles with age, his jaw protrudes,

ABOVE
Bette Davis × 2: looking like a born spinster (with Claude Rains) and transformed Hollywood Style into a woman of the world (with Gladys Cooper) in *Now, Voyager* (1942).

All made up—going against the Hollywood grain: Marlon Brando as a wily interpreter who moves and sounds as well as looks "Oriental" in *The Teahouse of the August Moon* (1956); Dustin Hoffman in not very convincing drag in *Tootsie* (1982); Jack Nicholson as the Joker in *Batman* (1989); and Brando as the aged Vito Corleone in *The Godfather*.

his nails grow, and his hair becomes stringy. As he hobbles crook-legged with the help of a knobby cane through the twisted streets of a studio Soho, he looks like Dr. Caligari.

As Ahab in *The Sea Beast* Barrymore also plays a before-and-after part. In the early scenes he's a Fairbanksian swashbuckler; shirtless and standing on the prow of a rowboat, harpoon firmly in hand as he hunts the great white whale, he has an exultant physicality. But the image of Barrymore as a ripe young hero is only a setup for his appearance after Ahab has been attacked by Moby Dick. A man possessed by a desire for revenge, he looks startlingly old and his eyes stare hollowly from a skull-like face.

Barrymore plays *Svengali* (1931) with a Pinocchio nose, a bushy wig and beard, thick fake eyebrows, and a phony Germanic accent. His stormy eyes stare at Trilby with a mesmerist's intensity. At the end, as an old man with a shuffling gait and muffled speech, Svengali himself seems mesmerized, or drugged.

After *Svengali*, his looks in ruins, the hopelessly alcoholic actor slipped into a self-parodying mode in which the only role he could really sustain was that of a self-dramatizing ham actor—the Great Profile in irreversible decline. Sometimes, as in *Twentieth Century* and *Midnight*, Barrymore's posturing is ripely amusing; sometimes, as in *Dinner at Eight* and *Grand Hotel*, it is touching despite the morbid grace notes; and sometimes, as in *Bill of Divorcement* (1932), it is excruciating.

Because he frequently changed his appearance and his voice from role to role, Paul Muni was not always easy to spot. An actor who trained on the Yiddish stage where as a young man he excelled in playing old geezers, Muni went against the American grain. Rather than creating a marketable screen persona to which he adhered, Muni had no identifiable image; he was an actor (a variable one, in truth) rather than a star. In *Scarface*

FROM LEFT
Determined to lose his looks: a dashing young John Barrymore confronts himself as Dr. Jekyll's monstrous alter ego in *Dr. Jekyll and Mr. Hyde* (1920). Eleven years later, an aging Barrymore uneasily eyes his Trilby (Marian Marsh) in *Svengali* (1931).

(1932), *The Good Earth* (1937), *The Life of Emile Zola* (1937), and *Juarez* (1939)—four of his numerous disguises—the actor creates four separate masks.

The difference between star acting and Muni's character acting can be gauged by comparing his Scarface to Cagney's Public Enemy. Where Cagney, without makeup and speaking in his own voice, seems like the real thing, Muni's gangster is an impersonation, an actor's skillful stunt. With a thick, indefinite accent, a false scar, makeup that gives him a simian appearance, and a strutting peacock walk, Muni shows us the character rather than fully inhabiting him. As Tom Powers, Cagney is a force of nature; Muni's Scarface is a stage Italian.

In *The Good Earth* Muni in full Oriental disguise replaces the thrusting staccato rhythms of Scarface with an Eastern lilt and bends his body in a Westerner's imitation of Oriental movement. But, as throughout his work, his voice throbs with feeling. In the locust attack when he cries out "We must keep fighting!" and when, his hands raised, he announces deliverance, "We beat them!" his voice quivers with an emotional fullness rare in American actors. When after his wife's death, he proclaims, "O-lan, you are the earth," his voice trembles with biblical force.

Muni's Emile Zola ages from a young man in a garret to a greying, heavyset author, a pipe-smoking, goateed patriarch who rises to the defense of Dreyfus and who speaks in the sepulchral tones of a man with his eye on history. Indeed, Muni plays the role as if Zola were already aware of what Anatole France was to say about him at his funeral: "[Zola] was a moment in the conscience of man."

As Juarez, Muni looks like an Indian icon and speaks with ostentatious dignity in a fanciful accent. His sanctimonious impersonation is abetted by the symbol-mongering

mise-en-scène: Juarez is often photographed in a low-angle ceiling shot; a portrait of Abraham Lincoln is placed prominently on the wall behind his desk; and to distinguish his democratic world from the palatial elegance in which his political opponents, Maximilian and Carlotta, are ensconced, the character is seen against rough stucco backgrounds. When Juarez, in a Lincolnesque top hat, walks through a firing squad to confront a Mexican traitor, the men lower their guns, as if zapped by his semidivine presence.

Muni's great-men figures—Zola, Juarez, Louis Pasteur—evoke an acting tradition that now seems outmoded. His simple, straightforward performance in *I Am a Fugitive from a Chain Gang* (1932), in which without makeup he enacts an American Everyman hounded by a corrupt judiciary system, is more appealing to contemporary tastes. Like the film itself Muni's performance is swift, terse, documentary-like: decidedly unactorly. But for all his calculating solemnity—Muni is no fun—his work offers a view of a theatrical tradition, the vibrant emotionalism of the Yiddish stage, that is virtually extinct today and that even at the time was an anomaly at the movies, where personality has a greater impact than versatility. The fact that in the thirties a performer like Muni could become a film star by exhibiting rather than concealing his rich acting heritage is another reminder of the bounties of Hollywood's Golden Age.

In interviews film stars often maintain that the "secret" of successful movie acting is in how they use their eyes. Through their eyes actors can deepen dialogue or action as well as quicken the viewer's attention. If screen players have had to learn how to use their eyes and faces, measuring at any particular moment how much or how little the camera demands of them, audiences too need practice in deciphering the facial codes that govern screen performance. Much Hollywood acting asks us simply to admire faces; the most vibrant acting demands that we go beyond merely looking at a face to studying it for clues about motive or identity. And to stimulate the audience's desire to explore their faces, the most cunning screen actors have developed a style in which emotion rumbles just beneath the surface, waiting to be expressed. Often the most provocative faces, the ones that engage the viewer in the most vital interchange, are both open and closed, secretive yet willing to be exposed.

FROM LEFT
Not always easy to spot: Paul Muni in disguise for *The Good Earth* (1937) and *Juarez* (1939) and overshadowed by a crucified Christ in *The Life of Emile Zola* (1937).

The Rustle of Language

"WHAT A DUMP!"
"The calla lilies are in bloom again."
"Gimme a whisky—ginger ale on the side. And don't be stingy, baby."
"Miz Scarlett, I don't know nothin' about birthin' babies."
"Beulah, peel me a grape."
"I coulda been a contender."
"Go ahead, make my day."
"Fasten your seat belts, it's going to be a bumpy night."

The Grain of the Voice (After Roland Barthes)

Everyone's listening to Jean Arthur's voice in *Mr. Smith Goes to Washington* (1939), as indeed they should: it's one of the most delightful sounds in movie history.

To focus on bodies and faces may seem to sever actors from their voices. But on film, where movement, gestures, glances, and wordless reactions not only amplify but often replace dialogue, speech is only one of the languages an actor uses. Further, such a focus helps to counter the popular assumption that the actor's voice is the inevitable fulcrum of his craft, the place from which he acts.

It's time now, however, to reunite actors with the words they speak. Since movies first began to talk, most of the major league players have had "star" voices, distinctive in pitch or rhythm or color, that are as immediately recognizable as their faces and bodies.

Consider: Bette Davis' staccato rhythm; Katharine Hepburn's fluted Brahminese; Humphrey Bogart's sibilance; James Stewart's stammer; W. C. Fields' growl; Groucho Marx's bark; Gregory Peck's whistle; Spencer Tracy's slur; Judy Garland's tremor; Gary Cooper's "yup"; Cary Grant's clip; John Wayne's sprawl; Elizabeth Taylor's high, scratchy breathiness. Montgomery Clift's hesitant, melancholy voice is as wounded as his face; Marilyn Monroe's fizzes like a bottle of uncorked champagne; Audrey Hepburn's floats, as regal as a swan; Kathleen Turner's smoky timbre oozes erotic invitation; Eddie Murphy's rapid-fire, high-pitched delivery crackles with savvy; Melanie Griffith's piping, kewpie-doll voice squeaks with vulnerability; Clint Eastwood's eerie, aspirate, dry voice promises a violent eruption; Barbra Streisand's Yiddish spritz has the comic crescendo of

a Borscht Belt entertainer; Mickey Rourke's voice seems lined with fur; William Hurt's is like glue, thick and coagulated; Al Pacino's is filled with porridge; Barbara Stanwyck's has a hide of leather. Jane Fonda's voice bristles; Jack Palance's curls; Shirley MacLaine's whooshes; Mae West's swivels as much as her hips; Margaret Sullavan's has a catch in the throat that mixes laughter with tears; Irene Dunne's has a tongue-in-cheek wryness; Claudette Colbert's brims; Bette Midler's flies; Grace Kelly's sails.

Reactions to voices are always subjective. One word from Lauren Bacall, who always sounds to me like a mean transvestite, and I'm steaming, whereas I'm jolted to delighted attention whenever I hear my favorite movie voice, the one that belongs to Jean Arthur. Raspy, surprised, sandpapery, flippant, plaintive, and nurturing, her voice dips and swoops, curves and ricochets, from whoops to whispers, from sighs to screams. Her completely one-of-a-kind voice often registers conflicting feelings at the same time— warmth and disapproval, say; or acceptance and suspicion, sturdiness and vulnerability. As it both enfolds and erases contradictions, Arthur's voice caresses and tickles, pokes and soothes. Listen to it.

At the beginning of the sound era stage actors with pristine diction and full, round tones—performers like Conrad Nagel—were regularly employed in the mistaken belief that movies should be well-spoken. But once the talkies hit their stride, and Hollywood lost its dependence on Broadway, the studios began to realize that their most popular genres required odd, imperfect, particular, or regional voices—voices oozing with personality and vernacular verity. The ticket was Cagney and Harlow rather than Nagel or Lunt and Fontanne. Harlow's twangy, nasal voice, the voice of a tootsie trying to put on airs, would have driven an elocution teacher wild. Nervous and quick, Cagney brought to movies the urgent pace of the big-city streets where he was raised.

Addressing multitudes: Chaplin as a mad German leader in *The Great Dictator* (1940). The world waits to hear the tyrant (and the actor) speak.

Many good film actors do not speak well. Shelley Winters has a coarse Chicago–cum–New York accent. Barbara Stanwyck never lost her flat Brooklyn "*a.*" James Dean talks in a muffled Midwestern drawl. Thelma Ritter speaks a plain-folks lower-class New York-ese. Robert De Niro sounds like a hoodlum. The fact that they do not have trained voices helps to brush their work with the sounds of the real world, though poor or merely ordinary speech is of course no proof in itself of acting mettle or an index of truthfulness. Betty Grable speaks in a thin, tinny, sloppy voice that is numbingly flat; without her legs and creamy complexion, she'd have been unemployable. Yet many stars like Grable and like Sally Field, who may well have the most untidy diction in movie history, have achieved popularity speaking a bland general American scarred with an unmistakable common touch.

While special voices have helped to boost many careers, studios in the Golden Age maintained diction coaches whose job, often perversely, was to remove traces of the exceptional as well as the ordinary from the voices of contract players. The coaches diligently scrubbed voices of burrs and scratches or of such incriminating evidence as lack of education or the residue of having grown up poor or on the wrong side of the tracks. Actors who graduated from studio training often emerged with a Voice from Nowhere, one from which the knots of their own backgrounds had been unbraided, a voice deflowered, punctured, aerated. Joan Crawford's is the prime example of a voice trained to emit Movie Speech. Where other divas like Hepburn and Davis maintained their own unique accents, Crawford's voice, like her face, remained masked.

Movie Speech has the same relation to reality as studio sets have. It's a form of verbal makeup, a coating of the voice—general American polished to a self-conscious sheen. Sounding like someone from whom the common touch has been scrupulously scraped clean, Rita Hayworth talks flawless Movie Speech. Her verbal "innocence"—the virginity of her proper pronunciation—is, however, suspect, as if she has been shoved into borrowing someone else's notion of good diction. Like masked faces and mannequin body language, Movie Speech is another way of imprisoning performers within the movies' manicured, made-up worlds. The actors who did not speak it, performers like Davis and Hepburn and Bogart who cultivated their own eccentric verbal styles, were rebels who defied the leveling process of studio grooming.

While British acting is clearly rooted in a tradition based on prodigious displays of the fluidly spoken word, American actors, and American film actors in particular, are popularly thought to be stranded in a verbal limbo. If its film stars have hardly proved their skill handling Shakespeare or Shaw, the American screen nonetheless has a considerable oral history of its own: many of the best screen actors have a decided way with words.

The first verbal mode is one represented by four beloved performers: Spencer Tracy, Henry Fonda, James Stewart, and Gary Cooper, all of whom speak in a resonant and specifically American idiom. Within their own individual styles they are all skillful orators who frequently play characters claiming authority by virtue of their rhetorical force. Many of their memorable scenes are in a forum of public address; in a courtroom or on a podium, or in a domestic setting in which as family patriarchs they issue homiletic wisdom, they embody the voice of decency, common sense, and American fair play.

For these actors language is deeply embedded in silence. Words are spoken only after issues have been thought about, and speech proceeds from an inner struggle. The fact that language does not come easily or quickly is marked by their well-known pauses and stumblings, their distinctively winding rhythms. It is in their measured, sometimes reluctant delivery that the scope of their victory with words can be gauged.

Standing alone in his garden at the end of *Guess Who's Coming to Dinner*, Matt Drayton (Tracy), his brow and face knitted in thought, stares intently into offscreen space. Respectful in the presence of Spencer Tracy thinking, the camera holds still for a long time while his character debates with himself about whether he should give his consent to his daughter's wish to marry a black man. Nodding his head to mark the segue between the end of thought and the beginning of action, Matt speaks aloud, "I'll be a son of a bitch," surprised at where his ruminations have taken him. In the following scene, the film's climax, he makes the speech of approval the characters as well as the audience have been waiting to hear.

At the end of his career, delivering the last word became Tracy's specialty. In *Inherit the Wind* (1960) and *Judgment at Nuremberg* (both produced, like *Guess Who's Coming to Dinner*, by Stanley Kramer) the action leads up to Tracy's statesman-like summations. Playing a lawyer based on Clarence Darrow in *Inherit the Wind*, Tracy confronts his

The actor as orator: patriarchal Spencer Tracy delivering the verdict in *Judgment at Nuremberg.*

opponents with pithy pronouncements ("Right has no meaning to me; truth does") and denunciations ("I pity you," he says to a cynical journalist. "What touches you? What warms you? You don't need anything . . . You're alone."). After he delivers his final speech, he places the Bible on top of a copy of Darwin's *Origin of Species* and walks out of a now-empty courtroom to the strains of "Glory, glory, hallelujah, His truth is marching on," a moment that conflates Spencer Tracy, American icon and truth-teller, with God the Father.

As the judge at the Nuremberg trial, Tracy has the responsibility of articulating the outrage of the civilized world at the abominations of Hitler's Germany. From initial neutrality tinged with disbelief that the Germans could be guilty of the crimes charged against them, his character moves to profound revulsion expressed in the voice of an American Everyman. In order to present the judge as a representative rather than a privileged moral witness, the film underscores Tracy's homespun image. "You had to beat the backwoods of Maine to come up with a hick like me," he says early on. To a worldly German (Marlene Dietrich), he says, "I don't think you realize what a provincial man I am." We see his character offstage, in casual clothes, devouring a hot dog and drinking beer. On the podium pronouncing final judgment, his thick, slow, grizzled voice vibrating with indignation, he is Lincolnesque, an American patriarch waiting to be carved on Mount Rushmore.

Even as a young actor in the thirties, before he had acquired his aura of an incorruptible lawgiver, a Voice to which all other characters defer, Tracy played leaders and orators, men of power. In this pre-hagiographic period, however, his characters were often fallible. In *Riffraff* (1935) he's a swelled-headed union leader who gets his comeuppance; in *The Power and the Glory* (1933), a proto–*Citizen Kane* saga, he is a railroad tycoon who is publicly lauded and privately detested; in *Mannequin* he is a poor boy who amasses a fortune only to lose his kingdom through greed. Tracy began acquiring a halo when he played sympathetic priests in *San Francisco* and *Boys Town* (1938) and a Portuguese fisherman in *Captains Courageous* (1937) who speaks folk wisdom ("I think the Savior He the best fisherman"). In *Captains Courageous* Tracy typically underplays the oratory, treating the character's gnomic utterances not as set speeches but as spontaneous insights. As in his later hortatory roles, his character's piety is firmly grounded, rooted in down-to-earth activity. Aphorism and metaphor—his character's speechmaking—grow out of natural behavior like eating, baiting, tacking, hauling, as he instructs the boy he profoundly influences in how to be a good fisherman. Saying is an adjunct to doing, a technique Tracy used throughout his career. Steeping words of wisdom in realistic action (like making coffee as he dispenses sage comment in *San Francisco*) helps to cut the corn and to convert oratory into the rhythms of real speech.

As a crusty paterfamilias in such M-G-M family fables as *Father of the Bride, Father's Little Dividend,* and *The Actress* (1953) Tracy also defuses speechifying by behaving like a regular guy. "I'd like to say a few words about weddings," he says straight to the camera at the beginning of *Father of the Bride*, as he puts on his shoes, leans back in his easy chair, and scratches his cheek. At the end of *The Actress*, when he releases his daughter to her dream by giving her permission to go to New York to seek her fortune, he delivers his Polonius-like speech as he eats his dinner, opening the ketchup, banging the table for emphasis, interrupting himself to speak curtly to his wife.

As a domestic bully who is really a softie, or as a fisherman who speaks blank verse, Tracy's voice remains unchallenged. His is the voice that makes decisions, awards permission and approval; his is the voice the other characters listen to. In *The Old Man and the Sea* (1958), in both dialogue and voiceover narration, his is in fact the only voice we hear. But whenever he teamed up with Katharine Hepburn, Tracy encountered a voice as sturdy and as commanding as his own. Most of the time his characters are skeptical of Hepburn's verbal excess, and they try to tone her down to his earthy level. Sometimes, however, as in *State of the Union* (1948), in which he is a politician who wages a false campaign, it is she who corrects him, making him recognize that his natural, straightforward self is the only one that works. But even with a well-matched opponent like Hepburn, Tracy usually gets the last word. At the end of *Adam's Rib*, in which they both play lawyers, Tracy fakes a crying scene during divorce proceedings and wins her over. "Us boys can do it too," he

Hearing the voice of the prairie: Henry Fonda addressing the community as *Young Mr. Lincoln* and reading a letter to Henry Morgan in *The Ox-Bow Incident* (1943).

Fonda's simple yet forceful way with words gives him presidential stature. (A color publicity still for *Young Mr. Lincoln*, a black-and-white film.)

says, demonstrating his fake cry later at home. "There ain't any of us don't have our little tricks." When she answers with a feminist broadside, "It proves what I said, that there's no difference between the sexes," Tracy rebounds with, "Only a little one: vive la différence," as he draws the curtain on their bed (and the film).

"I belong to the earth; I was raised in it, and I'm going to die in it," Henry Fonda as a backwoods boy in *The Trail of the Lonesome Pine* (1936) announces to the man from the city who has come to blast rocks in order to build a railroad. "I presume you know who I am . . . I'm plain Abe Lincoln," Fonda announces, as a nervous, physically awkward *Young Mr. Lincoln.* As Wyatt Earp in *My Darling Clementine* (1946) Fonda delivers a graveyard soliloquy to his slain brother, vowing "to clean up the country so kids like you can grow up safe." And in his most famous role, as Tom Joad in *The Grapes of Wrath* (1940), in a final speech to his mother before his departure he promises that "wherever there's a fight so hungry people can eat, I'll be there; wherever there's a cop beatin' up a guy, I'll be there."

Fonda's oratorical style—the lilting rhythms of his rural twang, his directness and simplicity—illuminates his most memorable roles. Like Tracy, Fonda plays characters other characters listen to. But unlike Tracy's, Fonda's forensic stance often comes out of reluctance or uncertainty rather than patriarchal assurance. Even in his rare victim roles (as in *Fury*, 1936) Tracy has the look and sound of a hero; Fonda often plays characters whose heroism is in some way punctured or compromised. Late in his career, Fonda ascended to an authoritative style reserved for veteran players of his stature—he plays the

Finding the words: James Stewart stumbles his way to victory as he argues a case to a jury in *Made for Each Other* (1938).

president of the United States in *Fail-Safe* (1964), and in *Fedora* (1978) he is the president of the Academy of Motion Picture Arts and Sciences. But in the thirties and forties and up through *The Wrong Man* (1956) his heroes were often physically as well as verbally vulnerable.

In his first scene in *The Trail of the Lonesome Pine* his wounded hero is lying in bed, as if marked for doom. And indeed the character is to be a sacrificial victim whose martyr-like death will heal an ancient feud between two backwoods clans. That "wound" lingers through much of Fonda's iconography, underlying many of his protagonists, from the fated ex-con in *You Only Live Once*, to the character in *The Wrong Man*, accused of a murder he did not commit. The first image of Fonda in *The Grapes of Wrath*—a solitary figure on an isolated highway—is demythicized once we learn that Tom Joad has just been released from jail for having killed a man who knifed him at a dance. Tom's famous speech to his mother at the end is similarly darkened by the fact that he is a man on the run, scarred in a fight that led to a murder for which he is now wanted. Violent ("Sometimes a man gets mad," he tells Ma), Tom also needs guidance ("That Casey, he was like a lantern; he helped me to see things").

In two Westerns, *My Darling Clementine* and *The Ox-Bow Incident* (1943), Fonda's characters slide hesitantly into leadership roles. In the former he's the ex-marshal from Dodge City who is whipped into fighting the Clanton gang only after they have stolen his cattle and killed his brother. In the latter he's a snarling, unshaven drifter who against his will is thrown together with vigilantes whose code he begins to question, although he doesn't speak out firmly enough against it. His character's strength is expressed only indirectly when, in a voice that conveys his own guilt, he reads a letter from one of the men they have hanged. As he reads, Fonda's slow country voice acquires a quiet moral authority; he sounds like an American folk poet who has risen up out of the Great Plains to stir the conscience of his listeners.

The actor's healing, homespun style is lionized in *Young Mr. Lincoln*. When Lincoln first speaks up, after mob violence has erupted at a July 4th fair, his words ("We lose our heads in times like this; we do things together we'd be mighty ashamed to do by ourselves") forestall an attempted lynching because he is so clearly one of the crowd, a man among his people. In the courtroom he defends the Clay boys, accused of murder, not through vigorous movements and a stentorian delivery but in an often relaxed posture as he tells stories of rustic humor in his plain folks drawl.

Folk heroes whose dreaminess is often contrasted with a tough streak and whose oratorical force is released only under pressure, Fonda's characters often achieve a spiritual transcendence. At the end of *The Grapes of Wrath* Tom walks off into the light of dawn, dispersing into the American air to become, in effect, an Emersonian Oversoul merging with the spirit of the Folk. At the end of *You Only Live Once*, staggering after he has been fatally shot, Eddie Taylor (Fonda) hears a voice ("You're free") which he interprets as a sign of his own release; swirling fog is pierced by heavenly light streaming down through the trees, and as the swelling sounds of a choir are poured over the image Fonda looks up, as if into the next world. At the end of *Young Mr. Lincoln* lighting and framing again lift him into the preordained role of Man of Destiny.

Fonda redeems the excesses of these last-minute metaphysical rushes by the note of rural innocence that sounds repeatedly in his voice. As with Tracy, a good part of his power as a speaker derives from his absolute simplicity. At its best his clean, plainspoken style, like Tracy's stripped of any legible traces of actorly technique, achieves an earthy lyricism.

Language does not come easily to James Stewart. "I . . . I . . . uh . . . can't help feeling there's . . . uh . . . been a mistake," he says, making his maiden public speech in *Mr. Smith Goes to Washington*. Typically Stewart's struggle to make words flow does not signal inarticulateness so much as it marks a respect for accuracy; aware of the power of words, he wants to be sure to choose the precise ones. In all his roles the actor's broken-backed rhythm, his stumbles and pauses—the way his words emerge from a thicket of nonverbal sounds—link dialogue to thought.

In his signature role as the freshman senator Jefferson Smith, Stewart asserts his heroism through his hard-won victory over words. At first he's tongue-tied. "I started to go toward [the Capitol Dome] . . . and that Lincoln Memorial . . . gee whiz, that Mr. Lincoln looking right at you as you go up those steps. . . . " Saunders (Jean Arthur), the sassy, cynical secretary whose job is to make sure he has no real power, rolls her eyes behind his back and calls his words "phony patriotic chatter." But the way he speaks begins to affect her. When, in his halting, modest style, he says, "Liberty is too precious a thing to be buried in books," she looks at him with real interest. And when, in a kind of folksy tone poem, he describes to her the virtues of his home state, she becomes teary. After Jefferson Smith is wised up to the fact that he was brought to Washington as a stooge—as someone who is not in fact supposed to speak up—he decides to return home to escape from the false words he is expected to utter and from the political theatre in which he is expected to play out a preassigned role. But he is saved now by Saunders' words ("Lincoln was waiting for you, Jeff"), which inspire him to continue. In the final filibuster on the Senate floor, with Saunders in the gallery coaching him, he spouts a river of words. "One lone and simple American holding the floor" (as a journalist describes him), Mr. Smith speaks in a voice vibrating with a novice's nerves and a novice's enthusiasm.

Like Mr. Smith, many of Stewart's most typical roles are about how his characters find their voice and, in mastering language, dispel the illusion of the innocent rube that trails them. "I can't describe her [his fiancée]; nobody can—here's a picture," his character says helplessly at the beginning of *Made for Each Other*. By the end he speaks up persuasively to the bosses who have given him a cut in pay. In *The Shop Around the Corner* (1940) he takes command of the shop in which for too long he has been an undervalued clerk.

In *It's a Wonderful Life* George Bailey (Stewart) finally gathers the nerve to speak up to Mr. Potter, a Scrooge-like banker who has held the town of Bedford Falls in his grip. "In the whole vast configuration of things, I'd say you were nothing but a scurvy little spider." Like most Stewart characters, George has to have his eyes opened. As a green young man he boasts that he is going to "shake the dust of this crummy town off my feet and see the world," little realizing that he is destined never to leave Bedford Falls. Later, still lacking in self-awareness, he tells his girlfriend, "I don't want to get married ever. I want to do what I want to do." George begins to see himself and his world with clarity only after he "dies" and an angel shows him what would have happened to Bedford Falls if he had never been born. "Get me back to my wife and kids; I want to live again," George prays. If you know how to see it properly, "It's a wonderful life."

Unlike Tracy and Fonda, who speak in an understated, monochromatic style, Stewart ranges from intimate whispers to shrieks of delight and rage, from a preternatural calm to hysteria. In impassioned moments tears coat his voice, and in epiphanies, as at the end of *It's a Wonderful Life*, his voice cracks with joy.

Later in his career, after audiences had become used to his idiosyncratic delivery, Stewart was cast as characters who are forensic aces. In *Rope* (1948), as a professor who solves a crime, and as a lawyer in *Anatomy of a Murder* (1959), he plays virtuoso public speakers whose attacking voices bristle with moral fervor. Both films are dominated by the sound of Stewart's voice as, rising and lowering for dramatic contrast, it steadily pursues the truth. Craggy, sometimes ornery, Stewart's parched voice is saturated with authenticity.

Gary Cooper's enduring image is as the strong, silent type. But in some of his best-known roles—in *Mr. Deeds Goes to Town*, *Sergeant York* (1941), *Meet John Doe*, and *High Noon*—the actor memorably breaks his silence. Where the words of a chatterbox are squandered, Cooper's are privileged by their scarcity—and by the impression he gives that, like Tracy and Stewart, he arrives at speech only after a period of debating with himself. Because they well up from so deep a silence, Cooper's words can have an eruptive force.

The climactic scenes in both *Mr. Deeds Goes to Town* and *Sergeant York* illustrate the actor's thoughtful relation to language. Locked in jail, mocked and humiliated by cynical urbanites, the folksy Mr. Deeds maintains his silence as a defense against the barrage of city slickers' words that have tricked him. As in *Mr. Smith* it is again Jean Arthur who recognizes the outsider's worth; recanting her earlier condescension toward Mr. Deeds ("I realized how real he was; if he's crazy the rest of us belong in a straitjacket"), she pleads with him to speak up. When at last he does, it is in a public forum, a courtroom, which like the Senate floor in *Mr. Smith* becomes the stage of his rhetorical triumph. Finding his voice, Mr. Deeds proves his sanity, while Gary Cooper certifies the fact that he can in fact speak quickly, wittily, and persuasively. Working the crowd as he mixes laugh lines with homely moral philosophy, he proves to be—proves himself by being—a shrewd orator who wins over an audience of skeptics. After he has made his point in words, Mr. Deeds feels entitled to nonverbal communication and punches the lawyer who has tried to get him committed.

Sergeant York's epiphany takes place on a mountaintop where he tries to reconcile the claims of his pacifist beliefs with his duties as a soldier. Cooper's face in this scene, as in all his best work, reveals the strain of silent contemplation. "I've thought things over," Sergeant York says out loud, as thought passes through silence into speech, "and I'd like to stay in this army. . . . There are things I don't understand but I must put faith in something bigger than me, like the parson says."

His role in *Meet John Doe* is constructed as an homage to the actor's natural way with words and to the impact of his iconography as a populist hero. Once again he plays a

Breaking silence: Gary Cooper proves to be a disruptively effective speaker in *Meet John Doe* (1941).

Bette Davis at full cry, lashing out at Charles Coburn in *In This Our Life* (1942).

country fella duped by city sophisticates. A slick, high-powered journalist (Barbara Stanwyck, following Marlene Dietrich, Miriam Hopkins, Jean Arthur, and Claudette Colbert who all, in films of the thirties, swindle and hoodwink Cooper, the perennial American innocent) hires him to pose as "John Doe," average American, who is to threaten to jump from a window in order to register his protest against modern civilization. When she writes a speech for his first broadcast, she cautions him, "All you have to remember is to be sincere." Handling the microphone clumsily, as if it might bite him, and repeatedly clearing his throat, "John Doe" speaks haltingly, like a man unused to the sound of his own voice. "I'm going to talk about us, the average guys . . . we are the meek who are to inherit the world . . . we're the people and we're tough," he begins, issuing platitudes in a flat heartland voice. But as he rises to the populist sentiments ("Tear down all the fences in the country and you'll really have teamwork"), his voice chokes up and by the end, like the other heroes in Frank Capra fables who speak authentically, he melts the cynical woman who has been using him.

In *High Noon*, as a man for whom deeds count more than words, Cooper speaks far less than in the Capra movies. As Will Kane, he says only what he feels and only as much as he has to. The character's few simple statements attain high moral force. Passed through Cooper's dry, lean, cracked voice, they sound like annunciations.

The film star as orator is a distinctly male tradition. Only two women in American pictures, Bette Davis and Katharine Hepburn, have had a substantial verbal impact, though neither was allowed the kind of public platform the populist actors assumed as if it was their birthright. For the women the arena in which their words have force is for the most part domestic—theirs are private as opposed to political voices. And unlike the men who command language, they have voices that are particular and extraordinary rather than representative. Hepburn's voice, indeed, is so antipopulist, so odd and extreme, that it has necessitated career-long special handling. Davis' vocal power contains such an assault on patriarchy that over and over her characters die or are punished—her upstarts don't share in the glory lavished on male good talkers like Mr. Smith, Mr. Deeds, and John Doe.

The Davis canon, to be sure, is stocked with arias in which at full volume the actress rips into men. She became a star the moment she lit into Leslie Howard at the end of *Of Human Bondage* (1934). "You disgust me!" she spits out in her faux-Cockney as the camera moves back to give her room in which to explode. In *Juarez*, as the Empress Carlotta, she lashes out at Napoleon III with torrential force, accusing him of having betrayed her and her husband, Maximilian. "You charlatan! . . . you murderer!" she hisses, as the monarch backs away from her into a corner. "I still love the man I killed!" she explodes at her pale-faced husband at the end of *The Letter*, spitting out her words like a succession of pounding blows. In *In This Our Life* (1942), as a Southern bad penny, she curses her rich old uncle for not bailing her out of her latest catastrophe.

These bravura passages highlight Davis' extroverted style, her sheer vocal power. Punching and throwing words, she uses language as a weapon, seizing it to strike out at the men her characters detest. Where, for actors like Tracy, Fonda, Stewart, and Cooper, speaking out brings movie sainthood, for Davis it is usually a transgression that earns disaster. Released in words, the accumulated rage her characters unfurl insures their demise. In *Of Human Bondage* Mildred's explosion precedes her death from tuberculosis. After she speaks the ugly, passionate truth, Leslie Crosby (in *The Letter*) wanders into her moonlit garden where, as if surrendering herself in expiation for her crimes of deed and word, she is killed by the wife of the lover she has murdered. After her explosion in *Juarez*, Carlotta disappears into an immense dark room, a visual foreshadowing of her imminent descent into madness. Reeling from her attack on her uncle, Stanley (in *In This Our Life*) drives like a wild woman to her death.

Davis' voice is not prepossessing. It is what she adds to it, how she makes it perform, that counts—the insistent way she uses and accents words ("What a *dump!*") and her canny timing (notice how she takes her time before she delivers the greatest line of her career, "Fasten your seat belts, it's going to be a bumpy night," and the pause that breaks the line into two equally weighted halves). Early on her voice can be thin and high and scratchy, as later, soaked with the effects of years of cigarettes and alcohol, it can be hoarse and growly, but her trademark staccato rhythm creates the illusion of vocal "quality."

The Davis verbal drumroll is abetted by physical mannerisms. Her circling, swinging arms, her huge, batting eyes, her twitching shoulders, her restless hands, her head-shakings—all are props to help her voice carry. Although she tried on a variety of accents—Cockney (sort of) for *Of Human Bondage*, British (sort of) for *The Letter* and for *The Private Lives of Elizabeth and Essex* and *The Virgin Queen* (1955), Southern for *Jezebel*, *In This Our Life*, *The Old Maid*, *Cabin in the Cotton* (1932), and *Hush, Hush, Sweet Charlotte* (1964)—the patented Bette Davis, so beloved of female impersonators, underlies them all.

Containing the overflow of the performer's own drive, her sheer enthusiasm for acting, the "Bette Davis" voice has to be repressed or chastened or silenced. If her character cannot be made to behave—in effect, to soften her voice—disaster waits in the wings. In the notorious *Beyond the Forest* Rosa Moline (Davis) dies, collapsing mysteriously but fatally near train tracks, as much as anything because she has not learned to lower her voice. But in the less typical *Jezebel* her spitfire is saved because she relaxes into a conventional movie heroine. Jezebel enters the film brazenly defying social codes: coming late to a reception, she is dressed in a mannish riding outfit and carrying a whip as her voice cuts assertively through the room. But by the end, as she goes off to help save the man who has spurned her (he has been struck by yellow fever), Jezebel has been humbled. Davis' big speech here is not a denunciation, eyes blazing, voice at full blast, but a whispered plea to her rival, the woman who married the man Jezebel loves. "I'm a better fighter than you," she argues, begging to be allowed to go to the quarantine camp. Though filled with urgency, Davis' voice is dimmed, its characteristic edge replaced by an unexpected softness.

This "other" Davis voice, subdued and declawed, a voice of sexual- and self-erasure, is the one she uses for her spinsters: tight-lipped Aunt Charlotte in *The Old Maid*, pretending to be her daughter's aunt rather than her mother; bitter Charlotte Vale, the ugly duckling at the beginning of *Now, Voyager*. When Charlotte Vale is transformed into a fashionably dressed woman of the world, she doesn't sound like "Bette Davis" in full cry but speaks instead in quiet, cultivated tones, in a voice with just the right inflection to deliver Davis' most romantic line: "Why ask for the moon, when we have the stars?"

When it is suppressed or held carefully in check, Davis' voice often sounds like an act. Indeed, it is the voice Davis uses when, as in *The Letter* and *Deception* (1946), her characters are lying. And when she plays conventional ingenue roles, as in *The Petrified Forest* and *The Man Who Came to Dinner* (1941), she sounds as if she's waiting for the chance to explode. In the former, as a waitress in a desert diner who reads poetry and yearns to go to France to become an artist, she speaks in a subdued voice that is nonetheless too grand for the character. Playing a young woman who cannot be other than naive, wistful, and idealistic, Davis keeps threatening to make her a twitchy neurotic and to unsweeten her vocally as well as physically. The strain is evident and her performance is as phony as Robert Sherwood's purple prose.

Davis' excess places her characters outside the romantic boundaries of Happily Ever After. Her "difference" is presented, variously, as sheer meanness, insanity (*What Ever Happened to Baby Jane?* and the other late Gothics), hypertension, illness (as in *Dark Victory*), or the claims of profession (as in *The Private Lives of Elizabeth and Essex*, *All About Eve*, and *The Star* [1952]). In her most overtly oratorical role, in *Elizabeth and Essex*, the queen voices the marginality and ostracism faced by most of Davis' characters: "To be a queen is to be less than human," Elizabeth complains. "Tell me, darling," she asks Essex in a moment of candor, "don't I sometimes wear on you?" And later, "I have a great affection for rebels, having been one often myself."

Davis then can't play regular folks. "Regular" simply isn't in her voice, which always contains a hint and usually a ton of acting. She doesn't dutifully recreate reality but at her best recharges it up to a ham-acting nirvana. Piling on effects with her voice and through makeup and gestures, she risked self-parody long before her late Grand Guignol phase, caricaturing herself as early as *Dangerous* in 1935. To give her audiences their money's worth, she is aggressively bigger than life. Which is why her greatest performance is as Margo Channing in *All About Eve*, a role in which her own urge to act is matched seamlessly to her character's penchant for acting. Whether on stage or off, in public or in private life, Margo is always on, turning each encounter into an acted scene. Like Davis, Margo projects her voice and displays her manner: the raised floor on which Davis delivers her most famous line is a kind of stage from which Margo can both survey and take command of the room, turning her party guests into spectators at a show. Only once in the film do the verbal gloves come off, in the scene in the back of the stalled car in which Margo talks about being unfulfilled as a woman. Physically confined—Davis can't do physical shtick in the back of a car—she speaks her character's (dated) sentiments with a no-frills simplicity.

Tracy, Fonda, Stewart, Cooper, and Davis represent high points in a specifically made-in-Hollywood oral tradition. Let's consider now some other performers whose very different negotiations with language exemplify two significant trends in American talking pictures: Carole Lombard, the whiz of screwball delivery, and Marlon Brando and James Dean, masters of Method naturalism.

Romantic comedies of the thirties and forties required writers who could write and actors who could speak a brand of native wit in which the lingua franca is the wisecrack, the one-liner, the riposte, and the thrust-and-parry. The comedies demanded actors who could deliver a lot of dialogue without sounding as if they were standing or sitting on a stage. Along with Lombard, the champion thirties screwball, Katharine Hepburn, William

Powell, Myrna Loy, Rosalind Russell, Barbara Stanwyck, Claudette Colbert, Jean Arthur, Melvyn Douglas, Robert Montgomery, Cary Grant, and Irene Dunne are among the prime talkers, actors who could tickle language and provide a glaze of verbal succulence even in undernourished scripts.

Freewheeling in spoken as well as body language, Carole Lombard, in typical high gear, strikes out in *Nothing Sacred* (1937).

A look at Lombard's way with words suggests how movie comedy in the thirties found its voice, one that alas is heard no longer. Lombard's speech is as freewheeling as her body. Actresses (*Twentieth Century; To Be or Not to Be,* 1942), liars (*True Confession; Nothing Sacred*), schemers determined to nab their man (*My Man Godfrey; Mr. and Mrs. Smith,* 1941)—Lombard's high-energy, quick-witted heroines are verbally eruptive. Plotting, fabricating, and masquerading, they speak in a rapid-fire lingo and turn on a dime from whispers to shrieks, while between words they interject an array of wheezes and snorts. Daringly, *My Man Godfrey* ends with a Lombard giggle.

A human volcano, she makes her entrance in *True Confession* racing up the stairs of a tenement building and jabbering excitedly to herself about the plan she has concocted to provide her lawyer-husband with a new case. For the rest of the film she remains in high gear. As she enacts characters who playact (in *Mr. and Mrs. Smith* she stages a scene to enflame her estranged husband's jealousy; in *To Be or Not to Be* she pretends to be interested in becoming a spy for the Germans; in *Nothing Sacred* she claims she's dying from radium poisoning), Lombard's own style is suitably playful. She makes words fizz and spin and sometimes runs them together so swiftly she creates verbal enjambment. With her light, swinging style and her daffy energy, she makes potentially unlikable characters (like her dizzy heiress in *My Man Godfrey,* oblivious to the havoc caused by the Depression) appealing. A verbal and physical live wire, she gooses her costars as well as her dialogue. Playing opposite her, William Powell (in *My Man Godfrey*) and Fred MacMurray (in *True Confession*) have never been livelier, and in *Nothing Sacred* she even manages to loosen up Fredric March.

Lombard's verbal expressiveness set the mode for screwball comedies, but her influence did not extend beyond the genre's life-span. Another oral tradition, Method spontaneity as popularized by Brando and Dean, reaches beyond a particular genre or era and remains a dominant influence on the way dialogue is delivered in American movies. Robert De Niro, Jack Nicholson, Geraldine Page, Ellen Burstyn, Sandy Dennis, Mickey Rourke, John Malkovich, Sean Penn, Meryl Streep, and Matt Dillon are among the many naturalists who adhere to the Brando-Dean mold.

In the early and mid-fifties, under the sway of the Method as it was articulated at the Actors Studio, the broken rhythms, the battles with words apparent in the work of actors like Stewart and Cooper, became a self-conscious tool for helping performers create an illusion of real behavior. Influential performances like Brando's in *A Streetcar Named Desire* and *On the Waterfront*, Clift's in *A Place in the Sun*, and Dean's in *East of Eden* and *Rebel Without a Cause* inspired a cult of verbal deconstruction.

Where Brando's and Clift's struggles with language are a character choice, Dean's seem to come directly from the actor himself. Unlike the others, Dean has only one verbal mode: inarticulateness. Words are insufficient to express the raw emotions from which his agonized adolescents are reeling. In key scenes in each of Dean's three films gestures, body language, tears, and verbal fragments replace full sentences. When in *Rebel Without a Cause* Jim Stark (Dean) sees his father dressed in an apron picking up food that has spilled from a tray, he pleads, "Dad . . . you . . . Dad . . . you . . . mustn't . . . " The character is so choked that he can't complete his thought, yet his fumbled, intercepted nonspeech is eloquent. At a later point, when he is deciding to report to the authorities the circumstances that led to the death of a fellow student, Jim wants his father to say something to him, to put into words a code of morality that can guide him and that he can respect. Unable himself to produce sturdy sentences, he nonetheless longs for the security they can provide.

Many of his character's actions in the film are nonverbal. We hear him first whining rather than speaking as he tries to imitate the sound of a fire engine; he presses a cool milk bottle against his face to enjoy a tactile sensation that does not need to be spoken; when his girlfriend, Judy, kisses him, his face fills with an erotic surge that transcends words; at the end he hugs his father's feet. Yet when pressure builds to a point he can no longer tolerate, he erupts in words: "You're tearing me apart!" he screams at his forever-squabbling parents.

Giant ends with Cal Trask (Dean) making a speech. Unlike the Capra heroes who in similar moments call on a native expressiveness, Cal collapses into a postverbal miasma. Blind drunk and unable to keep his head up, Cal "speaks" by breathing into a microphone and then emitting mumbles and incoherent fragments that empty the room. Mr. Deeds or Mr. Smith are applauded for talking well and for the obvious cost to them of doing so, yet Cal's unraveled speech is also a form of quite dramatic speechmaking. Here as in his other films, by not speaking clearly or fluently or even sensibly, Dean lacerates language with feeling and organically connects the production of words to his character's emotions.

In Brando's work, on the other hand, the struggle for coherence is only one of his approaches to language; unlike Dean, Brando has played roles in which his characters mesmerize others by the sound of their voice. His fiery revolutionary in *Viva Zapata!*, his elegant Napoleon in *Désirée*, his exceedingly well-spoken Antony in *Julius Caesar* (1953), his wandering minstrel in *The Fugitive Kind*, who seduces the women of a Southern backwater as much by his poetic imagery as by his body, are orators whose fluent speech commands attention.

His best-known verbal mode, nonetheless, is one of hesitation and delay in which thinking precedes speech—as in *On the Waterfront*, in which Terry's confusion is marked in Brando's jerky rhythms, his chopped-off words, his verbal stumblings wherein speech interrupts and turns back on itself. In a number of his films besides *Waterfront* Brando plays a man who undergoes a gradual change of heart; and along with the other characters we wait for him to speak, to put into words whatever has been rooting around in his mind.

In *The Men* (1950, Brando's film debut) he plays a paraplegic vet embittered into a silence broken only occasionally by words. "You're sorry, aren't you?" Ken (Brando) explodes at his bride, Ellie, during their first night together in their new home. They separate, Ellie returns to live with her parents, and after a period of silent brooding Ken goes in his wheelchair to see her to ask if she wants to go to a movie. The simple invitation seems to come from so far within the character that it has the force of a ceremony of remarriage.

In *Sayonara* (1957) Brando plays a Southern redneck who at first tells an army buddy not to marry a Japanese woman. Over the course of the film, however, his character becomes slowly acculturated as we see him thinking about and surprised by his shifting perspective. Like Brando's simple request to Ellie to go to the movies, his character's climactic question here—"Do you love me or don't you?" he asks his Japanese girlfriend—completes by putting into words the inner process of change we have witnessed. *Mutiny on the Bounty* pivots on the reactions of Fletcher Christian (Brando), first to the tyrannical Captain Bligh and then to postmutiny exile on Pitcairn Island. In both phases of the narrative the sailors try to interpret Christian's thoughts as they wait for him to speak. Showing what leads up to his character's public pronouncements, Brando deepens the role; his neurotic, foppish Christian is a far more compelling interpretation than Clark Gable's straightforward hero in the original version. "You remarkable pig! You can thank whatever pig-god you pray to you haven't turned me into a murderer!" Christian says when he finally turns against Bligh—an explosion that satisfies because Brando has made us wait for it. In exile, unable to solve his "private riddle," Christian sits in sullen silence alone in his cabin. When at last he speaks, it is to voice a decision the men this time will not

Struggling for language: too choked with feeling to be able to speak, James Dean confronts his parents (Ann Doran and Jim Backus) in *Rebel Without a Cause.*

heed. "Decency . . . we can't live without it . . . I didn't know until this moment the right way to proceed [to return to England to tell their story]."

The Young Lions offers a variation on the dramatically postponed Brando utterance. He's a German officer who becomes progressively de-Nazified. His first words are self-delusive: "I am not a Nazi. I am not political at all, but I think they stand for something hopeful in Germany." When he begins to apprehend the enormity of Nazi evil, however, he does not have the words to express his horror, and Brando's profound silence hovers over the end of the film. Only his eyes speak when a fellow officer tells him to kill the concentration camp inmates before the Americans arrive. His last action, wordless but eloquent, is to smash his gun, which in context becomes a symbolic gesture of disavowal.

The most delayed of Brando's speeches is in *Apocalypse Now* (1979), Francis Ford Coppola's transposition of Joseph Conrad's *Heart of Darkness* from Africa to Vietnam, in

FROM LEFT
Waiting for Brando to speak: as Fletcher Christian in *Mutiny on the Bounty* (1962) he takes the measure of his adversary, Captain Bligh (Trevor Howard); as Colonel Kurtz in *Apocalypse Now* (1979) he contemplates his crimes in the jungles of Vietnam.

which the actor is not seen until the long film is nearly three-quarters over. As Kurtz, an American officer who has gone over the edge in the jungles of Vietnam, he is the object of a quest by the narrating hero, Willard, sent on a secret mission to kill him. Moving upriver into the jungle, Willard puzzles over his quarry, seeing in Kurtz's fall into evil a mirror of his own potential. When Brando finally appears, he is indeed a striking presence—bald-headed, with a bull-like physique and a face that contains the record of a tormented life. As it is constructed, the film needs Kurtz to speak, either to explain or to deepen the enigma he represents. Instead Coppola's script provides mere fragments that Brando tries to cover over by mumbling, pausing, and looking intently into offscreen space; he encases the character in a fierce, silent concentration. His ultimate words (following Conrad), "The horror! the horror!" are under the circumstances too skeletal, "literary" rather than or-ganic. Brando and the film deserve more words.

Spectacles

The One and Only

Mae West, W. C. Fields, Judy Holliday, and Katharine Hepburn are four performers with voices that demand to be listened to. Their stardom is hinged to the way they sound, and indeed their movies are typically designed as showcases for their startling voices. While the careers of the first three players were both made and killed off by their trick voices—their movies are variations on a limited verbal keyboard—Hepburn has defied the odds to claim one of the longest star turns in film history.

Trapped by their voices, West and Fields are like flat Dickensian characters caught in a cycle of repetition. (Fields is ideally cast as Micawber in *David Copperfield* [1935]; to play a character created by Dickens, he simply brings on "W. C.") While locking them into personas with little "give," their theatrical vocal style turns them into spectacles, sideshow attractions. In old age in *Myra Breckinridge* (1970) and *Sextette* (1978), Mae West was still playing "Mae West," unable and apparently unwilling to escape from the voice that had made her famous on stage in the twenties and on film in the thirties. Where there are fleeting moments, of humiliation or collapse, in which Fields seems to "remove" his voice, West's voice never steps offstage. Steeped in irony and sounding as if their words are bracketed in quotes, their "stage" voices puncture bourgeois pieties about sex and sentiment. We know them by their pet phrases, their wisecracks and one-liners, but also by the

FROM LEFT
Can you hear these famous, one-of-a-kind voices? Mae West speaks her mind in *Goin' to Town* (1935, with Gilbert Emery); W. C. Fields emits a whine in *It's a Gift* (1934, with Kathleen Howard and Jean Rouverol).

noises they make between and around words, the marginal vocal notations, the hums and toots, that spice their verbal acts.

West broke the sexual rules by appropriating male prerogatives and casting men in the female role of sexual commodities to be ogled and appraised. Even more than her celebrated risqué one-liners, the daring of her sexual stratagems is expressed in the low growls and hums, the lip-smacking noises of sexual anticipation, with which she embellishes her double entendres. In these nonverbal but vocal asides, the embroidery of her hemming and hawing, she appraises potential lovers but also sizes up customers and adversaries, plays to her fans out front, and reveals the fact she herself is hot to trot. While the standard line on West—that she kids sex, poking at the layers of hypocrisy that surround it in American culture—is accurate as far as it goes, what is finally more interesting and subversive is her own enjoyment of sensual pleasures. Yes, Mae West burlesques sex, but despite her smashed-in face and beady eyes and the transvestite exaggerations of her figure and manner, she is really sexy too, as those dirty-minded sounds and her bawdy singing attest.

Far more than when she issues her aphoristic witticisms and bons mots, when Mae West sings, in a low, gravelly voice influenced by black jazz and blues, she sounds positively illegal. In *She Done Him Wrong,* in a voice throbbing with lust and oiled with lubricity, she

warbles three songs—"Easy Rider," "A Man That Takes His Time," and fragments of "Frankie and Johnny"—that stop the show. Watching and listening to her sing is like having access to a notorious after-hours club or a brothel—a place, in short, where attendance carries a risk of being arrested.

An unlikely Hollywood voice: Judy Holliday blasts Broderick Crawford in *Born Yesterday* (1950).

Where West kids but also believes in sex, Fields at his best is sublimely detached from all human desires—he's a man who really does hate children and family life and probably sex too. His flat voice disdains domesticity. In *The Fatal Glass of Beer* (1933) he breaks a water pitcher over his son's head and turns him out into a Yukon storm. "You kids are disgusting, reeking of lollipops and popcorn," his character snaps at a little brat in *You Can't Cheat an Honest Man* (1939).

Unlike West, who speaks a sharp-eyed common sense, Fields is often a verbal surrealist. As the security guard in *The Bank Dick* (1940) and the carny barker in *Honest Man* he plays characters who have an investment in misusing language, but Fields generally doesn't need a motive to confound and obscure. "I think I'll go out and milk the elk," he announces, à propos of nothing, in *Fatal Glass of Beer.* "You'll get your salary, and mustard and olives too," he tells his employees in *Honest Man.* Looking at a photograph of his deceased wife, he murmurs plaintively, "She was the first woman to wear jodhpurs."

West is always clear, nowhere more so than in her double entendres, whereas Fields' verbal code is often pixillated. Absurd names—Larson E. Whipsnade (*Honest Man*); Egbert Sousé (*The Bank Dick*); Harold Bissonnette, "pronounced Bisso*nay,*" as he continually reminds other characters in *It's a Gift* (1934)—tickle his fancy.

West uses her voice to seize control; Fields' whine often expresses his lack of it. As with the silent clowns, the world is his adversary, collapsing on him or preventing him from accomplishing even the simplest tasks. Objects conspire against him, insure his humiliation: in *My Little Chickadee* (1940) one of West's feather boas nearly strangles him; in *It's a Gift* he trips on a roller skate and slides into breakfast and, in an extended sequence, a series of interferences prevent him from attaining his modest goal of getting some sleep. He is often deflated by language as well. "You're all right; go ahead; nothing coming at all; street's clear as a whistle," he advises a blind man in *It's a Gift*—no sooner spoken than an inferno of traffic roars into sight. "I'm master of this house," he says, then jumps up when his wife shrieks for him.

West's vocal and figural persona remains statuesquely intact; Fields' is unstable, split between the fast-talking con artist waving words in a surreal collage to baffle and to sow disorder, as in *You Can't Cheat an Honest Man*, and the henpecked family man surrounded by a bevy of shrews who resorts to the mumble and the whimper, the sigh and the groan, to release his frustration, as in *It's a Gift*. West imitates only herself; Fields imitates the gentry, creating through his often ornate polysyllabic diction, pregnant with orotund Latinities, an illusion of propriety that is continually challenged. "What a euphonious appellation," he wheezes (in *Chickadee*) on learning the name of West's character, Flower Belle Lee, as West snorts. Where West's verbal style, then, is sober and overflows with authority, Fields' is sloshed.

Swiveling into a hotel lobby as she tosses her furs to the doorman, Judy Holliday as Billic Dawn makes a voiceless entrance in *Born Yesterday*. Silence hovers, as if waiting for a voice to fill it—and then it comes: "Whaa?" she shrieks, not quite intelligibly, at her sugar daddy. Shrill, brassy, deeply regional, her voice sounds like a put-on. The rest of the film, like Holliday's entire short-lived movie career, pivots on that seemingly mock voice that turns out to be the real thing, the way the character as well as the actress actually sounds. Holliday's achievement is to reveal a real person behind the show voice.

Garson Kanin's comedy, appropriately enough, is all about Billie Dawn's voice: the way she sounds, how she uses language. Harry, her crooked businessman-lover, comes to Washington to work a swindle, hires a well-spoken journalist to improve her speech after she has embarrassed him at their first Washington social. "Every time she opened her kisser tonight something wrong came out." Humbled, she confesses to her teacher, "I would like to learn how to talk good." Of course, in the tradition of such Pygmalion fables, she falls in love with her tutor, but unlike Eliza Doolittle she does not end up sounding like a duchess. Her vocabulary improves, she no longer says "ain't," she starts to question Harry's business practices, she comes to a realization that "there's a better kind of life than the one I have," but she still sounds the same as always, only a little less shrill. Billie Dawn remains herself. When Harry asks, too late, if he could find somebody "to make her dumb again," he misses the point. Billie was never dumb, she just needed a little push to be able to deliver her final message, "Would you do me a favor, Harry? Drop dead!"

Just as Billie's voice can't really change, neither could Holliday's. Unlike other stars under contract to Harry Cohn, the king of make-over moguls—performers like Rita Hayworth and Kim Novak—Holliday was immune to vocal rehabilitation, and even Cohn realized it. With her deep Brooklyn nasality, the way she rushes and blurs her words and raises and lowers her volume in sudden bursts and regressions, she is a hopelessly sloppy speaker—and a superb actress. Her untrained voice, pure Flatbush Avenue, sounds too real to be true: people in movies simply don't talk the way she does.

Her unreconstructed proletarian voice made Holliday the apotheosis of the absolutely ordinary, which is the premise of one of her pictures, *It Should Happen to You* (1954). She plays Gladys Glover, "an average American girl" who feels repressed by her anonymity. When she sees an empty sign on Columbus Circle, she decides to put her name on it. "Last week I was a nobody, now I have my name on a big sign, and dancing here where everybody's a somebody," she exults. "Look, there's Walter Winchell, that makes the seventh big name I've seen tonight." Under the slogan, "The Average American Girl Is

Unusual," she becomes a media celebrity and is asked to endorse products, to give interviews, and to pose for photos.

Though shrill and probably more nasal than any sound heard in movies before her, Holliday's voice contains humor, sensitivity, intuitive intelligence, and a welter of feelings trembling to find expression. Giving a new spin to the dumb-blonde archetype, her voice is surprisingly multicolored and perfectly poised for the kind of comedy that threatens to become serious—the bittersweet mode in which she specialized. Her forlorn quality darkens all her comic roles; she sounds as if tragedy might be imminent, and when it arrives, in a wrenching scene in *The Marrying Kind* (1952) in which one of her character's children drowns, it seems to fulfill the trepidation that always hovers over her.

But for all its flights and dips, its slides from bemusement to pathos, Holliday's voice typecast her as inescapably as Monroe's body or Garbo's face molded their careers. Holliday could only play variations on Billie Dawn or Gladys Glover, characters who can't really change and who end up where they started, only sadder and wiser. Although her career was terminated by her death from cancer at forty-five, she had already become a voice without a movie future.

When Katharine Hepburn makes her entrance in *On Golden Pond* (1981), greeting the loons in a voice of throbbing lyricism ("The loons are here again"), her exalted tone and the cadence of her dialogue recall a famous Hepburn line from *Stage Door* ("The calla lilies are in bloom again") that her character, an actress, intones during a performance on stage. Over four decades after *Stage Door*, in the trilling style that is her unmistakable vocal signature, Hepburn still speaks as if she is on a stage.

Katharine Hepburn, in oratorical flight, as a vagabond trouper in *Sylvia Scarlett* (1935). Here as in several other roles in her films of the thirties, Hepburn's blueblood voice is linked to sexual difference and ambiguity.

The history of Katharine Hepburn's career is in effect the history of the way her voice has been variously challenged and protected. Hers, manifestly, is a voice that does not blend in. Nor can it be disguised: Hepburn as a Chinese rebel in *Dragon Seed* (1944), a backcountry lass in *Spitfire* (1934), a British missionary in *The African Queen* (1951), or a Midwestern spinster in *The Rainmaker* (1956) sounds pure Yankee, take it or leave it. She sounds like Katharine Hepburn of Hartford, Connecticut, with a rinse of Bryn Mawr and a touch of something else entirely of her own invention.

Hepburn's thrusting, trumpeting voice clears—indeed, seizes—a space for its owner. If there is a more decisive voice in American movies, I don't know it; but is it sacrilege to suggest that it is also a voice that sometimes borders on the downright ludicrous? Unfazed by language, Hepburn is a distinctly vocal performer who speaks up forthrightly, with crisp attack, and some of her most vivid acting is in films (for instance, *Holiday, Bringing Up Baby, Philadelphia Story, Suddenly Last Summer,* and *A Delicate Balance* [1973]) in which her characters have a lot to say and for the most part say it rapidly, using language as self-declaration.

Since the late sixties Hepburn has been beatified, the most honored and perhaps even the most respected of all movie stars—respected not only for her talent but for her personal integrity, the American values of pluck and drive and unabashed egotism that she embodies. Yet it wasn't always so, and her career can be seen, in fact, as a progressive series of tamings: what it took to make her voice and her persona acceptable to a wide general audience.

In the first phase of her work, at RKO in the thirties, her individuality was given the chance to flourish. Rather than scraping away at her singularity of voice and manner, her studio presented her in vehicles tailor-made to display her cutting edge. Her roles proclaimed the fact that she was an American original, a patrician in a medium ringing with proletarian voices.

In *Morning Glory* (1933), *Alice Adams,* and *Stage Door* the extremity of Hepburn's voice is explained by the fact that her characters are actresses and therefore liable to fits of affectation. *Morning Glory* is the story of a brash, quickly successful young actress, a confident, talky New Englander (from Vermont, and Yankee to the core) who barrels her way into a producer's office and speaks her mind. "I'm either a very bad or a very good actress, nothing in between," she proclaims. We have to take her character's meteoric rise to stardom on faith, however, because her stage triumph is never shown, and her one performance—on a balcony at an opening-night party she recites passages from *Hamlet* and *Romeo and Juliet,* cowing the guests to a reverential silence—isn't nearly as accomplished as we're supposed to think it is.

In *Stage Door* and *Alice Adams* her accent becomes a topic of conversation. In the former she's an outsider in a boardinghouse of young theatrical hopefuls. Her chief adversary is played by Ginger Rogers, a tough-talking prole. "Fancy clothes, fancy language," Jean (Rogers) sniffs. "We speak pig Latin here." "I learned to speak English properly," Terry (Hepburn) counters. The others distrust her too. "Maybe she's a social worker doing a little slumming." "That new gal seems to have an awful crush on Shakespeare." When she fails to win their friendship, Terry says, "I'm beginning to feel there's something wrong with me. . . . I'm doing my best to pick up their slang." She's accepted only after she gives a good, realistic performance on stage, delivering her calla lilies line feelingly.

In *Alice Adams* her vocal excess is presented as the pose of an overeager small-town girl ("She's poor and hasn't any background"), a citizen of Booth Tarkington's America, trying to imitate the manners of the gentry. The film thus offers the spectacle of Hepburn, the real thing, playing a character who wants desperately to be the real thing. Again, as in *Morning Glory* and *Stage Door,* her bristling energy is regarded as the overflow of a theatrical temperament ("I want to go on the stage: I know I could act") but encompasses something more general as well, the character's desire to be different, to excel. This time she does not become a worldly success, but only herself—Alice Adams. "Stop it," her impatient boyfriend commands, silencing her "performance" for him. "I found out one thing," he tells her, "I love you, Alice," to which Alice, unmasked, replies, "Gee whiz!"

FROM LEFT
Taming Katharine Hepburn: in *Adam's Rib* (1949), as in most of their team efforts, Spencer Tracy cuts Hepburn down to size. In *Guess Who's Coming to Dinner* (1967) Hepburn is a dutiful wife.

In *Little Women* (1933) and *Sylvia Scarlett* her vocal difference is augmented by sexual ambiguities. In the latter she is an itinerant actress who performs in drag, and as Jo March, the second-eldest of the little women, she is a tomboy threatened by heterosexuality. To Meg, her marrying-kind sister, she pleads, "Why can't we stay as we are? Don't fall in love; don't go to marry that man." When Laurie proposes to her, she says, "I can't love you the way you want me to . . . I'll never marry." At her sister's wedding Jo stands apart, separated from the family circle by a fence post. When challenged for her transgressions, Jo declares, "I'll try to be a little woman and not be rough and wild, and do my duty at home, and not go off to war to help my father." While the film does not of course permit Jo to confront her sexual conflicts, neither does it suppress the impact on other characters of her offbeat, quixotic personality.

By the end of the thirties, after having played a number of formidable characters whose voices rustle with the silk of privilege and the snap of temperament, Hepburn was box-office poison, her image out of step with Depression America. She was able to recuperate her career only by submitting to having her feathers trimmed. Tellingly, her comeback vehicle, *The Philadelphia Story*, written for her first as a play by Philip Barry, begins with C. K. Dexter Haven (Cary Grant) shoving her onto the floor—a gesture that echoed the contemporary popular rejection of "Katharine Hepburn."

In *Philadelphia Story*, which begins Hepburn's M-G-M period—where RKO was a maverick studio that embraced its maverick star, M-G-M was the most conservative and family-oriented of the major studios—the actress is reprimanded. "You'll never be a first-class human being until you have some regard for human frailty," her former husband, Dexter, lectures Tracy Lord (Hepburn). Tracy's father says she's a prig, a spinster, and has "everything but an understanding heart." Forced to conspire in her own dislodging, Hepburn as Tracy admits, "I don't want to be worshipped; I want to be loved." Nonetheless, the Hepburn qualities celebrated in her RKO cycle are not forgotten here. The proletarian journalist (James Stewart), an outsider to Tracy's world who has come to her mansion to write about her upcoming wedding, salutes her "magnificence," which "comes out of your eyes and voice and the way you stand. You're the golden girl, full of warmth and delight . . . you have fires banked in you."

Hepburn's dethroning in the forties was sustained, of course, by pairing her with one of the screen's great democrats, Spencer Tracy, whose skepticism and wry underplaying periodically trim Hepburn's sails. Their partnership is spiced by the class differences

Following Hollywood tradition, John Malkovich as a French nobleman in *Dangerous Liaisons* (1988) appears in appropriate costume and makeup but speaks in his own distinctive American regional accent.

engrained in their voices—his broad, plainspoken American against her blue-blooded lilt; his legato against her staccato. On film she defers to him in a way she does to no one else; she allows him to dent and parody her autocratic manner. "Is that what they taught you at Yale?" he snaps during one of their pitched battles in *Adam's Rib*. "I'm old-fashioned, I like two sexes. I want to be married to a wife, not a competitor," he yells at her later before slamming the door on her. Imitating her accent, he exclaims in mock delight (in *Guess Who's Coming to Dinner*), "Oh, how wonderful, where are the roses to fill the rose bowl?"

In their first film together, *Woman of the Year*, Hepburn is Tess Harding, a crisp political journalist who speaks many languages, bosses a snippy male secretary, and hobnobs with world leaders, while Tracy is Sam Craig, a dry, down-to-earth sportswriter. Tess is an overachiever with star power, yet Hepburn in her post–*Philadelphia Story* phase dispels the character's sheer fabulousness with pratfalls and stumbles that, together with Sam's intermittent disapproval, soften her brittle edges. For the finale Tess tries to prove her wifely fealty by making breakfast for her estranged husband, but she knows nothing about navigating a kitchen and makes a mess. Sam is charmed by her utter incompetence, as indeed we are meant to be as well. Farce plus Tracy cuts Hepburn's character down to size, a formula that remained in place for most of their screen duets.

In succeeding decades Hepburn's iconography experienced in more muted ways the swings between transgression and containment that defined the first two phases of her career. Her vocal and physical difference in such fifties movies as *The African Queen*, *Summertime* (1955), and *The Rainmaker* is presented not as theatrical, as in the thirties, but as the marks of a born spinster. Since the late sixties, in her roles as the staunch wife of a physically failing husband (Tracy in *Guess Who's Coming to Dinner* and Henry Fonda in *On Golden Pond*), she has been chastened once again. As an old woman who bows to paternal authority, an upholder of tradition and the family, Hepburn is a more "lovable" presence than ever before. Ironically, then, the renegade of the thirties achieves her screen apotheosis as a model loyal wife, a woman who modestly serves her husband. These shamelessly sentimental films, in which Hepburn exploits the adoration of her fans, represent her ultimate taming.

Significantly, the two strongest female icons in American movies, Hepburn and Bette Davis, are both in varying ways "punished" for defying cultural norms. While Hepburn was becalmed, brought within the circumference of marriage and the family, Davis remained a permanent outsider, the queen of the Gothics.

Accents

As an eighteenth-century French nobleman in *Dangerous Liaisons* (1988) John Malkovich speaks in a slangy contemporary voice that makes no attempt to disguise his pure Chicago-ese. His impudent, vulpine characterization is chock-full of an actorly resourcefulness that clearly does not include work on his voice—in this period piece Malkovich sounds no different than he did on stage playing a modern lout in Sam Shepard's *True West*, the role that made him famous. That Malkovich does not play a French aristocrat with a French accent is not surprising, nor would it be necessary (audiences quickly accept vocal conventions), but that he makes no attempt to elevate his diction is a disappointment.

Nonetheless, in refusing to gild his voice with the patina of a different age and so in a sense to "historicize" it, Malkovich is simply following a Hollywood tradition. As Rhett Butler, a Southern gentlemen in *Gone With the Wind*, or as a British naval officer in *Mutiny on the Bounty*, Clark Gable speaks unadulterated Gable-ese. Playing the British Dr. Jekyll, Spencer Tracy retains his own American-eagle voice, and as a well-born Briton in the same film Lana Turner speaks pure American luncheonette. While in *Juarez* Paul Muni plays the Mexican leader sheathed in a Mexican-accented English, John Garfield's Porfirio Díaz is pure working-class New York. As Pierre in *War and Peace* (1956) Henry Fonda wears foreign-looking wire glasses but sounds exactly like Henry Fonda. The film's key scene is one in which Pierre, a pacifist overwhelmed by firsthand observations of the carnage of war, looks offscreen with an agonized expression. "Goddam Napoleon and the French!" Fonda says in his own casual prairie accent, sounding like Abe Lincoln adrift on the Russian steppes.

In Hollywood vocal changeovers are as rare as physical disguises. Star voices, like star faces and bodies, are expected, indeed virtually required, to remain the same for as long as they can. The only changes in most star voices are the ones imposed by time. Like faces, voices crack and wither, and while sometimes an aging voice acquires a deepened resonance (Paul Newman's, I think, is a case in point), sometimes it mars or perhaps even obliterates the qualities a performer projected when young. Old, Lucille Ball's tough, coarse voice barely contained a whisper of her beloved Lucy character.

Most screen actors simply bring on their own voices uncamouflaged by character accents or changes in the rhythms and inflections audiences are used to. Even when they play characters who require a "new" voice, many film stars don't bother, counting either like Malkovich on strong acting instincts or like Gable on sheer charisma to stifle possible

disbelief. Furthermore, when accents are added, they are rarely convincing and seldom disguise the famous voice to which they are shakily attached. For his Portuguese fisherman in *Captains Courageous* and his Mexican fisherman in *The Old Man and the Sea* Spencer Tracy makes slight alterations in rhythm, as if he is reciting poetry; his singsong cadence is intended to suggest an accent, or at least a departure from his regular delivery. Bette Davis' stabs at British and Southern only imperfectly cover her own Yankee staccato, just as Katharine Hepburn's New England brine continually punctures the faint Oriental accent she slips into for *Dragon Seed*. Hepburn's vocal illusion is as transparent as her Oriental makeup, and, finally, why not? Audiences paid to see and hear Katharine Hepburn, not Hepburn disguised as Anna May Wong. (For *Sylvia Scarlett*, in which she plays a French vagabond, Hepburn follows the usual mode by speaking in her own accent.)

In *The Lady Eve* Barbara Stanwyck plays (superbly) a card shark on the make who ensnares a rich American patsy (Henry Fonda, here vocally right at home). But Stanwyck has the challenge of a double role when her ever-inventive character disguises herself as her own aristocratic British cousin. Her masquerade succeeds—she fools Fonda's country bumpkin, but is she meant to fool us too? Stanwyck's own Brooklyn nasality continually pierces her vocal charade, and only audience goodwill—gratitude to Stanwyck for playing half her double role so vividly—can carry her over her vocal impasse.

Actors like Paul Muni, Dustin Hoffman, Marlon Brando, and Meryl Streep, who try on a variety of accents, clearly defy the Hollywood norm. Although Brando is best known for sounding like a thug, he is in fact an actor of many voices, an American master of vocal disguise. The voice that made him famous, that of Stanley Kowalski in *A Streetcar Named Desire*, is itself a mask—not the way Brando himself speaks but as he speaks in character as Stanley, wrestling with language, biting, chewing, and spitting his words, cutting them off in midsyllable. Brando as Stanley speaks in a slurred voice that sometimes rises to a howl that transcends language, as in his impassioned cry of "Stella!" and at other times diminishes to a whisper, as when he promises Stella to get "the colored lights" going. But why isn't Brando's accent Southern rather than working-class New York? His speech is fanciful, an actor's potent, if regionally inaccurate, artistic choice. So enduring is Brando's legacy that actors have continued to play Stanley as if he lived on the Grand Concourse rather than in the Vieux Carré.

FROM LEFT
Despite some attempts at visual authenticity, Henry Fonda as a Russian in *War and Peace* (1956) and Katharine Hepburn as an Oriental in *Dragon Seed* (1944) break the spell by retaining their own familiar accents.

Brando's accents have continued to be largely imaginative as opposed to naturalistic. As Napoleon in *Désirée* he assumes a clipped, faintly British accent, and in marked contrast to his early proles he is almost showily clear-spoken. Rather than breaking up his lines in the modern manner he made famous in *Streetcar* and *Waterfront*, he maintains a pseudo-classical decorum as he speaks in an elegant voice attuned to aphorism and proclamation, the lingua franca of Great Men in Hollywood epics. "I know what's ahead: I'm one of the men who make history," "I am the French Revolution and I know how to protect it," "Before next New Year's Eve I will sleep in Moscow," his Napoleon announces with suitable pomp.

Brando's Mark Antony in *Julius Caesar* speaks in a pure general American that instantly exposes the muffled voice of Kowalski and Terry Malloy as an actor's skilled masquerade. While John Gielgud as Cassius "sings" Shakespearean verse in the British style—his voice vibrates with the succulent pleasure of intoning great poetry—Brando speaks it without once slipping into modern naturalistic utterance. As befits a character who is a shrewd public speaker, an orator who calculates his rhetorical effects, Brando gives Antony a voice rumbling with leashed power.

His Japanese interpreter in *The Teahouse of the August Moon* also banishes any memory of Stanley Kowalski. For this role, and for virtually the only time, Brando sounds purely comic. Speaking Japanese and a convincing Japanese-accented English, he makes his voice seem weightless, without its usual knots and coils. To embody and "envoice" this charming Japanese con man—chorus to the action who sometimes speaks directly to the camera and who changes his tone and gestures to mirror those of the characters he is interpreting—Brando the Method heavy is utterly erased.

While Brando's vocal disguise for *Teahouse* is complete, it is oddly unfinished for two other experimental roles of this astonishing early period in his career: his revolution-

FOLLOWING PAGES, CLOCKWISE FROM TOP LEFT
Not sounding like a thug: as Napoleon in *Désirée* (1954, with Jean Simmons) Marlon Brando moves and speaks with an elegance that exposes his famous working-class accent in *A Streetcar Named Desire* and *On the Waterfront* as a skillful masquerade. As Mark Antony in *Julius Caesar* (1953) he uses his own voice, a pure, resonant general American that is good for Shakespeare but proves too rich for the brash gambler he plays in *Guys and Dolls* (1955). As the still here indicates, Brando is too brooding and introspective for the film's stylized, musical comedy mise-en-scène.

ary in *Viva Zapata!* and his Damon Runyon gambler in *Guys and Dolls*. For Zapata Brando uncharacteristically follows Hollywood tradition in playing a foreign character in his own unaccented voice. Though he is made up to look Mexican, with swarthy coloring and a florid handlebar moustache, he sounds disconcertingly American. Brando's Zapata needs more, either an accent or a non-American vocal color, while his Sky Masterson in *Guys and Dolls* needs less. In a brash musical comedy the actor's speaking voice is too resonant and too thoughtful, as his timing is too slow. His energy goes inside whereas the genre requires exactly the opposite thrust.

For *Sayonara, The Fugitive Kind, The Chase* (1966), and *Reflections in a Golden Eye* (1967) Brando rolls out the lush Southern drawl he withheld from *Streetcar*. For *The Young Lions*, as a Nazi who defects from the Third Reich, he has a menacing German accent. For *Mutiny on the Bounty* he speaks in a crisp British accent that bristles with irony and curls itself around the witticisms to which his character is partial: "I believe I did what honor dictated, which sustains me, except for a slight desire to be dead, which I'm sure will pass." For *The Godfather* he affects a wheezing, aspirate voice cracked with age, a voice that retains but a faint imprint of the character's former power and is yet engrained with the appalling crudeness of a Mafioso butcher. Little more than a croak, the Don's voice is one from which the sound of speech is beginning to slip away. In a lighter register Brando again uses the Don's voice in *The Freshman* (1990), a genial self-parody.

For *The Missouri Breaks* (1976) Brando concocts an indecipherable brogue that soon dwindles into a drawl mixed with a dollop of British and finally slouches off into an incoherent mumble. His shifting, inconsistent accent is presented frankly as a stunt, a turn that is as outrageous as his long, stringy hair, his shaggy, clownlike costume, his bloated size, and his character's loony actions such as kissing and sharing a carrot with his horse. In this disposable comic Western Brando is just horsing around.

In *Falling in Love* (1984), as a restless suburban housewife who slides into an affair, Meryl Streep uses her own unaccented voice, and "undressed" she sounds utterly ordinary. Her voice has no color or distinction or flavor whatever; yet with a coating, with layers added to it, it undergoes remarkable transformations. In *Silkwood* (1983) she puts on a working-class Southern drawl. In *Sophie's Choice* she speaks English with a heavy Polish accent. In *A Cry in the Dark* she has a working-class Australian accent. For *Out of Africa* she creates a lilting Danish accent, and for the voiceover narration in the prologue she ages her character's voice. For *Plenty* (1985) American intonations untypically slip through the cracks of an imperfectly mastered upper-crust British accent. In *Ironweed* she thickens her voice and deepens it to a growl to suggest her character's terminal alcoholism.

Streep has reversed the dominant Hollywood mode in which stars more or less play themselves. She is that rare thing, a star without a persona, and so she has no image to play into or against. Like British actors she seems to work from the outside in. For her, finding a voice for her character is a way to penetrate the character's surface and to begin to burrow within; rather than a display of technical virtuosity for its own sake, her vocal disguises are a way of seeping inside a role. Once she is in command of an accent (although there are conflicting views about her dialectal authenticity, she makes her accents seem credible and that is all that matters), she then plays from within rather than using the accent as a defense against doing any further acting.

In some of her earlier work Streep tended to show us her ideas for a part: her mean, dead-faced lesbian in *Manhattan* and her tough Karen Silkwood were primarily external. But again reversing a trend in star acting, in which temperament and manner become intensified over time, Streep has become less forced and her considerable technique has become less noticeable. Even in a slight comedy like *Postcards from the Edge* (1990), in which she is miscast, she delivers Carrie Fisher's glib wisecracks deftly; she doesn't push. In *A Cry in the Dark* her mastery of an Australian accent never looks like the masquerade of a clever guest artist from Hollywood but rather helps her to blend into the setting. As her fame has grown, her work has become increasingly seamless. She has her tricks, to be sure—a stammer, shifting eyes that make contact with an offscreen space or object—but she has learned how little the camera often needs. She's become a movie minimalist whose vocal sheathings help her to simplify and to be truthful.

Elaborate or finicky character accents, for the most part, are for the British: Olivier's sometimes bizarre but always theatrical American, German, and Middle European accents; Peter Sellers' virtuoso dialectal precision, unmatched by the record of any American actor. At the end of *The Pink Panther* (1964) Sellers as French-accented Inspector Clouseau, bumbling detective and would-be Lothario, happily disappears into a new role, that of a suave jewel thief, the Phantom, for whom he is mistaken, even though the masquerade carries the penalty of a term in prison. Like Clouseau melting into the Phantom, Sellers spent his career disappearing into vocal as well as physical disguises.

In his showiest performance, in *Dr. Strangelove or: How I Learned to Stop Worrying and Love the Bomb*, Sellers enacts three distinct characters with no slippage or skids from one to the other. As Colonel Mandrake he is a nerdy British officer whose thick accent is almost impenetrable. As President Merkin Muffley he masters a bland American voice that oozes with condescension whenever the president talks to the Russian premier, Dmitri Kissoff, in the tone of exasperated patience one reserves for a very slow child. And as Dr. Strangelove, wearing dark glasses and confined to a wheelchair, he portrays a menacing German whose voice rises toward hysteria as his paralyzed arm shoots up periodically in an atavistic Nazi salute. Presenting the three characters with pitiless detachment, Sellers seems to erase himself: we can't see the puppeteer pulling the strings behind his puppets.

In *Dr. Strangelove*, as in all his best work, Sellers' approach is exactly the opposite of the "American plan," in which stars transfer their own always-traceable personas onto their characters. Sellers seems to have no personality, no firm identity, to call on. That sense of emptiness, of being a man without a face or a voice except the ones he creates anew for each character, helps account for his immaculate chameleonism. No personal references mar the charade, as would have happened if any American star had attempted Sellers' *Strangelove* stunt.

His eeriest mask, because it seems like a metaphor for his own acting style, is in his last major film, *Being There* (1979). He plays a character who is a blank, a man with the mind of a child who is thrown out into the world when his employer dies. To enact this stranger in a strange land, Sellers empties his face and voice of any reference whatsoever: his dry, mechanical, oddly cadenced voice, with a touch of a foreign rhythm no one in the film can place, is without color or density, an endless "grey." And toward what twilight zone is his distant gaze directed? Lacking the code to read him, the people he encounters project onto him their own desires and contexts. When he speaks literally, they think he is talking in rich metaphors and impute gnomic wisdom to his every crabbed utterance. By doing nothing except remaining himself, a man without a past, he becomes a celebrity; a political cabal even wants to nominate him for the presidency.

FROM LEFT
Chameleon: Peter Sellers as Merkin Muffley, a flat-voiced American president, as a very British Colonel Mandrake, and as the title character, a mad German scientist, in *Dr. Strangelove or: How I Learned to Stop Worrying and Love the Bomb* (1964).

Sellers' matte performance is unsettling because he doesn't give us the comfort of detecting the actor behind his role. In *Being There* he seems to be showing us the blank slate from which he struck his earlier impersonations. His character's flat face and voice (Sellers completely suppresses his own British accent) are like empty vessels waiting to receive whatever any other character, or the actor himself, wants or chooses to place there.

One of the axioms of the Hollywood Style is that foreign accents, whether genuine or feigned, are more or less interchangeable. Hence, the spectacle of Garbo playing a Russian in *Ninotchka* or a French courtesan in *Camille* (in which, moreover, everyone else speaks in a flat American twang); Dietrich as a Spanish courtesan in *The Devil Is a Woman*, a gypsy fortune-teller in *Touch of Evil*, or a French countess in *The Garden of Allah* (1936); Ingrid Bergman as a Spanish Loyalist in *For Whom the Bell Tolls* (1943); the very Russian-sounding Vladimir Sokoloff as a Chinese farmer in *Dragon Seed*.

OPPOSITE, CLOCKWISE FROM TOP RIGHT

An actress of many voices: to play a terminal alcoholic in *Ironweed* (1987), Meryl Streep thickens and deepens her voice; in *Out of Africa* (1985) she has a Danish accent; and in *A Cry in the Dark* (1988) she hides out behind a working-class Australian accent. When, as in *Falling in Love* (1984, with Robert De Niro), Streep speaks in her own "undressed" voice, she sounds remarkably flat.

RIGHT

A voice and a face without a country or a past: Peter Sellers in a publicity still for his eerie tabula-rasa performance in *Being There* (1979).

While Hollywood, then, has been often notoriously tone-deaf in the matter of foreign accents, actors who don't speak American are problematic. Only a few foreign players—Garbo, Dietrich, Bergman, Charles Boyer, Maurice Chevalier, Hedy Lamarr—have had star careers, and because their accents have had to be in some way explained or accounted for, their employability was often of limited duration. When the kinds of stories that could accommodate them were used up, the stars either went home (like Chevalier), retired (like Garbo), faded into obscurity (like Lamarr), or de-exoticized their image (like Dietrich). In 1939 when both Dietrich and Garbo were labeled by exhibitors as box-office poison, they were forced in effect to become less "foreign." Garbo's role in *Ninotchka* as a frigid Russian who melts under the combined influence of Paris and Melvyn Douglas can be read as a metaphor for the taming of the star. The campaign to democratize her was continued less happily in *Two-Faced Woman.* Even its title implies that one face is no longer sufficient; split in two, as warring emblems of ice and fire, Garbo's image was undermined. She never acted again. On the other hand, Dietrich's Americanization in *Destry Rides Again* yielded the dividend of a prolonged career.

An unassimilated foreign performer like Anna Magnani, however, was destined to make only fleeting appearances in American movies. Startlingly homely, her eyes ringed

Not destined to be a Hollywood star: Anna Magnani, an unassimilated foreign actress, erupting in *The Rose Tattoo* (1955).

with dark circles, her body slack and untended, Magnani violated Hollywood codes in every possible way. Her foreignness is not picturesque like Garbo's and Dietrich's but explosive, unguarded, and in two of her four American pictures, *The Rose Tattoo* (1955) and *The Fugitive Kind,* both adapted from plays by Tennessee Williams, she erupts with a primal ferocity. In the former Magnani plays a passionate woman crazed by the memory of her dead husband. When she caresses her sleeping husband, she runs her hands over his bare back like a priestess worshipping at an altar. When neighbors come to tell Rosa (Magnani) about his death, she says in a choked, trembling voice as she stretches out her hand as if to ward off the devil, "Don't speak; don't speak." When she is infuriated by the sound of a player piano her daughter has turned on, she bolts into the room like an uncaged animal. When she bangs on a church door to demand that her priest tell her if her husband "gave her horns," she's like an exploding hand grenade. In these representative scenes Magnani's acting is vibrant and deeply rooted; by contrast Burt Lancaster's performance as a banana-truck driver with a Sicilian accent is a superficial stunt.

In *The Fugitive Kind,* as a woman chained to an embittered dying husband in a backwater Southern town, Magnani plays a character whose passion is suppressed but hardly becalmed—Lady Torrance's sexuality waits throbbingly to be released. This time Magnani has costars who match her feral intensity: Marlon Brando as the itinerant stud who ignites her, and Victor Jory as the husband she despises. In a confrontation on the stairs, when her dying husband admits that he and cronies caused a fire in which her father was killed, she growls at him, making sounds of rage that seem to come from primordial depths. Hollywood had no place for Magnani, no niche or category she could fit into. Beyond type, she was fated to be a visiting artist.

The only British actors who have had sustained Hollywood careers are the ones like Cary Grant, Richard Burton, Errol Flynn, Ronald Colman, and Deborah Kerr who seemed to become American—honorary citizens, in effect, whose accents seemed to lose their edge. (In the process of becoming a Hollywood star, Mel Gibson has more or less erased his Australian accent.) For the most part British accents have been an asset only in historical and biblical epics where they provide a rhetorical elevation most contemporary-sounding American actors can't reach. Among American stars only Charlton Heston, with his stentorian tones and statesman-like bearing, has a respectable epic-film dossier.

One of Hollywood's most intelligent epics, *Spartacus* (1960), cleverly pivots British against American speech to underline political conflict. Laurence Olivier, sounding gloriously patrician, is a decadent Roman aristocrat, a tyrant opposed by Spartacus, a proletarian upstart played by Kirk Douglas speaking a vigorous, earthy general American. The usual babble of British and American accents in the Hollywood epic is not usually so purposeful, however (and even *Spartacus* has Tony Curtis as a Roman slave speaking in his unreconstructed New York accent). Hence the aural dialectic in pageants like *Quo Vadis* (1951) or *The Robe* (1953) of proper British speakers such as Deborah Kerr, Jean Simmons, Peter Ustinov, and Richard Burton circulating freely with hollow-voiced Americans like Robert Taylor and Victor Mature.

Singing

Al Jolson's historic boast in *The Jazz Singer,* "You ain't heard nothin' yet," is misleading. While his words introduce a song, of greater consequence to film acting is the fact that as he sings his mother (played by Eugenie Besserer) makes little clucking noises. Her understated realistic reactions are more suited to the medium than Jolson's stage-bound musical performance. Talking pictures had a greater need of naturalists like Besserer who sound like real people than of minstrels like Jolson doing a turn. By and large singers like Jolson are happier on a stage than on a screen, and most singers imported from Broadway or the music hall or rock 'n' roll or opera have had only abbreviated screen careers.

Only singers who learned to act on film or who, like Doris Day or Frank Sinatra or Bette Midler, created a nonsinging persona have become more than specialty acts or sideshow attractions. In the history of American film only a handful of singers have also had major acting careers. Three performers of this rare group—Bing Crosby, Barbra

Streisand, and Judy Garland—not coincidentally speak as distinctively as they sing, phrasing dialogue as skillfully as they shape lyrics.

Crosby is not only the most relaxed singer in movies, he may well be the most relaxed actor too. Speaking and singing, his velvety, easy voice is wonderfully soothing. Sitting by a fireside and smoking his pipe as he croons "White Christmas" in *Holiday Inn* (1942), Crosby oozes a cozy intimacy that could calm even the most frazzled viewer. His nonchalant style is positively therapeutic. In his prime, as nerve-free actor and singer, Crosby is a smooth hypnotist who lulls children to sleep, banishes tensions in ardent young women, and resolves all narrative snags.

His most famous role, as the priest in *Going My Way* (1944), raises his reassuring blandness to mythic proportions. Remaining comfortably within his persona, and actually continuing the priestly aura he had always had, Bing Crosby with a turned-around collar dispenses wisdom and advice through dialogue and lyrics. Here his duties include teaching a runaway how to put thought into a song, being kindly to young thieves and a woman who can't pay her rent, coaching a baseball team, instructing a group of tough kids to sing and to enjoy singing "Silent Night," and becalming his adversary, a conservative older priest opposed to his progressive methods, by singing the old man to sleep with an Irish lullaby. At the end, after he has resolved all the problems in the parish, he steals away into the snowy night as he shakes his head in bemused affirmation: a magus surprised by his own healing powers.

In his *Road* movies with Bob Hope, Bing is the smoothie to Hope's comic patsy, the winner who gets the girls and puts one over on his unsuccessfully lecherous partner. While Hope grumbles and worries as he cracks wise, Crosby remains snugly above the fray, too cool to take the fabricated plots seriously; in *The Road to Rio* (1947), looking directly into the camera and winking, he says, "The world must never know what's in these papers."

Like Astaire's dancing, Crosby's singing seems effortless. But where Astaire's casual elegance is often presented as the result of a perfectionist drive, Crosby's carefree facade never crumbles. The difference between their styles is the subject of the self-reflexive *Holiday Inn:* Crosby's character wants to break up their song and dance partnership in order to retire on a farm where he can sit back, smoke his pipe, and watch the seasons change, while Astaire's character is a workaholic who wants to "dedicate [his life] to making people happy with [his] feet." Both entertainers, however, knowingly use their performing skills as a rite of courtship. "I'll capture her, singing," Bing boasts; "You haven't a chance when I go into my dance," Fred counters.

Except for *The Country Girl*, in which he plays, superbly, a washed-up alcoholic musical-comedy star making a comeback, Crosby is an unnervingly modest, one-note actor. Like Astaire, he doesn't have a true actor's tension or layers; his singing and his acting personas form an unbroken surface free of rumblings from within. Whatever demons may have haunted him in his private life (and his son Gary in his autobiography informs us that Bing was a cold father, a brutal disciplinarian, and an indifferent husband) are erased from his screen image. In the forties, as the country prepared for, entered, then recovered from the war, Crosby's low-pitched, steadying voice carried the assurance that all problems are solvable.

When Crosby sings "White Christmas," the camera sits quietly, as if stilled by the mellow sounds of his voice. Barbra Streisand's hard sell, on the other hand, often sends the camera into spasms. For "Don't Rain on My Parade," a big number placed right before the intermission in *Funny Girl* (1968), the apparatus goes into high gear as it tries to provide a visual accompaniment to match the star's soaring voice. Hectic intercutting that shreds the song into fragments is topped by a heroic, circling high-angle shot of Streisand belting up at the Statue of Liberty: epic shots for an epic voice. At the end of *Yentl* (1983), as on board ship heading to America Streisand sings "Papa, Watch Me Fly," the camera zooms up and away as if propelled by her sonic boom and races over the water to complete the leap of her voice.

Streisand sings the hell out of her songs even when she isn't facing the Statue of Liberty or heading for America. "People" (in *Funny Girl*) is an intimate number sung in an alleyway to a man her character loves, yet not once does Streisand look at her co-actor

FROM TOP
The most relaxed singer in movies: Bing Crosby crooning "White Christmas" in *Holiday Inn* (1942, with Marjorie Reynolds), a tonic for wartime nerves, and taking it easy on the set of *The Emperor Waltz* (1948), behaving as if he is in his own cozy den.

(Omar Sharif) but instead tortures the song into a show-stopping number. Her musical overkill transforms every song into a superstar spectacle in which sheer volume often clobbers lyrical intention.

In *Funny Girl*, her film debut, Streisand nominally plays Fanny Brice, Ziegfeld singer and Yiddish-flavored comic, yet the film is really all about Barbra, as Streisand upstages Brice. Dialogue and lyrics are riddled with paeans to her talent ("I ought to fire you but I love talent," Flo Ziegfeld tells her), to her brash self-assertiveness ("I'm the Greatest Star," trumpets one of her songs), to her command of the stage ("That's where I live . . . on stage," she tells her gambler-lover Nicky Arnstein early in their relationship). With her clarion voice and her crackerjack comic timing, Streisand is so obviously and abundantly talented that the star is born all too soon, leaving a narrative space that is filled by the soggy melodrama of Fanny's doomed romance.

When Streisand replayed the same basic story in the deeply obnoxious 1976 remake of *A Star Is Born*, her transparent arrogance topples the film. In her first scene, when she is an unknown singer, part of a trio called the Oreos, she's brassy and preening and already a smug pro. She's Barbra Streisand performing for her fans rather than a character named Esther Hoffman who is a would-be star, a singer perched nervously on the fringes of show business. When Esther protests, "I'm sorry, I'm not used to the rich and famous, it makes me stupid," she has the bearing of a big-leaguer, a woman who has already made it. Streisand is so far from being able to play a winsome show business outsider that the only way the film can squeeze a necessary vulnerability out of her is by cheating, placing her in a high-angle long shot, for instance, in which Esther stands deserted and forlorn at the end of a rock concert. Where Judy Garland, like Janet Gaynor, ends her *Star Is Born* announcing herself as Mrs. Norman Maine, for Streisand naming her character (an offscreen announcer calls out her name, Esther Hoffman Howard, as if he is heralding the Second Coming) is only a prelude to a musical double-header: a ballad, "With One More Look at You," in honor of her dead husband, which begins in a whisper and builds up to a teary finale, followed by an incongruous uptempo rock number—"Are You Watching Me Now?"—performed in a single take in tight closeup, a visual reprise of Streisand's bang-up rendition of "My Man" at the end of *Funny Girl*.

Verbally acquisitive, Streisand speaks at a rapid-fire tempo in a voice ready-made for quips and one-liners. Her movies are driven by the sound of her speaking as well as singing voice, and in vehicles like *What's Up, Doc?* (1972), *Hello Dolly* (1969), *The Owl and the Pussycat* (1970), *Yentl*, *A Star Is Born*, *Funny Girl*, and *Funny Lady* (1975) she plays characters whose vocal shrewdness impels them irreversibly toward success. Sometimes charmingly, sometimes improbably (in *Yentl* we are expected to believe that she can pass for a male Yeshiva scholar), and sometimes abrasively, like Katharine Hepburn she has appeared repeatedly in projects that celebrate her own energy and skill and the take-charge sound of her voice. It's no surprise that one of her best performances (in *What's Up, Doc?*) is in a remake of one of Hepburn's best films, *Bringing Up Baby*. Appropriating the power to rename the world according to her own decree, Streisand's character names the hero "Harvey" rather than calling him by his real name, Steve. "Listen," she tells him, "you can't fight a tidal wave," referring to her determination to nab him. This time Streisand's push is in perfect sync with the character's while remaining purely comic (Streisand is an ace comedienne who turns cloying in drama). There is a delicious musical moment when her character sings "As Time Goes By" to her "Harvey." Without a fuss, with no attempt to rouse the audience to a standing ovation, she sings with captivating simplicity.

Low-pitched and throbbing with feeling, Judy Garland's speaking voice is unusually rich. Like her singing voice it has a tremor with a tear in it, and so there's hardly a break in emotional pressure when she starts to sing. Unlike Streisand, Garland makes lyrics seem like the continuation and fulfillment of speech.

Garland makes her entrance in *The Wizard of Oz* (1939) in a state bordering on hysteria; holding nothing back, she at once establishes Dorothy as an emotional live wire. "You always get yourself into a fret over nothing," Aunt Em scolds her when she announces breathlessly that wicked Miss Gulch is after her dog, Toto. Beside herself with anxiety, filled to overflowing, what does Dorothy do? She sings. Out in the yard, looking wistfully up at the sky, she sings a wish song about a world that's easier and more tranquil than the one she has to contend with in Kansas, a make-believe realm that exists somewhere "Over the Rainbow."

When she sings "The Boy Next Door" in *Meet Me in St. Louis* (1944), she places the song deep within character and story. Although the director, Vincente Minnelli, gives the singer a performance frame, a "stage," by placing her within a window, music doesn't stop the show but continues the momentum of the scene. The song becomes the expression of the character's romantic longing, and when Garland looks offscreen (filling offscreen space in a way that is the inheritance of all born film actors) she seems to be conjuring an image of the boy she adores. When song springs from dramatic necessity, Garland is in her element, using music as intimate statement and binding the audience to her through its enchantment. She is America's foremost singing actress, a Method singer who acts rather than sells her songs. As she enhances melody with the improvisatory pauses and hesitations and the gestural reality with which she delivers dialogue, she makes lyrics sound like cadenced speech. Unlike Streisand, she is at her best when songs flow organically out of a scene, as with "Over the Rainbow" and "The Boy Next Door," rather than when music becomes more or less a spectacle in and for itself. Of course she can deliver this kind of musical showmanship too, as in the "Born in a Trunk" number in *A Star Is Born* or "Get Happy" from *Summer Stock* (1950), but more typically Garland looks and sounds strained in the kind of raucous Broadway style that is Streisand's forte. When she plays a new star on Broadway in *Presenting Lily Mars* (1943), in which we see musical excerpts from her starring vehicle, "Where There's Music," and in which the music is presented frankly as a showcase detached from narrative, Garland is working against her grain.

The use of song as a natural extension of the acted scene conforms to the homespun image M-G-M created for Garland. In film after film she is a small-town girl who embodies rural American values—the kind of character to whom the artifice and splash of show business are foreign. In the real world Garland was an unglamorous Frances Gumm; on screen she is the equally plain Esther Smith (in *Meet Me in St. Louis*), Hannah Brown (in *Easter Parade*, 1948), Susan Bradley from Ohio (in *The Harvey Girls*, 1946), Alice, a secretary (in *The Clock*, 1945). *In Strike Up the Band* she's Mary, a librarian; in *Girl Crazy* she's a mail carrier, seen first in the masculine activity of fixing a car; in *Summer Stock*, dressed in overalls and singing in the shower and on a tractor, she's a tomboy determined to rescue her failing farm from debt. Her one "exotic" character, Manuela in *The Pirate*, is nonetheless another version of her small-town girl next door, wide-eyed like Dorothy when she goes to the big city and so enters an unfamiliar realm.

In the idealized America created at Louis B. Mayer's M-G-M, Judy is everyone's kid sister or older sister, a wholesome plain Jane. Many of her roles safeguard and valorize her characters' folk values: Dorothy's discovery that "there's no place like home" resonates throughout Garland's career in the forties. In *Easter Parade* she can't release her musical and comic talent until her mentor (Fred Astaire) allows her to be herself. At first he tries to force her to become a facsimile of his erstwhile partner (Ann Miller), dressing Hannah Brown up in flounces and feathers and heavy glamorizing makeup, but of course Garland does "Ann Miller" awkwardly. But when she's permitted to be plain Hannah Brown she shines.

Minnelli designed *The Clock*, Garland's one nonsinging role in the forties, as a tribute to her beguiling simplicity and directness. In this wartime romance she plays a character whose story is meant to be but one in a million: she's Alice, Robert Walker is Joe, who meet by chance and fall in love without ever learning each other's last name. After a rushed marriage ceremony and a supper in a cafeteria, they go to a church where Alice reads the wedding service in a whisper: Minnelli holds the camera on her in a tight closeup that pays tribute to her luminous naturalism.

Considering her own turbulent history, her quietism on screen in the forties is remarkable. In her movies with Mickey Rooney it is often Garland who soothes his frazzled nerves or tames his compulsiveness. "The city is never quiet, there's always sounds underneath," Alice says in *The Clock*, a point that also applies to Garland, who of course

Everyone's kid sister: Judy Garland in one of her most famous homespun roles, as Esther Smith in *Meet Me in St. Louis* (1944), making eyes at the boy next door (Tom Drake) as her older sister (Lucille Bremer) watches.

was never *merely* quiet. Even in the most modest of her movies her persona is shadowed with the suggestions of a complicated or at least a full inner life. Her characters have undercurrents that sometimes erupt, as in Dorothy's ecstatic final speech, "It wasn't a dream, it was a place, a real, truly live place . . . We're home, I love you all . . . oh Auntie Em, there's no place like home," or in her dressing-room scenes in *Summer Stock* and *Presenting Lily Mars*, in which her characters have an attack of opening-night nerves. More typically, however, Garland's promise of emotional overdrive remains potential; only in the anomalous *The Pirate* does hysteria rise to the surface to saturate an entire performance. Playing a character who confuses illusion with reality, and who achieves her true self only on a stage—her final number, "Be a Clown," is a duet performed with Gene Kelly that celebrates acting, makeup, clowning, the world of entertainment—Garland emotes with an enthusiasm that seems to exceed even Manuela's fevered romanticism. *The Pirate* exposes her own frayed nerves in a way no other film in her M-G-M years does.

The dark side of Judy Garland—a pained look in the eye, a catch in the voice, the dramatic glints that are always there to deepen all her Hannah Browns—is released in her post–M-G-M comeback film, the Warner Brothers *Star Is Born*, to a degree that would never have been permitted in Culver City. Here both her talent and her unglamorous appearance are presented in a solemn, monumental way. "You're a great singer . . . you've got that little something extra—star quality," Norman Maine (James Mason) tells her after he discovers Esther Blodgett (Garland) singing "The Man That Got Away." She laughs, mumbling, "Nobody ever told me before that I'm a great singer." Like Streisand, Garland was already too mature and too established to play an unknown—her own star had long since been born—and considering the point in her career at which she plays Esther Blodgett, the film might more aptly be called *A Star is Reborn*. The big production numbers have a jarring self-reflexiveness not evident in her forties films. Her living-room performance for her husband is a kind of metamusical, a satire of M-G-M production numbers done in various styles including Brazilian, Chinese, African, Parisian, and Wild West. And "Born in a Trunk," a film within the film, glorious as it is, offers the disconcerting spectacle of Garland looking at and sometimes listening to herself as she studies her image.

At the studio, makeup artists scrutinize Esther Blodgett and talk about her as if she isn't there. "Give her the Crawford mouth," one says. We know from Garland's earlier films that the only mouth that will work will be her own. "What difference does it make how well I sing if my face is awful?" Garland, transformed into Vicki Lester, wails, evincing a note of self-pity that was always present but rarely given full-blown expression at

FROM LEFT
Garland insecurity, Streisand arrogance: in these parallel scenes from two versions of *A Star Is Born* (1954, 1976), which take place early in the story before the characters have become stars, Garland sings "The Man That Got Away" in character, as a performer whose talent has not yet been proclaimed, while Streisand is already a smug pro.

All about Barbra: Fanny Brice's name is up in lights, but *Funny Girl* (1968) is a celebration of a big new star.

M-G-M. In the teary last act of the movie Garland's dramatic power is unleashed in a continuous flood. In the famous dressing-room scene, perhaps using emotional memories of her own collapses, she falls apart as she tells her producer what it's like "seeing somebody you love destroy himself," then she dries her tears and returns to a sound stage to sing the final phrases of "Lose That Long Face." Mobbed by fans, she cracks up at her husband's funeral, then becomes hysterical again when she's asked to appear at a benefit to honor her husband. "Without him there's just nothing."

Immense as it is, her performance is also a dead end. Even if Garland's personal problems hadn't intervened, it is unlikely she could have found other musicals to star in (her last film, *I Could Go On Singing* [1963], is not really a musical). In *A Star Is Born*, and on TV and the concert stage, Garland institutionalized her suffering as well as her talent, overdoing her mannerisms as she brought to the surface the neurotic qualities that at M-G-M had provided a palpitant subtext.

While the quality of motion-picture exhibition has steadily declined, with theatres and screens becoming ever smaller, sound systems have improved. Dolby stereo is widely available in even the most uninviting mall cinemas, and as a result audiences can now hear movies better than ever. But if film sound has acquired increased volume, crispness, and dimension and if audiences are often surrounded and "embraced" by sound, actors' voices are only intermittently the aural focus.

Even in the most sophisticated sound tracks, dialogue is often muffled or obscured by other sounds—background noises, gunshots, screeching cars, explosions, bombastic musical annotations. With dialogue regularly layered into a dense, multilevel sound track, technology thus highlights the fact that the spoken word today seldom attains the primacy it enjoyed in the Golden Age. That there are fewer words in most of today's films than in the studio era and that these few have to compete for the spectator's attention corresponds to the fact that among contemporary stars there are fewer memorable voices than ever before. In the old days too, of course, there were plenty of dime-a-dozen-sounding Dorothy Lamours, but now there is a stronger tendency for stars to have voices that could belong to anybody. Actors with voices that can tickle or soothe or uplift, arouse or inspire, are rare—vocal distinction seems less acceptable, and today's movies are flooded with players like Kevin Costner or Kim Basinger or Julia Roberts who sound numbingly anonymous. Even a superior performer like Meryl Streep (unaccented) can sound dishearteningly bland. If, as the saying goes, "they had faces then," many of them had voices too. Alas, no longer.

Starstruck

Starmaking

THE HISTORY OF HOLLYWOOD ACTING IS INEVITABLY AN ACCOUNT of star acting—how the movies create, protect, sustain, and sometimes preside over the destruction of stars, and how the stars themselves variously conform to and chafe against, grow into and out of, the categories into which their looks and sometimes their voices place them. Hollywood's starmaking machinery is maintained in two basic and interconnected ways: through narrative formulas that celebrate the institution of stardom and through the time-honored system of typecasting.

First, what kinds of roles make or support stars? Here are three representative examples: Gary Cooper in *Morocco*, Claudette Colbert in *Since You Went Away* (1944), and Maurice Chevalier in *Love Me Tonight* (1932). Each of them faces the kinds of narrative burdens stars must carry successfully in order to win their spurs.

As a soldier in the Foreign Legion, Gary Cooper in *Morocco* is an innocent homme fatale who entices a bevy of native women, the captain's wife, and an ironic cabaret diva (Marlene Dietrich). Cooper is thus given the kind of challenge that could make or break a career: can he be as sexy as the story says he is? Can this tall, thin American knock Dietrich for a loop? There's a moment in a cafe scene that supplies the answer. As Tom Brown (Cooper) watches Dietrich perform, he eats a peach (Cooper was among the best eaters in movies: notice the zest with which he devours a sandwich in *Mr. Deeds Goes to Town*) while between bites he builds a slow smile that's loaded with erotic promise. If the audience doesn't see this in his smile, then Dietrich's obsession with Tom Brown and indeed the entire film are likely to appear incomprehensible.

In a voice rippling with feeling, Nazimova as a Russian refugee who works alongside Mrs. Hilton (Colbert) in a wartime factory (in *Since You Went Away*) turns to her and says, "You are what I thought America was," thereby loading the star with a do-or-die responsibility. Can we accept Nazimova's praise, that Colbert is indeed "America"? And if so, what kind of "America" does she represent? Holding down the home front while her husband is in the service, Mrs. Hilton lives with her two daughters (played by Jennifer Jones and Shirley Temple) in a house that looks like the Southern-mansion-style studio of David O. Selznick, who in fact produced as well as wrote the film. The Hiltons inhabit a hermetic world, one that is well insulated from the intrusions of the war; as in Greek drama, tragedy happens offstage. If Colbert is "America," she is an idealized version that many people, including Selznick, yearned for in 1944 in the midst of war. As this privileged American matron, a woman who resists the temptations of an attractive suitor in order to keep her hearth as it was for when her husband returns, Colbert with her warm voice and her knowing eyes is indeed comforting, among the best "America" has to offer.

Starstruck: Douglas Fairbanks, Sr., commands the attention of a vast crowd as he raises money for Liberty Bonds.

CLOCKWISE FROM TOP LEFT
Do you believe Gary Cooper (in *Morocco*, 1930) can turn Marlene Dietrich's head? Or that Claudette Colbert, Jennifer Jones, and Shirley Temple (in *Since You Went Away*, 1944) represent an ideal American family, the kind that American men were fighting a war to protect? Or that Maurice Chevalier (in *Love Me Tonight*, 1932) can dazzle a château full of aristocrats? Stars are made —or unmade—according to how audiences respond to such questions.

Love Me Tonight not only depends on but is actually all about Maurice Chevalier's fabled charm. The star plays a tailor (named Maurice) who masquerades as a baron. In order to retrieve money an irresponsible count owes him, Maurice goes in disguise to the count's château, where he not only gets back his money but awakens a sleeping princess. He so dazzles everyone that he is forgiven even after he is exposed as a mere tailor. Lifting his story to legend, a chorus of crones recites at the end, "Once there was a Prince Charming who was not a prince but who was charming."

In these roles the actors have to be as charismatic as the scripts claim they are: Chevalier has to be utterly disarming; Colbert has to incarnate a national ideal; Cooper has to be a sexual icon. In star roles, defined by the scale of their demands, performers must embody the power or talent or potency that earns their characters their stripes. We have to believe, for instance, that Sylvester Stallone in *Rocky* (1976) looks and moves like a champion boxer; that Edward G. Robinson in *Little Caesar* has the savvy to graduate in record time from obscurity to top of the gangland heap; that Katharine Hepburn in *Morning Glory* as a novice Shakespearean is good enough to silence a roomful of hardened Broadway professionals; that Ava Gardner in *On the Beach* is a knockout who can turn the heads of an entire submarine crew preoccupied with their imminent annihilation; that James Stewart in *Mr. Smith Goes to Washington* is a skillful orator who can turn the minds of congressional hardheads; that Rita Hayworth has the goods to become a leading model in *Cover Girl;* that Audrey Hepburn is a real princess in *Roman Holiday* (1953) or a plain intellectual who blossoms into a radiant cover girl with a new international style in *Funny Face* (1957) or a Cockney flower girl who can pass for a duchess in *My Fair Lady* (1964); that Katharine Hepburn in *Sylvia Scarlett* and Barbra Streisand in *Yentl* are convincing dressed up as young men, and that in drag Dustin Hoffman as *Tootsie* and Jack Lemmon and Tony Curtis in *Some Like It Hot* are believable women; that Lana Turner in *The Postman Always Rings Twice* and Barbara Stanwyck in *Double Indemnity* have the sizzling good looks that can fry nice guys like John Garfield and Fred MacMurray.

The star role compels the audience, like the characters within the film, to appreciate and to acknowledge the very qualities that helped the actor to get the part. Watching a performer in a starmaking or star-validating part is to be complicit with Hollywood's mythmaking apparatus, and nowhere is its self-referentiality more evident than in the Star Is Born theme. Hollywood's favorite story of the rituals of stardom, *A Star Is Born* (1937, 1954, 1976), has been miscast each time. Janet Gaynor (1937) isn't good enough; Garland's version is about the rebirth of a star; Streisand's arrogant self-canonization is about not the birth but the death of a star. Ideally the role should be cast with a performer who's an unknown or who has never before made a movie, so that along with the characters in the film we should participate in the excitement of discovering a newcomer who has the goods. But the system that creates stars never entrusted this plum role to a novice.

Once stars are born, they need to be looked after, to be cast in roles that make the audience love them. Three divas—Katharine Hepburn, Joan Crawford, and Mae West—in varying ways exemplify the adoration-of-the-star motif that underlies all star acting.

Throughout her long career, from her rebels in the thirties to her career women in the forties, her spinsters in the fifties, and her sturdy matriarchs at the finish, Hepburn has played characters the audience was forced to admire, characters who stand for Something of Value. Except for the drug-addicted mother in *Long Day's Journey into Night* (1962), who elicits sympathy if not admiration, only once has Hepburn notably departed from the worship-me formula, when she played the monstrous Mrs. Venable in *Suddenly Last Summer,* a Tennessee Williams Dragon Lady no one could possibly look up to. She's superb, yet it's easy to see why Hepburn reportedly detests the film and her role. An imperious matron who collapses into insanity when she cannot face the truth about her homosexual son, the character throws dark shadows onto Hepburn's luminous iconography.

Hepburn's other heroines are consistently admirable; Joan Crawford's, on the other hand, are often schizophrenic. Because Crawford's own hardness, which became increasingly difficult to conceal, warred with her desire, indeed her star's prerogative, to be loved by her fans, her vehicles are driven with internal contradictions as Crawford tries to sentimentalize the ambitious toughie she usually plays. The only framework in which her two-faced characters can be explained is that of two traditions of star acting: a star is supposed to be likable even if she is playing a "bad" character, and a "bad" character must reform if she is played by a certain kind of star (Crawford's kind), even if such transformation violates narrative logic. Crawford is a shrewd movie professional and, even if you don't like her, it's possible to see why she had a long career. But when she tries to elicit audience sympathy by "playing the star" she can lapse into what looks now like a parody of star emoting.

Unlike performers such as Hepburn and Crawford, nothing if not solemn in their stardom, Mae West seems to kid the adore-me star syndrome, but her burlesques also massage her hefty ego. Her elaborate preparations for her entrances set the stage as her stage, and hers alone. Before she appears in *She Done Him Wrong*, for instance, other characters sing her praises, and after the audience has been thoroughly primed, La West makes a regal entrance driven in a carriage. In *Myra Breckinridge* two rows of footmen part and trumpets blare to herald her arrival. Here the showcasing is surreal; in the thirties the gilded touches are a send-up of typical star vanity, but only up to a point. Writing her own scripts, West gives herself all the good lines; her coplayers, like the young Cary Grant, vanish into the negative space of the frame as West talks smart and resolves all conflicts through her wit and/or good-heartedness. The only time she shared screen space was when she appeared with W. C. Fields in *My Little Chickadee*, at a point when both their careers had begun to sag. The two performers so despised each other, however, that most of their dialogue scenes were filmed separately, with each of them delivering quips to the camera rather than to each other. For all her joking and self-parody, West was extremely self-protective and so enamored of her persona that she never once departed from it and continued to embrace "Mae West" long after she could play her.

Hooking stars up with the right partners is a frequent insurance policy. The prime example of successful mixing and matching is the Tracy/Hepburn team; at a time (the early forties) when her image most needed it, Tracy's earthiness helped to lessen the sting of her patrician style. When he pokes fun at her voice and manner, he relieves the audience of doing the same thing. Other performers who proved made for each other include William Powell and Myrna Loy, Fred Astaire and Ginger Rogers, Errol Flynn and Olivia de Havilland, Rock Hudson and Doris Day; almost invariably they are better together than when they are on their own.

Some combos, like Laurel and Hardy and the Marx Brothers, form so tight a unit that the actors are virtually inoperable on their own. Stan Laurel's thinness against Oliver Hardy's bulk, Laurel's whimper against Hardy's bluster, are perfectly paired oppositions. Yet many things in their personas are similar: their slow tumbles into speech (it takes them both a while to understand what is happening); their overgrown baby faces and their childlike vulnerability; their eagerness to get even and their resorting to violence, to kicking and shoving, to retaliate against their adversaries.

Groucho's and Chico's strategies of verbal deconstruction—the former's non sequiturs and word salads, the latter's puns and fractured English—are offset by Harpo's mime, just as Groucho's dead face and even deader eyes and Chico's tough mug are contrasted by Harpo's wonderfully mobile face, his wide, expressive eyes, the continual play of emotions that crosses his mask. Groucho and Chico are vaudeville clowns who perform turns while Harpo is a splendid actor who listens and reacts to everything his brothers say and do. The Marxes couldn't exist without him. As with Laurel and Hardy, however, there is much that links the three brothers, qualities that unite them against the world. All of them, of course, are archenemies of bourgeois decorum who wreak havoc wherever they are—on board ship, at the opera, at the races, on a college campus, in a doctor's office, in a Florida hotel—and who delight in surrealist collage and the destruction of sense. They are all also priapic. Like most comics they never discard their masks: Harpo never speaks (although, in real life, he could), Groucho never softens his growl, Chico never loses his fake accent. The mirror scene in *Duck Soup* (1933), with Groucho and Chico reflecting each other's moves and unable to tell if what they are seeing is an image of themselves or the body of another, is an apt metaphor for their symbiosis.

Changing image: Joan Crawford successfully concealing her hard-boiled look as a sweet secretary in *Grand Hotel* (with Lionel and John Barrymore); Katharine Hepburn, reluctantly departing from her "adore me" roles to play a monstrous matriarch in *Suddenly Last Summer*.

Aside from star partners, who bask in an evenly distributed limelight, there are also unsung partners, often men, who quietly support a star. Solid, undemonstrative actors like Joseph Cotten, William Holden, Glenn Ford, Joel McCrea, and Fred MacMurray, who know how not to compete and who serve the role and the star rather than themselves, have notably helped to frame star turns by Bette Davis, Gloria Swanson, Judy Holliday, Grace Kelly, Barbara Stanwyck, Katharine Hepburn, Carole Lombard, Jean Arthur, and Claudette Colbert.

OPPOSITE
Partners, lost without each other: Laurel and Hardy in *Liberty* (1929).

FROM LEFT
Supporting the star: note how Olivia de Havilland (in *In This Our Life*) and Fred MacMurray (in *Alice Adams*, 1935) focus their attention and thus ours on the divas, Bette Davis and Katharine Hepburn.

Though George Brent, Davis' frequent leading man, is often dismissed as a non-entity, in fact he was exactly the right partner for Davis: reserved where she is hyperbolic, soft-spoken and well-spoken where she is often shrill. Brent affords his co-performer the space within which to be "Bette Davis." Without erasing himself, Brent makes the doctor in *Dark Victory* a shrewdly underplayed foil to Davis' bravura performance. Most of Davis' female costars also realized that they helped both themselves and her by not overtly competing with her. As the best friend in *Dark Victory*, Geraldine Fitzgerald is a model supporting player. (At a 1989 Lincoln Center Tribute to Bette Davis, Fitzgerald said stars are people who never lower their voices, and no one wants them to.) In *What Ever Happened to Baby Jane?* Joan Crawford cannily holds herself in as Davis goes for broke. In *In This Our Life*, Davis acts up, playing a wicked Southern spitfire, while Olivia de Havilland as her genteel sister whispers her performance in sly and delicious counterpoint; as she sneaks sidelong disbelieving glances at Davis, she nearly steals the picture.

All About . . . Judy and Marlon and Jane

Late in their careers, or at a turning point, stars who have achieved a legendary status often appear in a film that seems to be all about them—as they really are, or at least as the public has been encouraged to think they really are. These ultimate vehicles draw not only on the stars' careers but on their offscreen lives as well—on the image that has been promoted through interviews on TV and radio, and in magazines, newspapers, and books.

A common aim of these self-reflexive vehicles is to construct scenarios for aging performers to prove they can still glitter. In *Limelight*, for example, Chaplin wrote and directed a fable in which as the "tramp comedian" Calvero he is doubly validated. Not only does his character have a theatrical success after a long retirement, but when Calvero dies his protégée, a young ballerina, dances gloriously; Calvero therefore proves he can still perform, and his legacy endures in the work of the dancer he has nurtured. Chaplin's performance is exquisitely valedictory—his voice and face are tipped with an elegiac radiance—but his onstage turns as Calvero don't achieve what they are supposed to. In all his

best work Chaplin's comedy was not isolated on a stage but sprang organically from the story. Among his major films Chaplin plays a performer (someone who stands on stage trying to elicit laughter from an audience) only once, in *The Circus,* where he passes the star test of convincing us of his character's comic gifts. But in *Limelight* he performs antediluvian material, circus songs and jokes about performing fleas, that seems to be a throwback not to his early movie slapstick but to his apprentice days in the British music hall.

In a less exalted mode, *The Color of Money* (1986) is a report from the front that informs the audience that Paul Newman also still has it. As pool shark Eddie Felson, Newman is returning to a role he created twenty-five years earlier in *The Hustler.* Now he is an old-timer who takes on a young, good-looking protégé (Tom Cruise). "He's got the eye, he's got the stroke, he's got the flake," Eddie says admiringly after he watches Vince (Cruise) perform at the pool table, reminding us that those are the qualities Eddie has too. Training Vince, teaching him the professional fine points ("The best is the guy with the most, in all walks of life"), he says, "I quit . . . I'm too old, my wheels are shot, it's a young man's game." But Eddie gets "hungry again." He plays Vince and wins; Vince accuses him, "You *used* me." "Yes I did," Eddie admits. And when the mentor and his student face off for their big game Eddie says, "Let's clean it up . . . I want your best game, I don't have that many games left in me." Then he speaks the line the whole film has been warming up to: "If I don't whip you now, I will next month in Dallas . . . I'm back." At the moment of the character's triumphant self-assertion the frame freezes while on the sound track we hear pool balls splitting. Coming from Paul Newman, who unlike Chaplin has never really left, "I'm back" really means "I'm still here," and, since the film is the opposite of a swan song, it also means "I'm ready for more." With its insistent double focus *The Color of Money* is a reminder that Newman, at sixty, with a creased face and a voice grown husky, is still a star.

I Could Go On Singing and *The Star* continually nudge the audience to identify the actresses, Judy Garland and Bette Davis, with their characters. Both play temperamental performers past their prime who have notably unhappy private lives, just like Garland and Davis themselves; yet art improves on life since their characters are reunited with estranged lovers and children. As Jennie Bowman, a misbehaving American singer in London, Garland allows herself to be presented unflatteringly as a spoiled diva who "gives more love than anyone, yet takes more than anyone could possibly give." As Garland herself often did, Jenny arrives late to a concert but with a droll wit tames the hooting mob

CLOCKWISE FROM LEFT
Stars playing stars, surrounded by their own images: Chaplin as Calvero in *Limelight* (1952); Bette Davis as former movie star Margaret Elliot in *The Star* (1952); Gloria Swanson as silent movie queen Norma Desmond in *Sunset Boulevard* (1950).

and then performs a hard-sell rendition of the title tune. Nakedly patterned on her own life, and making a spectacle of her turmoil, her fears about losing her voice, and the salvation her singing represents, the film is tabloid-level exploitation that Garland, aston-ishingly, manages to redeem by her truthful, low-key, improvisatory acting style. Her singing, however, is overstated. She has four numbers which she performs in her baroque late manner, chopping off the last syllables of words and running her hands through her hair as she turns songs into a display of her own emotional fragility. Nevertheless *I Could Go On Singing* proves that despite the tolls of her personal life and the uncertainties of her voice Jennie, like Garland herself, can still entertain her fans.

Absurdly, on the other hand, *The Star* retires its star. Bette Davis as a bruised has-been, Oscar-winner Margaret Elliot, leaves Hollywood behind to claim her "birthright, the glory and privilege of being a woman," and to set up house with her daughter and a former lover. (As if Bette Davis could ever quit acting!) Although written for Joan Craw-ford, the film is coated with references to Davis' life. And ten years later, in her 1962 autobiography, *The Lonely Life,* Davis returns to the concerns articulated in the film: the burden of supporting relatives; husbands who felt crushed by her success; the clash be-tween professional acclaim and bitter personal failures; the indignity of being offered tripe. Unlike Garland, who wisely underplays a dangerous role, Davis tries to salvage a poor script by going over the top, to prove that, unlike Margaret Elliot, Bette Davis still can act. But *The Star* is not an end-of-career testimonial like *Limelight* and *I Could Go On*

RIGHT
A star vehicle that assures us that Paul Newman at sixty still has star quality: in *The Color of Money* (1986) Newman holds his own against a contemporary star, Tom Cruise.

BELOW
In *Last Tango in Paris* (1972) we are teased with the illusion of seeing Marlon Brando himself misbehave.

OPPOSITE
Is this a scene from a movie or a photograph from a Judy Garland concert? An exploitative star vehicle like *I Could Go On Singing* (1963) deliberately confounds the boundaries between the star's role and her well-publicized private life.

Singing; rather it seems to confirm that after *All About Eve* its star is slipping, eager but rudderless and edging into the camp self-caricature that was to mar much of her later work.

In *Last Tango in Paris* (1972) Marlon Brando offers a variation on the self-referential star vehicle. Although the connection between actor and role is not as explicit as in the foregoing pieces—Brando plays Paul, an American in Paris whose wife has committed suicide—the film nonetheless teases us with the illusion that we are seeing aspects of the real live actor. Carrying on an anonymous affair ("I don't want a name, I'm better off with a grunt or a groan for a name") with a woman he has chosen to be his executioner, Paul embodies the peak of the voluptuous masochism that courses through Brando's career. Far from protecting his image the way most stars do, Brando reveals Paul's (and his own?) fear and loathing, his misogyny, fatal charm, black humor, scatological obsessiveness. Part of the film's shock value is the ultimate fantasy it seems to cater to, the spectacle of seeing a sex symbol actually Doing It. The action is not hard core, but the film creates an X-rated aura in which a famous actor breaks the barriers of sexual display. He talks dirty as he has sex with his topcoat on and when his girlfriend penetrates him anally with her fingers; he uses butter as a lubricant and takes down his pants during the transgressive title tango. The illusion that Brando is playing the dark side of himself is underlined by his ludic, improvisatory performance—he chews gum, he wipes his nose, he coughs—and by the sense that he seems to be making up his dialogue on the spot. Deliberately, Brando confuses the dividing line between acting and being.

Sunset Boulevard (1950) also throws a twist into the usual art-merges-with-life syndrome of the Great Star opus. As demented silent-movie diva Norma Desmond, Gloria Swanson is so persuasive that audiences assume she is simply "playing herself," as if writer-director Billy Wilder had lured her out of an obscure and disintegrating retirement with the role of her career. Though the film has autobiographical overtones—Norma's butler is played by silent film director Erich von Stroheim, who had directed Swanson in an aborted film of *Queen Kelly* (1929), and indeed Norma is surrounded by images of Swanson in her silent-picture heyday—the actress is not at all playing herself, and it is one of the film's tricks to make us think that she is. (In a picture that is narrated by a corpse, audiences should be wary of confusing movie illusion with reality.) Far from languishing in the cobwebs of memory, Swanson was an active businesswoman up until her death, a shrewd, practical woman who, when acting offers began to evaporate, declared that the world was a big place and she should find something else to do.

Movies like *The Star* and *I Could Go On Singing* promote the illusion that the star's own life is the raw material and preparation for the role. While trashing the lives of the legends they feed on—these movies have a built-in condescension toward their subjects, who are on the skids on screen and off—the films also sanctify them. That the performer actually lived the part, or that dramatic impact depends on audiences thinking that they did, elevates autobiography to Hollywood myth. In all the roles that we are encouraged to read as "all about" the stars who play them, two parallel texts interact, as the performer's screen image deliberately meshes with, echoes, or consolidates the publicly known facts of his or her life. Usually this movie/real-life symbiosis is reserved for stars at or near the ends of their careers, but sometimes if the performer's offscreen image generates enough buzz, the parallel-lives motif can occur in mid-career or earlier, as it did with Jane Fonda. In pictures like *Coming Home* (1978) and *The China Syndrome* (1979) Fonda is enacting a kind of double role.

As Fonda's characters undergo changes that evoke the general outline of her well-known real-life transformations, both films follow essentially the same narrative arc. Significantly, in her first scene in *Coming Home,* you don't notice her as she is sitting at a bar wearing an anonymous plastic sixties hairdo. Married to a gung-ho marine, her repressed character, Sally Hyde, cries out for an ideological overhauling, but the spectacle of Fonda playing a high school cheerleader type is paper thin. Speaking in a voice that's wised-up right from the start, Fonda inhabits the film's lower-class settings like a visiting celebrity. Nonetheless the film's agenda is to trace the way Sally gradually becomes a political activist. Working as a volunteer in a military hospital she learns about war's devastating toll, she changes her hair (a modish frizzy look replaces the earlier beehive), and she becomes liberated enough to have an affair. "My husband's not going to like the fact that I've changed," she tells her lover, a crippled vet. "I've never been on my own before."

The China Syndrome again recycles Fonda's offscreen radicalization. Here she plays a TV anchorwoman with bright red hair (her boss thinks she's a bimbo, "the red-head") who is given dimwit assignments. Kimberly Wells (Fonda) knowingly plays the female-object role to which the patriarchal system has confined her: she wears a lot of makeup as she delivers reports on hot air balloons and singing telegrams, and she speaks in a bright, chirpy voice. When she pleads with her boss for the chance to do some hard news, he tells her dismissively that she's "better at doing the soft stuff." After she finds a break-through story, a timely one about a nuclear power plant with a leak, she appears on camera to become an articulate advocate for closing the plant. It's her moment of glory, and for the first time in the film she erases her coy on-camera style—after years of her own public speaking, Fonda has the right clipped, forensic style for a no-nonsense TV journalist.

Behind the emergent heroism is of course Fonda's own real-life progress from playing roles like *Barbarella* (1968) while she was married to Roger Vadim, who turned her into a visual double of his ex-wife, Brigitte Bardot, to playing for real in the jungles of Vietnam as a vocal antiwar agitator. Whereas in the sixties she was typically encased in a waxen, stupid-Cupid milieu, in the seventies she began to play roles reflecting her own political evolution. Her offscreen convictions permeate these roles, but Fonda is a shrewd self-propagandist: her characters' feelings and the way they look (how they wear their hair, how they dress) rather than the issues (the war in Vietnam, nuclear disarmament) take up most of the screen time. In dramatizing her radicalization, her body remains central to her iconography—a through line in her career from the Vadim phase to her workout tapes in the eighties.

In the parallel texts of Fonda's work, life and art merged with climactic impact in *On Golden Pond,* in which she is the tense daughter of a remote father played by Henry Fonda. It was common knowledge that the Fondas had a troubled family history, but by 1981, with Jane's activism quieted and Henry's debilitating illness evident, they were reconciled. In dialogue that reverberates with real-life overtones the film rehearses the story of their estrangement and reconciliation. "It seems you and me have been mad at each other so long," Chelsea (Jane Fonda) says. Choked by her need for a loving father instead of the disapproving one she's had (as a real-life father Fonda was a notorious cold fish), she breaks down after she admits, "I want to be your friend. . . . " At the end, as father and daughter embrace tearfully, the Fondas seem to be playing out a scenario the audience has reason to believe is virtually synonymous with their own lives.

As they create the illusion that we are seeing the real thing, movies like *On Golden Pond* exploit our interest in stars' private lives—what we know about the Fondas' own family drama does in fact enhance the threadbare script. I know I'm entering risky terrain here, so let me say at once that being in the know about the lives of the stars is not a necessary tool for critical evaluation. Nonetheless, biographical information, even on the level of gossip, can help in penetrating the masks of star acting and can add another level on which to assess a performance. The desire to know about the stars—to compare and contrast the life with the works—is a perfectly natural extension of the voyeurism under-lying moviegoing. Seeing actors create an illusion within the limits of the frame provokes a counter-desire to see them beyond the borders of the screen, as themselves, surprised, caught off-guard—in short, not acting.

The celebrity interview, whether in print or on radio or TV, and books about movie stars are the usual ways in which the star is "revealed" to the public. Often, however, the image that is projected offscreen differs little from the movie image and so confirms the public's suspicion that most stars simply "play" themselves. Here are three celebrity inter-views in which the stars appearing as themselves seem little different from how they appear on film. In 1968, when she was in England making *Berserk* (aka *Circus of Blood*), Joan Crawford gave what may be the ultimate movie star interview, in which she remained securely hidden behind her by-then-terrifying mask. Grand, remote, terse, contemptuous of her smarmy interviewer, she is an almost perfect wall of resistance. As the television

camera probes her face in closeup, she remains within her star shield. As "herself" she is all fabrication—she even pretends to think before she gives stock answers to questions. And she flavors her dry comments with programmed sentiment, speaking of her gratitude to her many "friends" (she refuses to call them fans) to whom she personally writes 10,000 to 12,000 letters a month.

In April 1989, Bette Davis appeared on the David Letterman show to give what would be one of her last interviews. Unlike Crawford, she is spontaneous, sassy, self-deprecating, honest, and grateful for the applause of the audience. An old woman ravaged by illness, she is game and courageous and as feisty as Jezebel.

In *Meet Marlon Brando* (1966) the actor remains true to his image by demolishing the rituals of the celebrity interview. Plugging a film, *Morituri* (1965), that he knows is mediocre ("You have to see it, your life depends on it"), he flirts with the interviewer ("How do you know I'm attractive; have you ever seen me without my clothes on?") and through timing and charm takes charge of the proceedings. Only once, when he mentions his concern with the plight of American Indians, does he become serious. Underlying his sly mockery of the celebrity interview is the implication that making and selling movies is a silly way for grown-ups to earn a living.

In both their own memoirs and biographies written by others the stars are often presented as if they are appearing in one of their films. Life stories are made to conform to the narratives in which we have come to know them; so while pretending to tell all, many biographies perpetuate and protect their subject's image. In the post-studio era, however, there has been an attempt to demolish the myths about the stars created by ingenious studio public relations departments. Here are some of the categories of latter-day revisionism in recent biographies. The unexpected hot number: cool and regal Grace Kelly

FROM LEFT
From pinup (a publicity still for *Sunday in New York*, 1963) to social activist (playing a TV journalist with a raised consciousness in *The China Syndrome*, 1979), Jane Fonda's roles parallel her own real-life transformations.

revealed as a near-nymphomaniac who seduced her costars, most of whom were old enough to be her father. The compulsive Lothario: Gary Cooper. The secret lives of Hollywood bisexuals and homosexuals: Cary Grant, Tyrone Power, Rock Hudson exposed after years of speculation. Mommie and Daddy Dearest: in the rush to judgment sparked by Christina Crawford's scorching best-seller, which portrayed her mother, Joan Crawford, as a criminally insane parent, other abused Hollywood kids have spoken up; so far Bette Davis and Bing Crosby are the sweepstakes winners, the stars most feared or hated by their children. The smoking gun: Errol Flynn as a spy for the Nazis. The Great Lover debunked: Clark Gable as a disappointment in the boudoir; Valentino with two unconsummated marriages to lesbians.

But whether a biography celebrates or detonates, in selling the lives of the stars a few key themes reappear, as the echoing titles of books about stars indicate: *The Lonely Life, The Tragic Idol, The Hollow Man, The Reluctant Goddess, The Lonely Heart, The Last Star, The Story of a Survivor, No Bed of Roses, The Star-Crossed Lovers.* The titles conform to popular, reassuring myths that stardom isn't what it's cracked up to be, that good fortune inevitably carries a sting, that to achieve Hollywood success entails prostitution of the spirit as well as of the body and is insurance against being a loving spouse or parent or child. While insisting on and sometimes even fetishizing the ways in which stars are different—divinely favored and divinely punished—most biographies end up reminding readers that stars are really one of us, only mortal after all.

Typecasting

Actors become stars through repetition, playing the same basic character over and over. In the Hollywood system versatility is an all but useless commodity, perhaps even a violation of the American edict to Be Yourself. The biggest stars are their own genres, and seeing them in successive movies is in a sense to follow a continuing narrative, *The Further Adventures of . . .* . Each new entry in the canon is connected to each of the earlier entries, so that a star's career is coated with intertextual reference and citation.

From the beginning, typecasting has been the custom because it makes economic as well as artistic sense: the general public wants to see actors mining their special vein, playing the kinds of parts that made them famous in the first place, and American actors by and large are best at "playing themselves." Typecasting has been both good for actors—a guarantee of continuing employment if the type takes—and stifling.

Two vivid examples of fatal typecasting occur at the very origins of the star system, in the careers of Theda Bara and Mary Pickford. Bara was a major player for a mere five years, from 1915 to 1919. At the time, her vamp image was a fairly new type—a fresh way of projecting a luxuriant and wicked sensuality—that offered what acting often offers, a vicarious thrill. But her studio, Fox Film Corporation, overexploited her, putting her in too many similar films too quickly. She is Hollywood's first victim of overexposure, but her fall was all the more sudden because after the war more liberated attitudes and an emerging feminism made her vamp seem like a back number. Except for an unsuccessful comeback in 1925 Bara retired to a scandal-free private life.

Fatal typecasting: Theda Bara as the vamp (here, in *Cleopatra,* 1917).

A bigger star and a better actress, Mary Pickford is among the sorriest victims of typecasting in American films. Like Bara she played a character who had little "give." As America's Sweetheart she was also America's perpetual adolescent. Although the spectacle of a grown woman playing an adolescent seems now a recipe for a Carol Burnett skit, in her own time Pickford was a beloved performer whose audience demanded that she continue to be Little Mary and rejected her periodic attempts to shake the character.

While it will never be possible to resuscitate Little Mary other than as a historical curiosity—even in 1916 the character was a throwback—within the limits of the role that ultimately silenced her, Pickford found ways of playing against the image the public loved while at the same time satisfying that public by not carrying her clever demolition work to an extreme. America's Sweetheart was a cunning termite.

Poor Little Rich Girl (1917) and *Stella Maris* (1918) reveal typical Pickford strategies for undermining her characters' saintly aura. As Gwendolyn, the Poor Little Rich Girl, Mary is a girl in curls, discovered skipping rope on the marble floors in her family's mansion. Playing with dolls and teddy bears, she is a prisoner in "the home of Everything—except the Love she longed for." Like the actress herself the character dreams of escaping, and of becoming a "free little poor girl." To disturb the sweetness expected of her, Pickford in a ploy that runs throughout her career gives the character a sneaky, mischievous humor and an active physical life. Pickford is a slapstick clown who uses pratfalls, spills, and tumbles to break the sugar-spun coating. Another typical way out for her is through cross-dressing—in one section Gwendolyn dresses up and walks like a boy and gets into a mud fight with a gang of roughnecks.

In *Stella Maris* Pickford escapes from Little Mary by playing a double role. As the title character she is another entrapped rich girl, a bedridden recluse who has been "tenderly shielded from all the sordidness and misery of life." As Unity Blake, she is the ugly duckling of a London orphanage. A waif in pigtails and a plain dress, Unity is a hunchback with terrified eyes who bows and scrapes and walks backwards whenever she leaves a room and who stands as if she expects to be beaten. The film is one of Pickford's showiest ways of sneaking around Little Mary: as Unity she vividly plays a character part while satisfying her public with the sickly sweet title character, a saintly princess who greets her subjects and well-wishers with a radiant smile.

In *Dorothy Vernon of Haddon Hall* (1924), as a young woman who saves the lives of Queen Elizabeth and Queen Mary and who is preoccupied with her own romantic concerns, Pickford tried to play a grown-up role, but her audience was so disappointed that

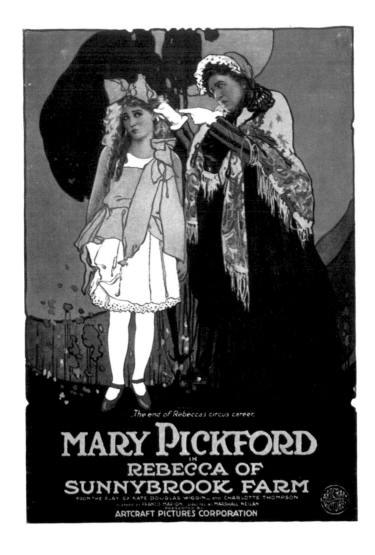

CLOCKWISE FROM LOWER LEFT
Mary Pickford as Little Mary, a perpetual adolescent, in characteristic poses in *How Could You, Jean?* (1918) and a poster for *Rebecca of Sunnybrook Farm* (1917). When Pickford tried to escape from Little Mary, as in *Kiki* (1931), her fans did not accept her.

she returned to familiar ground in her next film, *Little Annie Rooney* (1925), a big hit in which she's once again a presexual, hell-raising adolescent. A tomboy and a live wire, Annie Rooney is far removed from the world of adult romance. Talking pictures made Little Mary an impossibility—Pickford's mature voice would have exposed her real age. Technology killed off her persona once and for all, and Pickford was unable to find another her fans could accept.

Many stars added mileage to their careers by doing successfully what Pickford failed at, playing with new colors that subvert or modify the personas that won them fame. Often the most enduring stars have leaks within their iconography that permit variation: Henry Fonda, James Stewart, James Cagney, John Wayne, Barbara Stanwyck, and Humphrey Bogart are among the players with usable cracks in their facade. (In contrast to actors with a dual register are performers like Mae West, the Marx Brothers, and Fred Astaire from whom audiences wouldn't expect or want modification or complication.)

Throughout their careers Fonda and Stewart played heroes with qualities that continually threatened to undermine their heroism; weakness, uncertainty, emotional and physical vulnerability, are a standard part of their protagonists' makeup. Fonda has a softness in his voice and body and around the corners of his mouth that makes him a convincing victim, as in *You Only Live Once* and *The Wrong Man*. Even when he has played powerful characters, leaders and men of destiny, as in *The Grapes of Wrath, Young Mr. Lincoln*, and *Mister Roberts* (1955), a lingering instability haunts his presence. His martinet in *Fort Apache* is a Western hero gone bad, a man whose need to be in control is so great that his "strength" evokes doubts in other characters as well as the audience. It is rare for Fonda to play a stalwart, entirely clear-headed character, as he does in *Jezebel*, where his hero stands up firmly to the willful heroine.

Fonda's image is thus interestingly unpredictable. His characters could either triumph or dissolve, either seize or lose control. This "double" quality is effectively used in

Daisy Kenyon (1947), in which he is cast as a vet suffering from nightmares who wins a career woman (Joan Crawford) away from his worldly adversary (Dana Andrews), then loses her, only to regain her in the end. Fonda gives the character a double-edged quality—he's a pushover who has strength in reserve; he's a neurotic with boyish charm. He's a man, in short, who could either win or lose, and as a result the ending—who will Daisy Kenyon wind up with?—is up for grabs.

James Stewart's heroes often suffer from neurotic or "unmanly" symptoms. Before he claims his victory, Mr. Smith collapses emotionally, verbally, and physically. Stewart's character in *It's a Wonderful Life* teeters on the brink of self-destruction before he regains his place as the hero of his hometown. In the fifties, in his work with both Hitchcock (*Rear Window* and *Vertigo*) and Anthony Mann (*Bend of the River*, 1952; *The Naked Spur*, 1953), negative aspects of his persona were deepened as the actor began to play characters with breaks in their moral armor. His Hitchcock heroes are physically as well as emotionally wounded. In *Rear Window* he's a voyeuristic photojournalist with a broken leg who is afraid of making a real commitment to his fiancée. In *Vertigo* he's a detective with a fear of falling who is determined to mold a mousey secretary into the image of the dead aristocratic beauty with whom he has become obsessed. In his Westerns with Mann he plays characters with shadowed pasts. In *Bend of the River*, for instance, he is a grizzled wagonmaster with a violent streak who was a former raider. "A man can change," says the wagonmaster when he yearns to become part of a new community of settlers upriver.

When it comes to typecasting, John Wayne and James Cagney are complementary performers: Wayne often plays heroes with villainous or menacing possibilities, Cagney frequently enacts gangsters touched with heroism. Wayne's misanthropy and Cagney's warmth were emphasized in two midcareer films: in *Red River* (1948) Wayne is the heavy, in *Yankee Doodle Dandy* (1942) Cagney elicits audience sympathy. In *Red River* Wayne is a tyrant, a rigid reactionary who incites mutiny among the men he leads on a cross-country trek. Though Wayne didn't have much give as a screen presence, a number of his later cowboys carry the dark tones released in *Red River*. Except for *White Heat*, Cagney's bad guys, as most typically in *The Public Enemy* and *Angels with Dirty Faces* (1939), are gilded with a lovable streak. The pure and rather sickly sentimentality released at full blast in Cagney's completely sanitized version of George M. Cohan in *Yankee Doodle Dandy* is but the fulfillment of the gleam in the actor's eye, and the bounce in his body, apparent from the start of his career.

CLOCKWISE FROM LEFT
Tampering with Hollywood heroism: Henry Fonda (in *The Wrong Man*, 1956, with Vera Miles), James Stewart (in *Vertigo*, 1958, with Kim Novak), and John Wayne (in *Red River*, 1948, with Montgomery Clift) sometimes take on roles that modify their iconography. In *The Wrong Man* Fonda is a passive victim; in *Vertigo* Stewart is a neurotic detective; in *Red River* Wayne is a tyrant who must be supplanted by a liberal, new-style Western hero.

Like Cagney, Barbara Stanwyck, a nice tough cookie, typically performs in a double mode in each of her films. Except for *Double Indemnity*, she's the warmest hard-boiled dame in American movies. Stanwyck's tough egg with the soft center, more convincing than Joan Crawford's, is best highlighted in *Remember the Night* (1940) in which she is a brittle jewel thief who melts when a sympathetic district attorney (Fred MacMurray) falls for her. The film's point is to reveal the gentleness beneath the character's (as well as the actress's) facade; when the D.A. takes her home to his mother for Christmas, her voice loses its edge, her face and body become less angular.

Stanwyck's dual register—loud and soft, brash and sensitive—is not as neatly sustained in *Stella Dallas*, in which she plays a vulgarian we are prodded to look down on, feel sorry for, laugh at, and admire, sometimes all at once. Stella Dallas is a mill hand's daughter who marries out of her class, then loses her husband and daughter because of her atavistic vulgarity and their snobbism. Sometimes her commonness is clearly an act, sometimes it is genuine, and sometimes Stella erases all traces of it—the role is conceived with more skids and contradictions than Stanwyck can cover over.

If long-lasting stars play with a flexible doubleness or sometimes slide gradually into new personas over the course of their careers, sometimes careers are rejuvenated in a single role that dramatically challenges a performer's official iconography. Casting against type depends, of course, on the complicity of the audience, who are expected to have a knowledge of how the star in this new guise unsettles his or her earlier image. Since we are never really allowed or even supposed to forget that the star in this new role is being re-

presented, made over, playing against type is ultimately a reminder of type. Here are five performances in which stars drastically and effectively change.

Except for *The Clock,* a nonmusical in which nonetheless she plays her usual character and seems, moreover, always on the verge of breaking into song, Judy Garland's career at M-G-M was entirely in musicals. Though her gifts as a straight dramatic actress were always apparent, it wasn't until *Judgment at Nuremberg* that she departed from her persona. Her performance as a Nazi victim is a knockout. Garland's entrance is delayed until just a moment before intermission, when we see her first in silhouette with her back turned away from the camera. When she moves into the light, she looks startlingly worn— clearly there is no song in this character. (Later in the film the presiding judge holds up a picture of a young Irene Hoffman [Garland] and remarks, rather cruelly, "She really was sixteen once, wasn't she?") An investigator has searched for Irene Hoffman to inquire if she would testify at Nuremberg. After a long pause, her voice trembling with suppressed emotion, and in a sturdy German accent, she says one line only, the final words before the intermission: "We've always known it would come to this."

In Part II, on the stand, she is hounded by the German defense counsel. Slowly going to pieces, she protests her innocence—she was thrown into a concentration camp for having slept with a Jew, though she claims the man was like her father, not her lover. The character's breakdown is so shattering it compels a Nazi (played by Burt Lancaster in a casting gamble that, unlike Garland's, does not work) to admit his guilt.

Like Garland, Chaplin always acted with an emotional ripeness that chafed against generic limits, and part of the challenge of his evolving comic style was in the way it acquired potentially contradictory elements like pathos and social consciousness. Although Chaplin never did play a straight role, his first part after his farewell to the Tramp in *Modern Times* had the same shock of the new as Chaplin in a dark dramatic role would have had: in *Monsieur Verdoux* the most charming actor in movies is a man who courts and kills rich women. His performance has, in fact, a double shock, for not only is Chaplin in a role that reverses his usual alignment with his audience, but he does not play it according to popular preconceptions. Instead he presents a monster as a charming dandy, fastidious at all times in voice and bearing. His Verdoux is a solid bourgeois, a man who has worked for a bank for thirty years and who embarks on a life of crime to support his crippled wife and cherubic blonde son. "These are desperate days, with millions starving . . . it's not easy for a man of my age to make a living," he explains. Monsieur Verdoux makes his entrance clipping roses and taking special care to preserve the life of a caterpillar. He's a dapper boulevardier with a flower in his buttonhole, a poseur who checks out his image in mirrors and leans seductively against a piano in order to attract a lady's attention. Before he kills one of his victims, he pauses and in a dreamy voice delivers an ode to the moon.

Periodically Chaplin entertains us with moments of delicious, unexpected slapstick that recall earlier routines and are included here to break down our resistance to the character. While as a moral philosopher toying with notions of good and evil Chaplin may be overreaching, his against-type performance as a villain of impeccable delicacy is formidable.

To appreciate Cary Grant in *Suspicion* (1941), you have to be familiar with the Grant of *Topper, The Awful Truth* (1937), *Holiday,* and *The Philadelphia Story,* a man who seemed more at ease in a tuxedo than any other actor in Hollywood. In *Suspicion,* qualities that audiences had come to expect and to desire from "Cary Grant"—glamor, deftness, easy charm—are cleverly submitted to close scrutiny. The film asks, is Cary Grant playing his usual part, or is he playing a cad capable of murder? Making his entrance in pitchblackness—his voice startles the spinsterish heroine Lina (Joan Fontaine) whom he will marry and terrorize—Grant plays an ambiguous character. His Johnny Aysgarth has the shifty eyes of a man who looks as if he is being cornered, and his voice can turn suddenly hard and icy. "You shouldn't interfere in my affairs," he snaps at his new wife in a sharp tone. Sometimes, when she isn't looking, Johnny has private moments that suggest his bad faith and arouse our suspicion that he may indeed be what his increasingly terrified wife suspects him to be, a man capable of murdering her. Grant gives Johnny hooded looks and a masked voice only to disarm our doubts with a return to his familiar persona, as when he asks charmingly at a dinner party, "Do I look like a murderer?" "No," answers the mystery writer to whom the question is addressed, temporarily allaying our suspicions as well as the heroine's.

During a climactic car ride on cliffs, during which Lina thinks she is about to be killed, Grant's face looks hard and set as he spins the car around hairpin curves. When the car door opens, Lina thinks he is pushing her to her death, but no, his outstretched hand is meant to save her from falling. Her scream provokes a confession: "I'm no good," Johnny says, admitting that the poison she had discovered was intended not for her but for himself—he was going to kill himself because he'd gotten so deeply into a financial hole. Johnny's a rotter, but he's no killer, and a relieved heroine asks him to turn back and head toward home. Reluctantly he turns the car around as, protectively but ominously, his arm reaches out to cover her shoulder.

In the novel from which the screenplay was adapted, Johnny is a murderer— Hitchcock's happy ending was apparently dictated because the studio feared that audiences would not accept Cary Grant as a villain. But the finale, surely among the edgiest, most unstable "happy" endings in movies, seems to be Hitchcock's private joke on his bosses, for while apparently explaining everything, Johnny's confession is unconvincing. Grant and Hitchcock don't make it easy for us; it isn't clear whether the confession is the truth or yet another of Johnny's lies. After arousing our qualms about the character, the film deliberately fails to resolve or erase them, and we're left wondering, and feeling distinctly suspicious.

Filtering Grant's fabled charm through a glass darkly, *Suspicion* exploits the actor's dark side. But it was neither the first nor the last film to do so—Grant tampered with and disavowed his image probably more often than any other actor of his stature. In *Only Angels Have Wings* (1939) he is a tough boss of an air carrier that flies mail into the jungle. "You're a hard man," another character tells him, and Grant, suppressing the charm, proves the aptness of the comment. But in *None But the Lonely Heart* (1944) Grant—as an Oedipally attached London slum tough who slips into a criminal life but who ultimately reforms— looks tortured, as if he has wandered into the wrong film. He tries to subdue his natural ebullience but "Cary Grant" keeps thrusting across the surface. "Cary Grant" is more effectively suppressed in *Penny Serenade* (1941), in which he plays a father whose life and marriage collapse when his young daughter dies. And in *Notorious* (1946), as in *Suspicion*, Hitchcock again uncovers a bedeviled other side to his sparkling leading man.

In *Once Upon a Time in the West* (1969), Sergio Leone's spaghetti Western and an outsider's tribute to an American genre, Henry Fonda is cast disruptively against the image that had sustained his long career. The star is given a grand delayed entrance as a circling camera discloses his profile and moves in to reveal cold blue eyes and a menacing, enigmatic half-smile. He spits tobacco, then shoots a little boy, the sole survivor of the rampage he and his gang have just waged. It's startling to hear the voice of Tom Joad and Young Mr. Lincoln speak lines like, "People scare better when they're dying," and when making love to Claudia Cardinale, "I begin to think I might be a little sorry killing you . . . you like to feel a man's hands all over you, don't you, even if they're the hands of the man who killed your husband?" His soft voice takes on a sinister undertone, and his body language—he's a tall, lean figure in a black hat and black coat—is threatening. The fact that a beloved American icon plays a demon in the West gives the film a continuous frisson.

In *Hush, Hush, Sweet Charlotte* Olivia de Havilland shreds the sweetness that had been her career-long stock-in-trade. Hollywood's ultimate lady, de Havilland was almost always pious; her Melanie in *Gone With the Wind* is the best-acted goody-two-shoes in American movies, a performance so securely pitched that it never once topples into bathos. Here in a role originally to be taken by Joan Crawford, which would have been predictable casting, de Havilland's presence gives the film a jolt. She plays a character whose masquerade of poisonous pleasantness is exposed when she drops her mask and confesses to being the mastermind behind a plot to drive Cousin Charlotte (Bette Davis) crazy. "You'll do exactly as I say," she spits out at Charlotte, who cowers fearfully in the presence of her unleashed fury. As if making up for a career of being meek and repressed,

of smiling coyly at Errol Flynn and of supporting stars like Bette Davis, de Havilland performs her juicy role to the hilt.

They don't make stars the way they used to—they can't. The full-fledged star-making apparatus declined with the passing of the studio system. Today's studios don't have the same long-term investment in individual performers and so don't groom or coddle or even promote stars in ways that were customary during the studio era. But while today's free-lance market isn't designed to develop stars as the studios could, movies nonetheless continue to produce them. Stars are what the medium and the audience demand. Performers who incite audience desire, fantasy, identification, and admiration still rise to the top and once there replay the kind of role that earned them their popularity.

What *has* changed is the style of stardom: the royal trappings with which vigilant studio publicists bolstered the image of contract players are passé, and stars now are more "real" and down-to-earth both on screen and off. In publicity outlets like magazine profiles and the omnipresent television interview, what the stars reveal about themselves and what the public will accept as "the truth" have become less idealized and remote. But if star deportment and the public's perception of stars have shifted, the star system itself is a permanent fixture of the film industry. The power of stars to attract customers is still the central artery of the business of making and selling movies.

CLOCKWISE FROM TOP LEFT
Playing against type: a distinctly older, unmusical Judy Garland in *Judgment at Nuremberg,* a sinister Cary Grant in *Suspicion* (1941, with Joan Fontaine), an unsweetened Olivia de Havilland in *Hush, Hush, Sweet Charlotte* (1964), and a villainous Henry Fonda in *Once Upon a Time in the West* (1969).

Imitations of Life

"LOOK AT HIM!" A YOUNG WOMAN GASPED WITH ADMIRATION AS Tom Cruise made his entrance in *Days of Thunder* (1990). Her companion's knowing laugh seemed to signal agreement, and both women settled back, content to be dazzled. In this calculated star vehicle Cruise has been presented to elicit exactly the response the two young women provided. He is groomed and coiffed like a strictly top-of-the-line high-fashion model. His skin glows, his white teeth flash, his nose crinkles seductively, his clear blue eyes gaze with unshakable assurance at friend and foe alike.

Not the Hollywood Style: a real little boy, Richie Andrusco, in a real setting, a luncheonette in Brooklyn, in *Little Fugitive* (1953).

The film's manufactured story, about a heroic racing-car driver, is a thin pretext for glorifying the star. And even though its mechanisms for eliciting audience approval are so transparent that *Days of Thunder* presents almost a parody of star acting, the two sophisticated Manhattanites seemed quite willing to be taken in. They clearly recognized the movie for the silly confection it is but were willing to endure it for the pleasure of looking at Cruise, whose authentic star quality survives. Even in claptrap he delivers.

"Her legs go on forever," a man said enthusiastically but perhaps not tactfully to his date, as the camera slowly traveled up Julia Roberts' body in the opening shots of *Pretty Woman* (1990), another synthetic star vehicle, but unlike *Days of Thunder* a big commercial hit. A modern-day Cinderella story about yet another good-hearted whore, *Pretty Woman* evidently provides many viewers with the kind of fairy tale they desire. In this archetypal Hollywood allegory, appearance not only guarantees social acceptance but incites spiritual transformation as well. The film assures us that clothes and the proper makeup do indeed make the woman. When she's dressed like a whore, the title character is treated like a whore; when she appears in Rodeo Drive finery, she evokes awe from observers within the film and, by extension, from the audience.

In the Hollywood Style, as these two recent films forcibly demonstrate, surfaces count. Form *is* content. As surrogate for the audience, the camera inspects the stars, peering closely at faces and bodies. Julia Roberts' legs that go on forever and her big smile, Tom Cruise's enticingly crooked nose and ingratiating grin, are key factors in their accession to the Hollywood big time.

Screen acting in the Hollywood Style, then, is often a medium for projecting glamor and personality. And even performers who don't trade as conspicuously as Cruise and Roberts on qualities of youth and beauty still must present a performing self that attracts a wide general audience. In leading roles, Hollywood acting is star acting, whether the actor's style is primarily realistic or artificial, primarily internal or external, and whether the star is a specific type like Marilyn Monroe or a chameleon like Meryl Streep.

That stars seem to play themselves—or, more accurately, their personas, which of course might differ markedly from their own unadorned, real-life personalities—should not discount the rigors of the profession. The ability to project for the camera is a lot harder than it may appear. One of the illusions in a medium stocked with them is that the actor's task is a simple one: to behave in a natural fashion in front of the camera. In fact, knowing how to hold the camera's eye and to fill the space of the frame is an exacting art.

If film stars are popularly thought to play themselves, isn't that in one sense what all actors do? "The actor is his own instrument," one of the cornerstones of Method acting, is an inevitable factor in the acting process: all actors "use" themselves, either their own histories or their imaginative recreation of emotions or circumstances they may never have experienced directly. In building characters, actors draw on the way their "instruments"—their bodies, faces, and voices and their storehouse of emotional and sensory memories—conceive and project "good" or "evil," "heroism" or "romance."

Like the film image itself, screen acting creates a convincing imitation of life, and despite their literal absence the great stars saturate the frame with a bewitching illusion of presence. The imprint of themselves that remains when continuous strips of celluloid are projected onto a screen presents audiences with a ripe copy of the "real." It's an article of faith that movies demand a realist performing style, and that despite aberrant examples like Bette Davis and Katharine Hepburn, who do a great deal of visible emoting, the medium inherently forbids too much acting. Yet what kind of "realism" is it that most film acting provides?

Writing in 1857 about characters in novels, Herman Melville discovered a formula that applies with uncanny accuracy to the level of realism expected of screen performers. "The people in a fiction," he writes, "like people in a play, must dress as nobody exactly dresses, talk as nobody exactly talks, act as nobody exactly acts. It is with fiction as with religion: it should present another world, and yet one to which we feel the tie." "Another world, and yet one to which we feel the tie": isn't that an apt description of Hollywood realism, the parallel realm created in movies, which the work of actors helps to sustain?

Acting is never just like life, and even the most naturalistic film performer, who may seem "merely" to be living or being, is all the while building an illusion, weaving a spell over the camera and us. And since screen actors' work is subject to more interruptions, and to greater technical and mechanical enhancements, than stage actors', acting for the movies is actually more remote from real life than acting on stage. Like every other element of the film image, acting tricks the spectator as it heightens, distorts, and runs rings around reality.

Consider how James Stewart, a seminal movie realist, solved an acting problem. To achieve the hoarseness required for his filibuster scene in *Mr. Smith Goes to Washington*, Stewart used a mercury solution provided by his physician which irritated and inflamed his vocal chords. "I'm sure the Method people wouldn't have approved of it, but I was in trouble," Stewart recently confessed. Does this revelation lessen his achievement? No, certainly not, for it is the measure of Stewart's art that he has made an acting trick, a subterfuge, seem like the real thing. He fooled us.

As Melville writes about fiction, acting, like the movies in which it is embedded, represents "nature unfettered, exhilarated, in effect transformed." The means of "transforming" and "exhilarating" nature are vastly increased in movies—through musical underlining, lighting, camera choreography, editing, all the elements, in short, of mise-en-scène. Nonetheless, even with all the assistance they receive, actors exude an irreducible essence that ultimately cannot be camouflaged. No matter how skillfully or deceitfully the resources of film technology are employed, actors still have to act; "film" cannot finally create and sustain an illusion of good acting. No amount of fancy filmic footwork can protect a performer who hasn't mastered the art of speaking to the camera.

In his experiments with editing in Russia in the twenties, Sergei Eisenstein theorized that movies did not require trained actors, and he hired people who looked the part regardless of whether or not they could act. Eisenstein has been followed by other filmmakers working against the Hollywood grain of "realism"; such mavericks as Vittorio de Sica, Andy Warhol, Robert Flaherty, and John Cassavetes have sometimes used non-professionals rather than actors.

The authenticity that amateur acting sometimes attains can provide a jolting alternative to Hollywood's star acting, even in its most realistic manifestations. One of my favorite performances is that of an amateur, Richie Andrusco, a real Brooklyn boy who plays exactly that in an enchanting film, *Little Fugitive* (1953), made by New York filmmakers Ray Ashley, Morris Engel, and Ruth Orkin. As opposed to movie-trained moppets like Shirley Temple and Margaret O'Brien, Andrusco is the real thing, a "found object," who is placed in real places, a dingy Brooklyn apartment and playground and Coney Island. Andrusco is a natural, but would he have seemed as real if he had continued to make films? Wouldn't he have lost his innocence, begun to repeat himself, to employ techniques of seeming to be real? It's likely that a performance like his in *Little Fugitive* is not repeatable.

Amateur acting—at any rate, the spectacle of real people playing themselves—can have only a limited use in Hollywood narratives. In *The Killing of a Chinese Bookie* (1976), for instance, John Cassavetes cast a waitress from a Hamburger Hamlet restaurant in Los Angeles because she looked the part and had a fresh quality Cassavetes felt he would be unlikely to find in a professional. On screen the novice performer, Virginia Carrington, shares her scenes with Ben Gazzara, and her nonprofessional status is palpable. She's interesting, but even in a Cassavetes film she is *too* real, too unvarnished, and she doesn't have the energy to hold her part of the frame. Her scenes with an accomplished under-player like Gazzara are oddly off-kilter. Nonetheless, her hesitant, untutored performance doesn't seriously disrupt Cassavetes' experimental movie, whereas in a more regular inflection of the Hollywood Style it would be likely to stop the show.

Technique—command of craft and of the camera—is essential for the actor working in the Hollywood marketplace. On-screen actors are in fact less protected than stage actors, who are shielded by their distance from the spectator. Two representative failed performances highlight the differing requirements of performing on stage and on film: movie star Kathleen Turner stumbling as Maggie the Cat in a 1990 Broadway revival of Tennessee Williams' *Cat on a Hot Tin Roof;* stage star Ethel Merman collapsing in the 1953 film version of her 1950 Broadway musical comedy hit, *Call Me Madam.*

In Act I of *Cat on a Hot Tin Roof* Williams has written a series of set speeches in which Maggie harangues her distracted husband. There are no cuts; time is continuous and filled with Williams' lushly orchestrated, incantatory language. Tackling these prose arias, Turner's "instrument" seemed to freeze—her voice flattened, her vocal rhythms became monotonous. She lacked the lyric quality and the sheer vocal stamina needed to drive Williams' virtuoso writing. When has Turner needed to be lyrical in movies, and when has she had to sustain long passages of rhetorically heightened dialogue? Yet on film, in short takes and delivering the staccato bursts of movie dialogue, Turner is a vital performer. On stage she was able to regain the spontaneity of her film work only in Act III, when Maggie's dialogue consists of short, jabbing interjections. Here, in the quick give-and-take typical of film acting, she rose above the memorized quality of the rest of her performance.

While with a lot of work Turner might become an acceptable stage performer, Ethel Merman had no resources whatever for film acting. Recreating a role she had played on stage for hundreds of performances, Merman on screen seems hopelessly stagebound. Belting her dialogue as well as her songs, she often faces front in the posture of a stage performer who is "cheating" by playing to the house. In the theatre Merman in fact was known to play front, with her eyes and her focus on the audience rather than on her fellow actors. Waiting for laugh lines and freezing for applause at the end of musical numbers, she retains her stage timing. She never appears to think about what her character is saying or doing or singing, and the camera—which is clearly for her an inadequate substitute for a live audience showering her with the laughs and applause she is used to—exposes her performance as a canned reconstruction. She doesn't adjust her brassy style for the camera, and closeups reveal her utterly blank eyes. More than the fact that her face didn't have the contours the camera likes, it was her dead eyes that insured Merman's failure on film.

What do film actors do for us? Reciprocally, what do we do for them? If we can accept the by-now-traditional designation of Hollywood as a dream factory, then the audience is linked to actors in a relation that parallels that of the dreamer to the dream. Movies of course aren't really our own dreams; they're the ones concocted by filmmakers who are either recreating their own or ones they think moviegoers want or need to see. As the embodiments of mass-market fantasies, actors are sexier, emotionally and physically freer, and more expressive than most people in the real world. Enacting dreamlike scenarios on a screen that magnifies (and sometimes shrinks) their real-life dimensions, they always represent more than their own individual selves. They are the custodians, in a sense the living historians, of contemporary American values and myths. A star like Bette Davis, whose characters are punished for not conforming to bourgeois norms, reflects then-current social attitudes toward strong-willed women, just as Jane Fonda's heroines of a later vintage suggest a more enlightened view of the culture's expectations of women. (This, of course, does not mean that Fonda is a better actress than Davis; in the movies artistry does not necessarily keep pace with ideology.) James Dean's tortured adolescents and Brando's hoods reveal cracks in the surface of fifties homogeneity. Katharine Hepburn's heroines embody notions of how Our Betters think and sound and move. Shirley Temple represented a childhood ideal cherished by enough parents to have catapulted her to the position of the nation's top box-office star in the mid-thirties. Similarly, the top-earning stars of 1990—Sylvester Stallone, Arnold Schwarzenegger, Eddie Murphy, Jack Nicholson, Bruce Willis, Sean Connery, Michael J. Fox, Tom Cruise, Michael Douglas, and Harrison Ford (notice the absence of women in the top ten)—incarnate various contemporary tensions, goals, and ideals.

The impact of screen acting is tied to the power of photographed images, to their often erotic appeal and their intoxicating sense of the momentary and the actual. For the audience the illusion of reality summoned by movies creates illusions of intimacy and presence. Watching moving pictures, we feel we "own" the image; film's magical flexibility in manipulating space and time gives viewers the fantasy that we too can cut and sever and restructure. For as long as the movie continues, we have the feeling that we are in the driver's seat. "Ownership," however deceptive, includes a sense of possession over the people who act "our" scenarios. Seeing screen actors in the flesh, don't we think, at least momentarily, that we already know them and that we are therefore entitled to a sign of recognition in return? Paradoxically, since we "know" them through their larger-than-life images, in the flesh film actors look different, oddly diminished, even perhaps denatured.

Just as viewers see film players in a double focus, actors too compete with their screen twins. If images are forever, the actors are bound by their own mortality, their merely human bodies. Only the imprint of themselves on film can outwit time. A star's negotiations with real time were provocatively highlighted in Greta Garbo's legendary wish to be alone, to be allowed to shed her Garboesque alter ego in private. Only the periodic publication of candid photographs offered a trace of the real-life Garbo. These photographs—a series of testaments to the fact that "Garbo," screen icon of the twenties and thirties, no longer existed in the real world—revealed a dead-faced woman who refused to play to the camera as she had in her films. Shielding or averting her face from the prying camera, who was she protecting, herself or us? Did she perhaps wish to preserve for us an illusion that "Garbo" had defied time? Did she wish to spare us from the inevitable fact that this other person, not in fact the Garbo we knew and so in a sense not even "Garbo" at all, had grown old like everyone else on the *other* side of the screen?

Other icons, like Marilyn Monroe and James Dean, did not grow old, but if they had, how could they ever have competed with the widely distributed images of their perennially youthful selves? Even now, decades after their deaths, they remain a conspicuous part of our visual culture; their images beckon from store windows, calendars, greeting cards. They don't date or wear out their welcome, and fresh pictures, renewed evidence of their ability to speak to the camera, seem to surface periodically. How could the real-life performers have withstood the impact of their iconization? Would they have felt that these images of themselves robbed them of their own, nonmythic identities?

If spectators want to or think they claim possession of actors while watching them on screen, actors too have strong possessory rights, over the characters they have created. Doesn't Vivien Leigh forever "own" Scarlett O'Hara? Can anyone besides Clark Gable ever "be" Rhett Butler? Would anyone dare to? Tom Joad, the hero of John Steinbeck's *Grapes of Wrath,* is forever stamped with the features of the young Henry Fonda. Ma is forever crusty, pumpkin-shaped Jane Darwell, as Casey is the elongated face and El Grecoesque figure of John Carradine. Their presence supersedes and appropriates the author's originals, encased within written language, to become part of a collective national consciousness. One of the reasons a 1990 Broadway production of *Grapes of Wrath* failed was that the images that have become attached to the characters were missing: audience memories of the film inevitably hovered over the stage, and though the play was well performed by Chicago's acclaimed Steppenwolf Company, the stage actors could not measure up, literally or figuratively, to the size of their film predecessors. On stage *Grapes of Wrath* without Fonda and Company seemed diminished, a threadbare imitation.

"We made you what you are," exclaimed a fan besieging Katharine Hepburn for an autograph. "Like hell you did," Hepburn retorted. Yet if we do not in fact "make them what they are," we do do something for screen actors. Acting is always a two-way process, a series of negotiations between the viewer and the viewed. There is no acting without an audience; a performance is completed only when it is received by the viewer. Being receptive to acting—looking, listening, interpreting—is itself creative, a skill audiences develop intuitively over time. Allowing actors to trigger our feelings, we "act" too. And as we respond to the work of actors, we are in fact often more moved, more carried away, than the performers, who after all must remain in conscious control of the emotions they are seeking to arouse in us.

"Reality" as depicted in Hollywood's Golden Age is different from the image of the real that prevails in current movies. "Back then" audiences accepted, and probably didn't even notice, a greater degree of stylization in sets and performances, and many Golden Age films were glazed with an innocence and sentimentality no longer likely to be tolerated. In a general sense the conception of human nature was more idealized in the past than it is in today's cynical movies besotted with violence and profanity. Films still construct a parallel world, a place necessarily different from the real world, but if in the past the movie world tended to be finer, prettier, more artful and ennobling, than the world outside the theatre, today's movies frequently confront audiences with settings that are harsher, more brutal and dangerous, than the ones most spectators are likely to live in. The fantasies movies supply have changed, inevitably, as have the actors who envoice and embody them. Nonetheless, just as the post-studio system can still produce some good movies and persuasive acting can crop up even in mediocre formula pictures, the history of acting in Hollywood is primarily one of continuities rather than disruptions and departures.

Types endure, remolded to fit the spirit of the times. In storytelling as well as acting, imitation and repetition remain the rules of the game. All of today's major stars have clear-cut antecedents; they conform to categories set in the Golden Age or before even as they inject hip, postmodern variations on them. The Hollywood Style is rooted in tradition—repetition creates patterns that in turn attain the status of pop myths. It is those patterns, as they are influenced by the process of moviemaking and by the actors' instruments, that I have attempted to define and illustrate here. My hope is that this book has provided a framework within which to gauge your own responses to film actors; to determine how latter-day performers like Tom Cruise and Julia Roberts, for instance, employ the tools of their trade to get you to like them; to assess the way actors use their bodies and faces and eyes and voices to create whatever illusion the script calls for. Standards of beauty and realism shift, but underlying the superficial changes are recurrent strategies screen actors use or misuse in their attempts to pierce the flatness of the screen, to reach the strangers assembled in the dark who have paid to look at and listen to them.

A long shot.

Two figures walk away from the camera down a road that seems to stretch to infinity through a bare landscape: Charlie Chaplin and Paulette Goddard in the most famous walk in movies, at the end of *Modern Times*. The image has been read as representing the indomitability of the human spirit, which it certainly does—survivors, the Tramp and the Girl dust themselves off, arrange their features into a smile, and confront whatever the highway of life may have in store for them. But the shot might also serve a more immediate purpose here, as a reminder of what, at its best, acting in the movies can give us. Taking us back to the story we have just seen, that final walk lifts the characters into a timeless realm, the silent Everyman and his Girl facing their future, and watching them we are given what strong acting always bestows, a deepened insight into the human condition. The sense that we know these characters and care about them; the ways the actors have charged our emotions, indeed inflamed our ability to respond; the enlightenment and clarity they have offered—these are among the reasons why we go to movies and what, often enough, we can continue to find there even in the years after Hollywood's Golden Age.

Selected Bibliography

Affron, Charles. *Cinema and Sentiment.* Chicago: University of Chicago Press, 1982.

——. *Star Acting: Gish, Garbo, Davis.* New York: Dutton, 1977.

Agee, James. *Agee on Film: Reviews and Comments.* Boston: Beacon Press, n.d.

Althusser, Louis. *Lenin and Philosophy and Other Essays.* New York: Monthly Review Press, 1971.

Altman, Rick. *The American Film Musical.* Bloomington: Indiana University Press, 1987.

Andrew, Dudley. *Concepts in Film Theory.* New York: Oxford University Press, 1984.

Anger, Kenneth. *Hollywood Babylon.* New York: Dell, 1981.

Arliss, George. *My Ten Years in the Studios.* Boston: Little, Brown, 1940.

Auerbach, Erich. *Mimesis: The Representation of Reality in Western Literature.* Garden City, N.Y.: Doubleday Anchor, 1957.

Barrymore, John. *Confessions of an Actor.* 1926. Reprint. New York: Arno Press, 1971.

Barthes, Roland. *Camera Lucida.* New York: Farrar, Straus & Giroux, 1981.

——. *Empire of Signs.* New York: Hill & Wang, 1982.

——. *The Grain of the Voice.* Farrar, Straus & Giroux, 1985.

——. *The Pleasure of the Text.* New York: Farrar, Straus & Giroux, 1975.

——. *The Rustle of Language.* New York: Farrar, Straus & Giroux, 1986.

——. *Writing Degree Zero.* New York: Farrar, Straus & Giroux, 1968.

Bates, Brian. *The Way of the Actor: A Path to Knowledge and Power.* Boston: Shambhala, 1987.

Bazin, André. *What Is Cinema?* 2 vols. Berkeley: University of California Press, 1967.

Bell-Metereau, Rebecca. *Hollywood Androgyny.* New York: Columbia University Press, 1985.

Benjamin, Walter. "The Work of Art in the Age of Mechanical Reproduction." In *Illuminations,* edited by Hannah Arendt, pp. 217–51. New York: Schocken, 1969.

Bergman, Andrew. *We're in the Money: Depression America and Its Films.* New York: New York University Press, 1971.

Bergman, Ingrid, and Alan Burgess. *My Story.* New York: Delacorte, 1980.

Bordwell, David, Janet Staiger, and Kristin Thompson. *The Classical Hollywood Cinema: Film Style and Mode of Production to 1960.* New York: Columbia University Press, 1985.

——. *Making Meaning.* Cambridge, Mass.: Harvard University Press, 1990.

Braudy, Leo. *The World in a Frame: What We See in Films.* Garden City, N.Y.: Doubleday Anchor, 1976.

Britton, Andrew. *Cary Grant: Comedy and Male Desire.* Newcastle upon Tyne: Tyneside Cinema, 1983.

——. *Katharine Hepburn: The Thirties and After.* Newcastle upon Tyne: Tyneside Cinema, 1984.

Brooks, Louise. *Lulu in Hollywood.* New York: Knopf, 1982.

Brown, Peter H. *Kim Novak: Reluctant Goddess.* New York: St. Martin's, 1986.

——, and Jim Pinkston. *Oscar Dearest.* New York: Harper & Row, 1987.

Brownlow, Kevin. *The Parade's Gone By.* Berkeley: University of California Press, 1968.

Butler, Ivan. *Silent Magic.* New York: Ungar, 1988.

Callow, Simon. *Charles Laughton: A Difficult Actor.* London: Methuen, 1987.

Capra, Frank. *The Name Above the Title.* New York: Macmillan, 1971.

Carey, Gary. *All the Stars in Heaven: Louis B. Mayer's MGM.* New York: Dutton, 1981.

——. *Cukor & Co.* New York: Museum of Modern Art, 1971.

——. *Doug and Mary.* New York: Dutton, 1977.

——. *Judy Holliday: An Intimate Life Story,* New York: Seaview, 1987.

Carney, Raymond. *American Vision: The Films of Frank Capra.* Cambridge: Cambridge University Press, 1986.

Carroll, Noel. *Demystifying the Movies.* New York: Columbia University Press, 1988.

Caughie, John, ed. *Theories of Authorship.* London: Routledge & Kegan Paul, 1981.

Cavell, Stanley. *Pursuits of Happiness: The Hollywood Comedy of Remarriage.* Cambridge, Mass.: Harvard University Press, 1981.

——. *The World Viewed: Reflections on the Ontology of Film.* Enlarged edition. Cambridge, Mass.: Harvard University Press, 1979.

Cole, Toby, and Helen Krich Chinoy. *Actors on Acting.* New York: Crown, 1970.

Crane, Cheryl, with Cliff Jahr. *Detour: A Hollywood Story.* New York: Arbor House, 1988.

Croce, Arlene. *The Fred Astaire and Ginger Rogers Book.* New York: Dutton, 1987.

Crosby, Gary, and Ross Firestone. *Going My Own Way.* New York: Ballantine, 1984.

Dalton, David. *James Dean: The Mutant King.* New York: St. Martin's, 1974.

Dardis, Tom. *Harold Lloyd: The Man on the Clock.* New York: Viking, 1983.

——. *Keaton: The Man Who Wouldn't Lie Down.* New York: Scribner's, 1979.

David, Lester, and Irene David. *The Shirley Temple Story.* New York: Putnam, 1983.

Davidson, Bill. *Spencer Tracy: Tragic Idol.* New York: Dutton, 1987.

Davies, Marion. *The Times We Had.* Indianapolis: Bobbs-Merrill, 1975.

Davis, Bette. *The Lonely Life.* New York: Putnam, 1962.

——, with Michael Herskowitz. *This 'n That.* New York: Putnam, 1987.

De Mille, Cecil B. *Autobiography.* New York: Prentice Hall, 1959.

DiOrio, Al. *Barbara Stanwyck.* New York: Coward-McCann, 1983.

Doane, Mary Ann. *The Desire to Desire: The Woman's Film of the 1940s.* Bloomington: Indiana University Press, 1987.

Dooley, Roger. *From Scarface to Scarlett: American Films in the 1930s.* San Diego: Harcourt Brace Jovanovich, 1979.

Durgnat, Raymond. *The Crazy Mirror: Hollywood Comedy and the American Image.* New York: Dell, 1970.

——. *Films and Feelings.* Cambridge, Mass.: M.I.T. Press, 1967.

Dyer, Richard. *Heavenly Bodies: Film Stars and Society.* New York: St. Martin's, 1986.

——. *Stars.* London: British Film Institute, 1979.

——, ed. *Star Signs.* London: British Film Institute, 1982.

Eisenstein, Sergei M. *Film Form.* New York: Harcourt Brace, n.d.

——. *The Film Sense.* New York: Harcourt Brace, n.d.

Everson, William K. *American Silent Film.* New York: Oxford University Press, 1978.

Farber, Manny. *Negative Space.* New York: Praeger, 1971.

Ferguson, Otis. *The Film Criticism of Otis Ferguson.* Edited and with a preface by Robert Wilson. Philadelphia: Temple University Press, 1971.

Flynn, Errol. *My Wicked, Wicked Ways.* New York: Putnam, 1959.

Fonda, Henry, with Howard Teichmann. *My Life.* New York: NAL, 1981.

Foucault, Michel. *The History of Sexuality, Volume I: An Introduction.* New York: Random House, 1978.

Fountain, Leatrice Gilbert, with John R. Maxum. *Dark Star: The Untold Story of the Meteoric Rise and Fall of the Legendary John Gilbert.* New York: St. Martin's, 1985.

Francisco, Charles. *Gentleman: The William Powell Story.* New York: St. Martin's, 1985.

Franklin, Joe, with William K. Everson. *Classics of the Silent Screen.* New York: Cadillac, 1959.

Funke, Lewis, and John E. Booth, eds. *Actors Talk About Acting.* New York: Random House, 1961.

Fussell, Betty Harper. *Mabel: Hollywood's First I-Don't-Care Girl.* New Haven: Ticknor & Fields, 1982.

Gallagher, Tag. *John Ford: The Man and His Films.* Berkeley: University of California Press, 1986.

Gish, Lillian, with Ann Pinchot. *Lillian Gish: The Movies, Mr Griffith and Me.* Englewood Cliffs, N.J.: Prentice-Hall, 1969.

Griffith, Richard. *The Movie Stars.* Garden City, N.Y.: Doubleday, 1970.

Hancock, Ralph, and Letitia Fairbanks. *Douglas Fairbanks: The Fourth Musketeer.* New York: Henry Holt, 1953.

Hansen, Miriam. "Pleasure, Ambivalence, Identification: Valentino and Female Spectatorship." *Cinema Journal* 25, no. 4 (Summer 1986): 6–32.

Harris, Warren. *Cary Grant: A Touch of Elegance.* New York: Doubleday, 1987.

Hart, William S. *My Life East and West.* Boston and New York: Houghton Mifflin, 1929.

Harvey, James. *Romantic Comedy in Hollywood.* New York: Knopf, 1987.

Haskell, Molly. *From Reverence to Rape: The Treatment of Women in the Movies.* New York: Holt, Rinehart & Winston, 1974.

Heath, Stephen. *Questions of Cinema.* Bloomington: Indiana University Press, 1981.

Hepburn, Katharine. *The Making of The African Queen*. New York: Knopf, 1987.

Higham, Charles. *Audrey: The Life of Audrey Hepburn*. New York: Macmillan, 1984.

————. *Brando*. New York: NAL, 1987.

————. *Kate: The Life of Katharine Hepburn*. New York: Signet, 1981.

————. *Marlene: The Life of Marlene Dietrich*. New York: Norton, 1977.

Hill, James. *Rita Hayworth: A Memoir*. New York: Simon and Schuster, 1983.

Hollander, Anne. *Moving Pictures*. New York: Knopf, 1989.

Houston, David. *Jazz Baby: The Shocking Story of Joan Crawford's Tormented Childhood*. New York: St. Martin's, 1983.

Huston, John. *An Open Book*. New York: Knopf, 1980.

Irigaray, Luce. *This Sex Which Is Not One*. Ithaca: Cornell University Press, 1985.

Kael, Pauline. *5001 Nights at the Movies*. New York: Henry Holt, 1984.

Kanin, Garson. *Tracy and Hepburn*. New York: Viking, 1971.

Kaplan, E. Ann. *Rocking Around the Clock: Music Television, Post-Modernism, and Consumer Culture*. New York: Methuen, 1987.

Kay, Karyn, and Gerald Peary, eds. *Women and the Cinema: A Critical Anthology*. New York: Dutton, 1977.

Kazan, Elia. *A Life*. New York: Knopf, 1988.

Kerr, Walter. *The Silent Clowns*. New York: Knopf, 1979.

Kiernan, Thomas. *Jane Fonda: Heroine for Our Time*. New York: Delilah, 1982.

Kobal, John. *The Art of the Great Hollywood Portrait Photographers*. New York: Harrison House, 1980.

————. *Hollywood: The Years of Innocence*. New York: Abbeville, 1985.

————. *People Will Talk*. New York: Knopf, 1985.

Kotsilibas-Davis, James. *The Barrymores: The Royal Family in Hollywood*. Garden City, N.Y.: Doubleday, 1981.

————, and Myrna Loy. *Myrna Loy: Being and Becoming*. New York: Knopf, 1987.

Kuhn, Annette. *Women's Pictures: Feminism and Cinema*. London: Routledge & Kegan Paul, 1982.

Lacan, Jacques. *Ecrits: A Selection*. New York: Norton, 1977.

La Guardia, Robert. *Monty: A Biography of Montgomery Clift*. New York: Arbor House, 1977.

Lambert, Gavin. *On Cukor*. New York: Putnam, 1972.

Lang, Robert. *American Film Melodrama: Griffith, Vidor, Minnelli*. Princeton: Princeton University Press, 1989.

Lawrence, Jerome. *Actor: The Life and Times of Paul Muni*. New York: Putnam, 1974.

Levin, Martin, ed. *Hollywood and the Great Fan Magazines*. New York: Castle, 1970.

Levy, Emanuel. *And the Winner Is . . . The History and Politics of the Oscar Awards*. New York: Ungar, 1987.

Lindsay, Cynthia. *Dear Boris: The Life of William Henry Pratt a.k.a. Boris Karloff*. New York: Knopf, 1975.

Lloyd, Harold. *An American Comedy*. 1928. Reprint. New York: Dover, 1971.

McGilligan, Patrick. *Cagney: The Actor as Auteur*. San Diego: Oak Tree, 1982.

Madsen, Axel. *Gloria and Joe: The Star-Crossed Love Affair of Gloria Swanson and Joe Kennedy*. New York: Arbor House, 1988.

————. *William Wyler*. New York: Thomas Crowell, 1973.

Mailer, Norman. *Marilyn*. New York: Grosset & Dunlap, 1973.

Mandelbaum, Howard, and Eric Myers. *Screen Deco: A Celebration of High Style in Hollywood*. New York: St. Martin's, 1985.

Marx, Arthur. *The Nine Lives of Mickey Rooney*. New York: Stein and Day, 1986.

Mast, Gerald. *The Comic Mind: Comedy and the Movies*. 2nd ed. Chicago: University of Chicago Press, 1979.

————, and Marshall Cohen, eds. *Film Theory and Criticism*. 3rd ed. New York: Oxford University Press, 1985.

Metz, Christian. *The Imaginary Signifier: Psychoanalysis and the Cinema*. Bloomington: Indiana University Press, 1977.

Mix, Paul E. *The Life and Legend of Tom Mix*. Cranbury, N.J.: A. S. Barnes, 1972.

Mordden, Ethan. *The Hollywood Studios: House Style in the Golden Age of the Movies*. New York: Knopf, 1988.

————. *Movie Star: A Look at the Women Who Made Hollywood*. New York: St. Martin's, 1983.

Morin, Edgar. *The Stars*. New York: Grove Press, 1960.

Moss, Robert F. *Karloff and Company: The Horror Film*. New York: Pyramid, 1974.

Mulvey, Laura. "Visual Pleasure and Narrative Cinema." *Screen* 16, no. 3 (Autumn 1975): 6–18.

Naremore, James. *Acting in the Cinema*. Berkeley: University of California Press, 1988.

Neale, Stephen. *Genre*. London: British Film Institute, 1980.

Newquist, Roy. *Conversations with Joan Crawford*. Secaucus, N.J.: Citadel, 1980.

Nichols, Bill, ed. *Movies and Methods*. Vol. II. Berkeley: University of California Press, 1985.

Olivier, Laurence. *On Acting*. New York: Simon & Schuster, 1986.

Pastos, Spero. *Pin-Up: The Tragedy of Betty Grable*. New York: Putnam, 1986.

Paul, William. *Ernst Lubitsch's American Comedy*. New York: Columbia University Press, 1983.

Peary, Danny, ed. *Close-Ups: The Movie Star Book*. New York: Galahad, 1981.

Pickford, Mary. *Sunshine and Shadow*. New York: Doubleday, 1955.

Poitier, Sidney. *This Life*. New York: Knopf, 1980.

Powdermaker, Hortense. *Hollywood, the Dream Factory*. Boston: Little, Brown, 1950.

Pratt, George C. *Spellbound in Darkness: A History of the Silent Film*. Greenwich, Conn.: New York Graphic Society, 1973.

Pudovkin, V. I. *Film Technique and Film Acting*. New York: Grove Press, 1976.

Ramsaye, Terry. *A Million and One Nights: A History of the Motion Picture Through 1925*. New York: Simon & Schuster, 1964.

Ray, Robert B. *A Certain Tendency of the Hollywood Cinema, 1930–1980*. Princeton: Princeton University Press, 1985.

Robbins, Jhan. *Everybody's Man: A Biography of James Stewart*. New York: Putnam, 1985.

Robinson, David. *Chaplin: His Life and Art*. London: Collins, 1985.

Rosen, Marjorie. *Popcorn Venus*. New York: Coward, McCann, 1973.

Rosen, Phil, ed. *Narrative, Apparatus, Ideology: A Film Theory Reader*. New York: Columbia University Press, 1986.

St. Johns, Adela Rogers. *Love, Laughter and Tears: My Hollywood Story*. New York: Doubleday, 1978.

Sarris, Andrew. *The American Cinema*. New York: Dutton, 1968.

Schatz, Thomas. *The Genius of the System: Hollywood Filmmaking in the Studio Era*. New York: Pantheon, 1988.

Schickel, Richard. *His Picture in the Papers*. New York: Charterhouse, 1973.

————. *Intimate Strangers: The Culture of Celebrity*. New York: Doubleday, 1985.

————. *The Stars*. New York: Bonanza, 1962.

Scott, Evelyn F. *Hollywood: When Silents Were Golden*. New York: McGraw-Hill, 1972.

Sennett, Ted. *Great Movie Directors*. New York: Abrams, 1986.

Shepherd, Donald, and Robert Slatzer with Dave Grayson. *Duke: The Life and Times of John Wayne*. New York: Doubleday, 1985.

Shipman, David. *The Great Movie Stars: The Golden Years*. New York: Da Capo, 1982.

Shulman, Irving. *Harlow*. New York: Bernard Geis, 1964.

————. *Valentino*. New York: Trident Press, 1967.

Silverman, Kaja. *The Subject of Semiotics*. New York: Oxford University Press, 1983.

Sontag, Susan, ed. *A Barthes Reader*. New York: Hill & Wang, 1982.

————. *On Photography*. New York: Farrar, Straus & Giroux, 1977.

Spada, James, *Grace: The Secret Lives of a Princess*. New York: Doubleday, 1987.

Spoto, Donald. *The Dark Side of Genius: The Life of Alfred Hitchcock*. Boston: Little, Brown, 1983.

Stine, Whitney. *Mother Goddam: The Story of the Career of Bette Davis*. New York: Hawthorn, 1974.

Swanson, Gloria. *Swanson on Swanson*. New York: Random House, 1980.

Swindell, Larry. *The Last Hero: A Biography of Gary Cooper*. Garden City, N.Y.: Doubleday, 1980.

————. *Screwball: The Life of Carole Lombard*. New York: William Morrow, 1975.

Thomas, Bob. *Astaire: The Man, the Dancer*. New York: St. Martin's, 1984.

Tyler, Parker. *The Hollywood Hallucination*. New York: Simon & Schuster, 1970.

————. *Magic and Myth of the Movies*. New York: Simon & Schuster, 1970.

Von Sternberg, Josef. *Fun in a Chinese Laundry*. London: Columbus Books, 1987.

Walker, Alexander. *The Celluloid Sacrifice*. New York: Hawthorn, 1966.

————. *Garbo*. New York: Macmillan, 1980.

————. *Peter Sellers*. New York: Macmillan, 1981.

————. *The Shattered Silents: How the Talkies Came to Stay*. London: Harrap, 1978.

————. *Valentino*. New York: Stein & Day, 1976.

Warshow, Robert. *The Immediate Experience*. Garden City, N. Y.: Doubleday Anchor, 1964.

Wayne, Jane Ellen. *Gable's Women*. New York: Prentice Hall, 1987.

Weales, Gerald. *Canned Goods as Caviar: American Film Comedy of the 1930s*. Chicago: University of Chicago Press, 1985.

Webb, Michael, ed. *Hollywood: Legend and Reality*. Boston: Little, Brown, 1986.

Weis, Elisabeth, and John Belton, eds. *Film Sound: Theory and Practice*. New York: Columbia University Press, 1985.

———— and Stuart Byron, eds. *The Movie Star: The National Society of Film Critics on the Movie Star*. New York: Penguin, 1981.

Windeler, Robert. *Sweetheart: The Story of Mary Pickford*. New York: Praeger, 1974.

Zierold, Norman. *The Child Stars*. New York: Coward, McCann, 1965.

————. *The Moguls*. New York: Coward, McCann, 1969.

————. *Sex Goddesses of the Silent Screen*. Chicago: Henry Regnery, 1973.

Index

Acknowledgments

and

Photograph Credits

Charles Silver, Film Study Center at the Museum of Modern Art; Pat Sheehan, Joe Balian, and the staff of the Motion Picture Division of the Library of Congress; The Kobal Collection, London and New York; Photofest; Bill O'Connell; Margaret Kaplan; Margaret Donovan; John Crowley; Dirk Luykx; Jerry Vermilye; Lillian Friedman; Ted Sennett; Kristofer Batho; Michael Bavar; Susan Grode.

Photograph Sources

Courtesy of the Academy of Motion Picture Arts and Sciences: 39, 42 above, 63 below, 71, 102–3, 106, 124 above, 209, 210, 264 right. The Kobal Collection: 2–3, 6, 16–17, 26, 27, 28, 32, 33, 37, 38, 42 below, 43, 44–46, 48 left, 49, 52 right, 53, 54–57, 59–61, 63 above, 65–68, 70, 76, 78, 80 above left, 80 below right, 82, 83, 85, 86–87, 89, 92, 94–97, 98, 99, 101, 104 below, 105, 108, 110–11, 113, 116–19, 120 left, 121, 122, 124 below, 126–28, 131, 132, 135–40, 142, 143, 145, 146, 148–49, 151–54, 156, 161, 162, 164, 165, 167–73, 175 left, 176, 177, 181, 183–87, 190, 192, 193 above, 194, 195, 196 left, 197, 200, 204 above, 205, 206, 216, 222, 224, 225, 228, 229, 230 below, 231, 233, 235, 236, 239 below, 242–43, 244–45, 246, 249 below, 250–52, 254, 255, 258–60, 262 below, 263, 264 left, 268, 269, 276–77. Lake County (Illinois) Museum, Curt Teich Postcard Archives: 22. Photofest: 19, 21, 24, 35, 36, 41, 47, 48 right, 52 left, 62, 69 right, 79, 80 below left, 80 above right, 88, 90, 104 above, 109, 125, 130, 144, 158, 163, 166, 174, 175 right, 178, 180, 188, 191, 193 below, 196 right, 198–99, 202, 204 below, 215, 217, 218, 219, 220, 226, 234, 239 above, 240–41, 249 above, 253, 262 above, 270–71. Jerry Vermilye: 8–9, 69 left, 74, 93.

Film Copyrights

2–3: *Life With Father,* © 1947 Katherine B. Day, Howard Lindsay & Russell Crouse. All Rights Reserved. 6: *Queen Christina,* © 1934 Turner Entertainment Co. Ren. 1961 Metro-Goldwyn-Mayer Inc. All Rights Reserved. 8–9: *City Lights,* Chaplin films © and property of Roy Export Company Establishment. 16–17: *Queen Christina,* © 1934 Turner Entertainment Co. Ren. 1961 Metro-Goldwyn-Mayer Inc. All Rights Reserved. 18: *The Seven Year Itch,* © 1955 Twentieth Century Fox Film Corporation. All Rights Reserved. 19: *Viva Zapata,* © 1952 Twentieth Century Fox Film Corporation. All Rights Reserved. 24: *Queen Elizabeth,* 1912, Copyright © by Universal Pictures, a Division of Universal City Studios, Inc. Courtesy of MCA Publishing Rights, a Division of MCA Inc. 26 above right: *The Wind,* © 1928 Turner Entertainment Co. Ren. 1956 Loew's Inc. All Rights Reserved. 26 below: *Dark Victory,* © 1939 Turner Entertainment Co. All Rights Reserved. 27 above: *The Taming of the Shrew,* © 1929 United Artists. 27 below: *On the Waterfront,* © 1954, renewed 1982 Columbia Pictures Industries, Inc. 28 left: *City Lights,* Chaplin films © and property of Roy Export Company Establishment. 28 right: *The Jazz Singer,* © 1927 Turner Entertainment Co. Ren. 1955 Warner Bros. Pictures, Inc. All Rights Reserved. 32, 33: *Rear Window,* 1954 Paramount Pictures Corporation. All Rights Reserved. Courtesy of Paramount Pictures. 35: *Gone With the Wind,* © 1939 Turner Entertainment Co. Ren. 1967 Metro-Goldwyn-Mayer Inc. All Rights Reserved. 36: *Dr. Jekyll and Mr. Hyde,* 1931, Copyright © Universal Pictures, a Division of Universal City Studios, Inc. Courtesy of MCA Publishing Rights, a Division of MCA Inc. 37: *You Only Live Once,* 1937, © 1937 Walter Wanger. Renewed 1964 United Artists Associated, Inc. All Rights Reserved. 38: *It Happened One Night,* © 1934 renewed 1962 Columbia Pictures Corp. 39: *Young Mr. Lincoln,* © 1939 Twentieth Century Fox Film Corporation. All Rights Reserved. 41 above left: *I Wake Up Screaming,* © 1941 Twentieth Century Fox Film Corporation. All Rights Reserved. 41 above right: *Criss Cross,* 1948 Copyright © by Universal Pictures, a Division of Universal City Studios, Inc. Courtesy of MCA Publishing Rights, a Division of MCA Inc. 41 below: *Mildred Pierce,* © 1945 Turner Entertainment Co. All Rights Reserved. 42 above: *Top Hat,* © 1935 RKO Radio Pictures, Inc. Ren. 1962 RKO GENERAL, INC. All Rights Reserved. 42 below: *How to Marry a Millionaire,* © 1953 Twentieth Century Fox Film Corporation. All Rights Reserved. 43 left: *The Petrified Forest,* © 1936 Turner Entertainment Co. All Rights Reserved. 43 right: *Sea of Grass,* © 1946 Turner Entertainment Co. Ren. 1973 Metro-Goldwyn-Mayer Inc. All Rights Reserved. 44: *Beyond the Forest,* © 1949 Turner Entertainment Co. All Rights Reserved. 45: *Anna Christie,* © 1930 Turner Entertainment Co. Ren. 1957 Loew's Inc. All Rights Reserved. 46: *The Little Foxes,* 1941, © 1941 Samuel Goldwyn, Jr. Courtesy Samuel Goldwyn, Jr. and the Samuel Goldwyn Company. 47: *East of Eden,* © 1955 Warner Bros. Pictures, Inc. Renewed 1982 Warner Bros. Inc. All Rights Reserved. 48 left: *A Streetcar Named Desire,* © 1951 Charles Feldman Group Productions. Renewed 1979 Deane F. Johnson & The Motion Picture and Television Fund. All Rights Reserved. 48 right: *A Place in the Sun,* Copyright © 1951 by Paramount Pictures Corporation. All Rights Reserved. Courtesy of Paramount Pictures. 49: *Bhowani Junction,* © 1956 Turner Entertainment Co. Ren. 1983 MGM/UA Entertainment Co. All Rights Reserved. 52 left: *To Catch a Thief,* © 1955 Paramount Pictures Corporation. All Rights Reserved. Courtesy of Paramount Pictures. 52 right: *Rear Window,* 1954 Paramount Pictures Corporation. All Rights Reserved. Courtesy of Paramount Pictures. 53: *The Swan,* © 1956 Turner Entertainment Co. Ren. 1984 MGM/UA Entertainment Co. All Rights Reserved. 55 above: *Blonde Venus,* 1932, Copyright © by Universal Pictures, a Division of Universal City Studios, Inc. Courtesy of MCA Publishing Rights, a Division of MCA Inc. 55 below: *The Devil Is a Woman,* 1935, Copyright © by Universal Pictures, a Division of Universal City Studios, Inc. Courtesy of MCA Publishing Rights, a Divison of MCA Inc. 56: *The Scarlet Empress,* 1934, Copyright © by Universal Pictures, a Division of Universal City Studios, Inc. Courtesy of MCA Publishing Rights, a Division of MCA Inc. 57: *Blonde Venus,* 1932, Copyright © by Universal Pictures, a Division of Universal City Studios, Inc. Courtesy of MCA Publishing Rights, a Division of MCA Inc. 59: *Raging Bull,* © 1980 United Artists Corporation. 60 above left: *Taxi Driver,* © 1976 Columbia Pictures Industries, Inc. 60 above right: *Mean Streets,* © 1973 Warner Bros. Inc. All Rights Reserved. 60–61 below: *Raging Bull,* © 1980 United Artists Corporation. 62: *Jimmy the Gent,* © 1934 Turner Entertainment Co. All Rights Reserved. 63 above: *The Wild One,* © 1953 The Stanley Kramer Company, Inc. International Copyright Secured. All Rights Reserved. 63 below: *One-Eyed Jacks,* © 1960 by Pennebaker, Inc. All Rights Reserved. 65: *Top Hat,* © 1935 RKO Radio Pictures, Inc. Ren. 1962 RKO GENERAL, INC. All Rights Reserved. 66–67: *A Streetcar Named Desire,* © 1951 Charles Feldman Group Productions. Renewed 1979 Deane F. Johnson & the Motion Picture and Television Fund. All

Rights Reserved. 68 below: *I'm No Angel*, 1933, Copyright © by Universal Pictures, a Division of Universal City Studios, Inc. Courtesy of MCA Publishing Rights, a Division of MCA Inc. 69 left: *Ziegfeld Girl*, © 1941 Turner Entertainment Co. Ren. 1968 Metro-Goldwyn-Mayer Inc. All Rights Reserved. 69 right: *Twentieth Century*, © 1934 Columbia Pictures Industries Inc. All Rights Reserved. 70: *There's No Business Like Show Business*, © 1954 Twentieth Century Fox Film Corporation. All Rights Reserved. 71: *Mr. Skeffington*, © 1944 Turner Entertainment Co. All Rights Reserved. 74: *Ruby Gentry*, 1953, © 1983 CBS/Fox, 1980 American Broadcasting Companies. 75: *Pretty Woman*, © 1990 Touchstone Pictures. 76 above: *White Heat*, © 1949 Turner Entertainment Co. All Rights Reserved. 76 below: *East of Eden*, © 1955 Warner Bros. Pictures, Inc. Renewed 1982 Warner Bros. Inc. All Rights Reserved. 77: *Rebel Without a Cause*, © 1955 Warner Bros. Pictures Inc. Renewed 1983 Warner Bros. Inc. All Rights Reserved. 78: *One Flew Over the Cuckoo's Nest*, 1974, Copyright © 1975 N. V. Zwaluw, All Rights Reserved. Released through United Artists Corporation. 79: *Five Easy Pieces*, © 1970 Five Easy Pieces Productions, Inc. 80 above left: photo of Claudette Colbert Copyright © by Universal Pictures, a Division of Universal City Studios, Inc. Courtesy of MCA Publishing Rights, a Division of MCA Inc. Photo by E. R. Richee. 80 below right: *Gilda*, © 1946, renewed 1973 Columbia Pictures Industries, Inc. 82: *Pal Joey*, © 1958 Columbia Pictures Industries, Inc. Courtesy Columbia Pictures, Inc. 83 left: *Cover Girl*, © 1944 Renewed 1972 Columbia Pictures Industries, Inc. Courtesy Columbia Pictures Industries, Inc. 83 right: *Dinner at Eight*, © 1933 Turner Entertainment Co. Ren. 1960 Metro-Goldwyn-Mayer, Inc. All Rights Reserved. 85: *Niagara*, © 1953 Twentieth Century Fox Film Corporation. All Rights Reserved. 86–87: *How to Marry a Millionaire*, © 1953 Twentieth Century Fox Film Corporation. All Rights Reserved. 88: *Don't Bother to Knock*, © 1952 Twentieth Century Fox Film Corporation. All Rights Reserved. 89: *The Prince and the Showgirl*, © 1957 Marilyn Monroe Productions Inc. Renewed 1985 Warner Bros. Inc. All Rights Reserved. 90: *Rambo*, © 1985 Tri-Star Pictures. All Rights Reserved. 92: *Monsieur Beaucaire*, 1924, Copyright © by Universal Pictures, a Division of Universal City Studios, Inc. Courtesy of MCA Publishing Rights, a Division of MCA Inc. 93: *Blood and Sand*, 1922, Copyright © by Universal Pictures, a Division of Universal City Studios, Inc. Courtesy of MCA Publishing Rights, a Division of MCA Inc. 94: *Red Dust*, © 1932 Turner Entertainment Co. Ren. 1959 Loew's Inc. All Rights Reserved. 95: *Susan Lenox: Her Fall and Rise*, © 1931 Turner Entertainment Co. Ren. 1958 Loew's Inc. All Rights Reserved. 96: *Hud*, 1963, © 1962 Paramount Pictures Corporation, Salem Productions, Inc. and Dover Productions, Inc. All Rights Reserved. Courtesy Paramount Pictures Corporation. 97: *Butch Cassidy and the Sundance Kid*, © 1969 Twentieth Century Fox Film Corporation. All Rights Reserved. 98: *I Was a Male War Bride*, © 1949 Twentieth Century Fox Film Corporation. All Rights Reserved. 99: *Holiday*, © 1938 Columbia Pictures Industries, Inc. All Rights Reserved. 102–3: *Mark of Zorro*, © 1920 Douglas Fairbanks/United Artists. 104 above: *Robin Hood*, © 1922 Douglas Fairbanks/United Artists. 104 below: *The Adventures of Robin Hood*, © 1938 Turner Entertainment Co. Ren. 1965 United Artists Television, Inc. All Rights Reserved. 105: *The Westerner*, © 1940 Samuel Goldwyn. 108: *The Searchers*, © 1956 CV Whitney Pictures, Inc. Renewed 1984 Warner Bros. Inc. All Rights Re-

served. 109: *Fort Apache*, © 1948 Argosy Pictures Corporation. Ren. 1975 RKO GENERAL, INC. All Rights Reserved. 110–11: *The Good, the Bad, and the Ugly*, © 1966 P.E.A. Produzioni Europee Associate, © 1990 MGM/UA Home Video, Inc. 113: *You'll Never Get Rich*, Copyright © 1941 Columbia Pictures Industries, Inc. All Rights Reserved. 114 15: *The Gay Divorcee*, © 1934 RKO Radio Pictures, Inc. Ren. 1961 RKO RADIO PICTURES, a division of RKO General, Inc. All Rights Reserved. 116: *The Pirate*, © 1948 Turner Entertainment Co. Ren. 1975 Metro-Goldwyn-Mayer Inc. All Rights Reserved. 117: *A Midsummer Night's Dream*, © 1935 Turner Entertainment Co. Ren. 1962 United Artists Associated, Inc. All Rights Reserved. 118: *Strike Up the Band*, © 1940 Turner Entertainment Co. Ren. 1967 Metro-Goldwyn-Mayer Inc. All Rights Reserved. 119: *Jailhouse Rock*, © 1957 Turner Entertainment Co. and Avon Productions, Inc. Ren. 1985 MGM/UA Entertainment Co., Lawrence Weingarten, Pandro S. Berman and Kathryn Berman. All Rights Reserved. 121 left: *One A.M.*, Chaplin films © and property of Roy Export Company Establishment. 121 right: *Easy Street*, Chaplin films © and property of Roy Export Company Establishment. 1916. 122: *Go West*, © 1940 Turner Entertainment Co. Ren. 1967 Metro-Goldwyn-Mayer Inc. All Rights Reserved. 124 above: *The General*, 1927 © 1926 Joseph M. Schenck. 124 below: *The Freshman*, 1925 © Harold Lloyd/Pathé Exchange. 125: *Gold Rush*, Chaplin films © and property of Roy Export Company Establishment. 126–127: *Stella Dallas*, © 1937 Samuel Goldwyn. 127: *The Fugitive Kind*, © 1960 United Artists. 128: *Broken Blossoms*, © 1919 D. W. Griffith/United Artists. 130: *Way Down East*, © 1920 D. W. Griffith/United Artists. 131: *Orphans of the Storm*, © 1921 D. W. Griffith/United Artists. 132: *Frankenstein*, 1931, Copyright © by Universal Pictures, a Division of Universal City Studios, Inc. Courtesy of MCA Publishing Rights, a Division of MCA Inc. 135: *Dracula*, 1931, Copyright © by Universal Pictures, a Division of Universal City Studios, Inc. Courtesy of MCA Publishing Rights, a Division of MCA Inc. 136: *The Hunchback of Notre Dame*, 1923, Copyright © by Univeral Pictures, a Division of Universal City Studios, Inc. Courtesy of MCA Publishing Rights, a Division of MCA Inc. 137 below: *The Phantom of the Opera*, 1925, Copyright © by Universal Pictures, a Division of Universal City Studios, Inc. Courtesy of MCA Publishing Rights, a Division of MCA Inc. 138: *Anna Karenina*, © 1935 Turner Entertainment Co. Ren. 1962 Metro-Goldwyn-Mayer Inc. All Rights Reserved. 139, 140: *The Little Colonel*, © 1935 Twentieth Century Fox Film Corporation. All Rights Reserved. 142, 143: *Two-Faced Woman*, © 1941 Turner Entertainment Co. Ren. 1968 Metro-Goldwyn-Mayer Inc. All Rights Reserved. 144: *Mutiny on the Bounty*, © 1935 Turner Entertainment Co. Ren. 1962 Metro-Goldwyn-Mayer Inc. All Rights Reserved. 145: *The Hunchback of Notre Dame*, © 1939 RKO Radio Pictures, Inc. Ren. 1967 RKO GENERAL, INC. All Rights Reserved. 146: *A Place in the Sun*, Copyright © 1951 by Paramount Pictures Corporation. All Rights Reserved. Courtesy of Paramount Pictures. 148–49: *The Heiress*, © 1949 Paramount Pictures, Inc. Renewed 1977 EMKA. All Rights Reserved. 151: *Sophie's Choice*, 1982, Copyright © by Universal Pictures, a Division of Universal City Studios, Inc. Courtesy of MCA Publishing Rights, a Division of MCA Inc. 152: *The Letter*, © 1940 Turner Entertainment Co. Ren. 1968 UNITED ARTISTS TELEVISION, INC. All Rights Reserved. 153: *Bad Day at Black Rock*, © 1954

Turner Entertainment Co. Ren. 1982 Metro-Goldwyn-Mayer Film Co. All Rights Reserved. 154: *Rain Man*, © 1988 United Artists Pictures, Inc. All Rights Reserved. 156: *This Gun for Hire*, 1942, Copyright © by Universal Pictures, a Division of Universal City Studios, Inc. Courtesy of MCA Publishing Rights, a Division of MCA Inc. 158: *Double Indemnity*, 1944, Copyright © by Universal Pictures, a Division of Universal City Studios, Inc. Courtesy of MCA Publishing Rights, a Division of MCA Inc. 161: *A Woman's Face*, © 1941 Turner Entertainment Co. Ren. 1968 Metro-Goldwyn-Mayer Inc. All Rights Reserved. 162: *Joan of Arc*, © 1948 King World. 163: *Autumn Sonata*, © 1978 ITC/New World. 164: *The Palm Beach Story*, 1942, Copyright © by Universal Pictures, a Division of Universal City Studios, Inc. Courtesy of MCA Publishing Rights, a Division of MCA Inc. 165: *Cleopatra*, 1934, Copyright © by Universal Pictures, a Division of Universal City Studios, Inc. Courtesy of MCA Publishing Rights, a Division of MCA Inc. 166: *The Petrified Forest*, © 1936 Turner Entertainment Co. All Rights Reserved. 167: *Casablanca*, © 1943 Turner Entertainment Co. Ren. 1970 UNITED ARTISTS TELEVISION, INC. All Rights Reserved. 168: *Camille*, 1936, © 1936 Turner Entertainment Co. Ren. 1963 Metro-Goldwyn-Mayer Inc. All Rights Reserved. 169: *Flesh and the Devil*, © 1927 Turner Entertainment Co. Ren. 1954 Loew's Inc. All Rights Reserved. 170: *Grand Hotel*, © 1932 Turner Entertainment Co. Ren. 1959 Loew's Inc. All Rights Reserved. 171: *Camille*, 1936, © 1936 Turner Entertainment Co. Ren. 1963 Metro-Goldwyn-Mayer Inc. All Rights Reserved. 172, 173: *Ninotchka*, © 1939 Turner Entertainment Co. Ren. 1966 Metro-Goldwyn-Mayer Inc. All Rights Reserved. 174: *Judgment at Nuremberg*, Copyright © 1961 Roxcom Films, Inc. 175 above left: *On the Waterfront*, © 1954, renewed 1982 Columbia Pictures Industries, Inc. 175 above right: *The Godfather*, © 1972 by Paramount Pictures Corporation. All Rights Reserved. Courtesy of Paramount Pictures. 176 above: *Cat on a Hot Tin Roof*, © 1958 Turner Entertainment Co. Ren. 1986 MGM/UA Entertainment Co., Weingarten Dec. 12, 1967 Trust, and Pandro C. Berman and Kathryn Berman. All Rights Reserved. 176 below: *Cleopatra*, © 1963 Twentieth Century Fox Film Corporation. All Rights Reserved. 177: *Suddenly Last Summer*, © 1959 Columbia Pictures Industries, Inc. All Rights Reserved. 178: *Who's Afraid of Virginia Woolf?* © 1966 Warner Bros. Pictures Inc. All Rights Reserved. 180: *Key Largo*, © 1948 Turner Entertainment Co. Ren. 1975 UNITED ARTISTS TELEVISION, INC. All Rights Reserved. 181: *Mississippi Burning*, © 1988 Orion Pictures Corporation. All Rights Reserved. 183: *High Noon*, 1952, Courtesy of Republic Films Corporation. 184: *Whales of August*, © 1988 Nelson Entertainment, Inc. 185: *Emperor Jones*, © 1933 United Artists Corporation. All Rights Reserved. 186: *Blackboard Jungle*, © 1955 Turner Entertainment Co. Ren. 1983 MGM/UA Entertainment Co. All Rights Reserved. 187: *The Defiant Ones*, © 1958 Lomitas Productions, Inc. and Curtleigh Productions, Inc. Renewed 1986 United Artists Corporation. 188: *Richard III*, © 1955 London Films. 190: *Dr. Jekyll and Mr. Hyde*, © 1941 Turner Entertainment Co. Ren. 1968 Metro-Goldwyn-Mayer Inc. All Rights Reserved. 191: *Now, Voyager*, © 1942 Turner Entertainment Co. Ren. 1969 UNITED ARTISTS TELEVISION, INC. All Rights Reserved. 192 above: *The Teahouse of the August Moon*, © 1956 Turner Entertainment Co. Ren. 1984 MGM/UA Entertainment Co. All Rights Reserved. 192 below: *The Godfather*, © 1972 by Paramount Pictures Corporation. All

Rights Reserved. Courtesy of Paramount Pictures. 193 above: *Tootsie*, © 1982 Columbia Pictures Industries, Inc. All Rights Reserved. 193 below: *Batman*, © 1989 Warner Bros. Inc. All Rights Reserved. 194: *Dr. Jekyll and Mr. Hyde*, 1921, Copyright © by Universal Pictures, a Division of Universal City Studios, Inc. Courtesy of MCA Publishing Rights, a Division of MCA Inc. 195: *Svengali*, © 1931 Corinth Films. 196 left: *The Good Earth*, © 1937 Metro-Goldwyn-Mayer Corporation. Ren. 1964 Metro-Goldwyn-Mayer Inc. 196 right: *Juarez*, © 1939 Turner Entertainment Co. All Rights Reserved. 197: *The Life of Emile Zola*, © 1937 Turner Entertainment Co. All Rights Reserved. 198–99: *Mr. Smith Goes to Washington*, © 1939, renewed 1967 Columbia Pictures Corp. 200: *The Great Dictator*, Chaplin films © and property of Roy Export Company Establishment. 202: *Judgment at Nuremberg*, Copyright © 1961 Roxcom Films, Inc. 204 above: *Young Mr. Lincoln*, © 1939 Twentieth Century Fox Film Corporation. All Rights Reserved. 204 below: *The Ox-Bow Incident*, © 1943 Twentieth Century Fox Film Corporation. All Rights Reserved. 205: *Young Mr. Lincoln*, © 1939 Twentieth Century Fox Film Corporation. All Rights Reserved. 206: *Made for Each Other*, © 1939 Renewed © 1966 American Broadcasting Companies, Inc. All Rights Reserved. 209: *Meet John Doe*, © 1941 Liberty Films. 210: *In This Our Life*, © 1942 Turner Entertainment Co. All Rights Reserved. 213: *Nothing Sacred*, © 1937 David O. Selznick. 215: *Rebel Without a Cause*, © 1955 Warner Bros. Pictures Inc. Renewed 1983 Warner Bros. Inc. All Rights Reserved. 216. *Mutiny on the Bounty*, © 1962 Turner Entertainment Co. and Arcola Pictures Corp. All Rights Reserved. 217: *Apocalypse Now*, Copyright © 1979 Omni Zoetrope. 218: *Goin' to Town*, 1935, Copyright © by Universal Pictures, a Division of Universal City Studios, Inc. Courtesy of MCA Publishing Rights, a Division of MCA Inc. 219: *It's a Gift*, 1934, Copyright © by Universal Pictures, a Division of Universal City Studios, Inc. Courtesy of MCA Publishing Rights, a Division of MCA Inc. 220: *Born Yesterday*, © 1950 Columbia Pictures Industries, Inc. Courtesy of Columbia Pictures Industries, Inc. 222: *Sylvia Scarlett*, © 1936 RKO Pictures, Inc. All Rights Reserved. 224: *Adam's Rib*, © 1949 Turner Entertainment Co. Ren. 1976 Metro-Goldwyn-Mayer Inc. All Rights Reserved. 225: *Guess Who's Coming to Dinner*, © 1967 Columbia Pictures Industries, Inc. Courtesy of Columbia Pictures Industries, Inc. 226: *Dangerous Liaisons*, © 1988 Warner Bros. Inc. 228: *War and Peace*, © 1956 by Paramount Pictures Corporation. All Rights Reserved. 229: *Dragon Seed*, © 1944 Turner Entertainment Co. Ren. 1971 Metro-Goldwyn-Mayer Inc. All Rights Reserved. 230 above: *Désirée*, © 1954 Twentieth Century Fox Film Corporation. All Rights Reserved. 230 below: *Guys and Dolls*, © 1955 Samuel Goldwyn. 231: *Julius Caesar*, © 1953 Turner Entertainment Co. Ren. 1981 Metro-Goldwyn-Mayer Inc. All Rights Reserved. 233: *Dr. Strangelove*, 1964, © 1963 Hawks Films, Ltd. 234 above left: *Falling in Love*, © 1984 Paramount Pictures Corporation. All Rights Reserved. Courtesy of Paramount Pictures. 234 above right: *Ironweed*, © 1987 Taft Entertainment/Keith Barish/Home Box Office. 234 below left: *A Cry in the Dark*, © 1988 Evil Angels Films Pty., Ltd. All Rights Reserved. 234 below right: *Out of Africa*, 1985, Copyright © by Universal Pictures, a Division of Universal City Studios, Inc. Courtesy of MCA Publishing Rights, a Division of MCA Inc. 235: *Being There*, © 1979 Lorimar Pictures. 236: *The Rose Tattoo*, © 1955 Paramount Pictures Corporation. All Rights Reserved. Courtesy of Paramount Pictures. 239 above: *Holiday Inn*, 1942, Copyright © by Universal Pictures, a Division of Universal City Studios, Inc. Courtesy of MCA Publishing Rights, a Division of MCA Inc. 239 below: *The Emperor Waltz*, © 1948 by Paramount Pictures Corporation. All Rights Reserved. Courtesy of Paramount Pictures. 240–41: *Meet Me in St. Louis*, © 1944 Turner Entertainment Co. Ren. 1971 Metro-Goldwyn-Mayer Inc. All Rights Reserved. 242 above: *A Star Is Born*, © 1954 Warner Bros. Inc. Renewed 1982 Warner Bros. Inc. All Rights Reserved. 242–43: *Funny Girl*, © 1968 Columbia Pictures Industries Inc. All Rights Reserved. 243 above: *A Star Is Born*, © 1976 Barwood Films Ltd., The First Artists Production Company Ltd. and Warner Bros. Inc. All Rights Reserved. 246 above left: *Morocco*, 1930, Copyright © by Universal Pictures, a Division of Universal City Studios, Inc. Courtesy of MCA Publishing Rights, a Division of MCA Inc. 246 above right: *Since You Went Away*, 1945, © 1945 David O. Selznick. Released through United Artists Assoc. Inc. All Rights Reserved. 246 below: *Love Me Tonight*, 1932, Copyright © by Universal Pictures, a Division of Universal City Studios, Inc. Courtesy of MCA Publishing Rights, a Division of MCA Inc. 249 above: *Grand Hotel*, © 1932 Turner Entertainment Co. Ren. 1959 Loew's Inc. All Rights Reserved. 249 below: *Suddenly Last Summer*, © 1959 Columbia Pictures Industries, Inc. All Rights Reserved. 251 left: *In This Our Life*, © 1942 Turner Entertainment Co. All Rights Reserved. 251 right: *Alice Adams*, © 1935 RKO Pictures, Inc. All Rights Reserved. 252 left: *Limelight*, Chaplin films © and property of Roy Export Company Establishment. 252 right: *The Star*, © 1952 Twentieth Century Fox Film Corp. Renewed 1980 Warner Bros. Inc. All Rights Reserved. 253: *Sunset Boulevard*, Copyright © 1950 Paramount Pictures Corporation. All Rights Reserved. Courtesy of Paramount Pictures. 254 above: *The Color of Money*, © 1986 Touchstone Pictures. 255: *I Could Go on Singing*, © 1963 United Artists Corporation. 258: *Sunday in New York*, © 1963 Turner Entertainment Co. All Rights Reserved. 259: *The China Syndrome*, © 1979 Columbia Pictures Industries, Inc. 260: *Cleopatra*, © 1917 Twentieth Century Fox Film Corporation. All Rights Reserved. 263: *Kiki*, © 1931 Mary Pickford/United Artists. 264 left: *The Wrong Man*, © 1957 Warner Bros. Pictures, Inc. Renewed 1984 Warner Bros. Inc. All Rights Reserved. 264 right: *Vertigo*, © 1958 Alfred J. Hitchcock Productions, Inc. All Rights Reserved. 265: *Red River*, © 1948 Monterey Productions. Renewal 1975 United Artists Corporation. All Rights Reserved. 268 above left: *Judgment at Nuremberg*, Copyright © 1961 Roxcom Films, Inc. 268 above right: *Suspicion*, © 1941 RKO Radio Pictures Ren. 1969 RKO GENERAL, INC. All Rights Reserved. 268 below: *Once Upon a Time in the West*, Copyright © 1969 by Paramount Pictures Corporation. All Rights Reserved. 269: *Hush, Hush, Sweet Charlotte*, © 1965 Twentieth Century Fox Film Corporation. All Rights Reserved. 276–77: *Modern Times*, Chaplin films © and property of Roy Export Company Establishment.